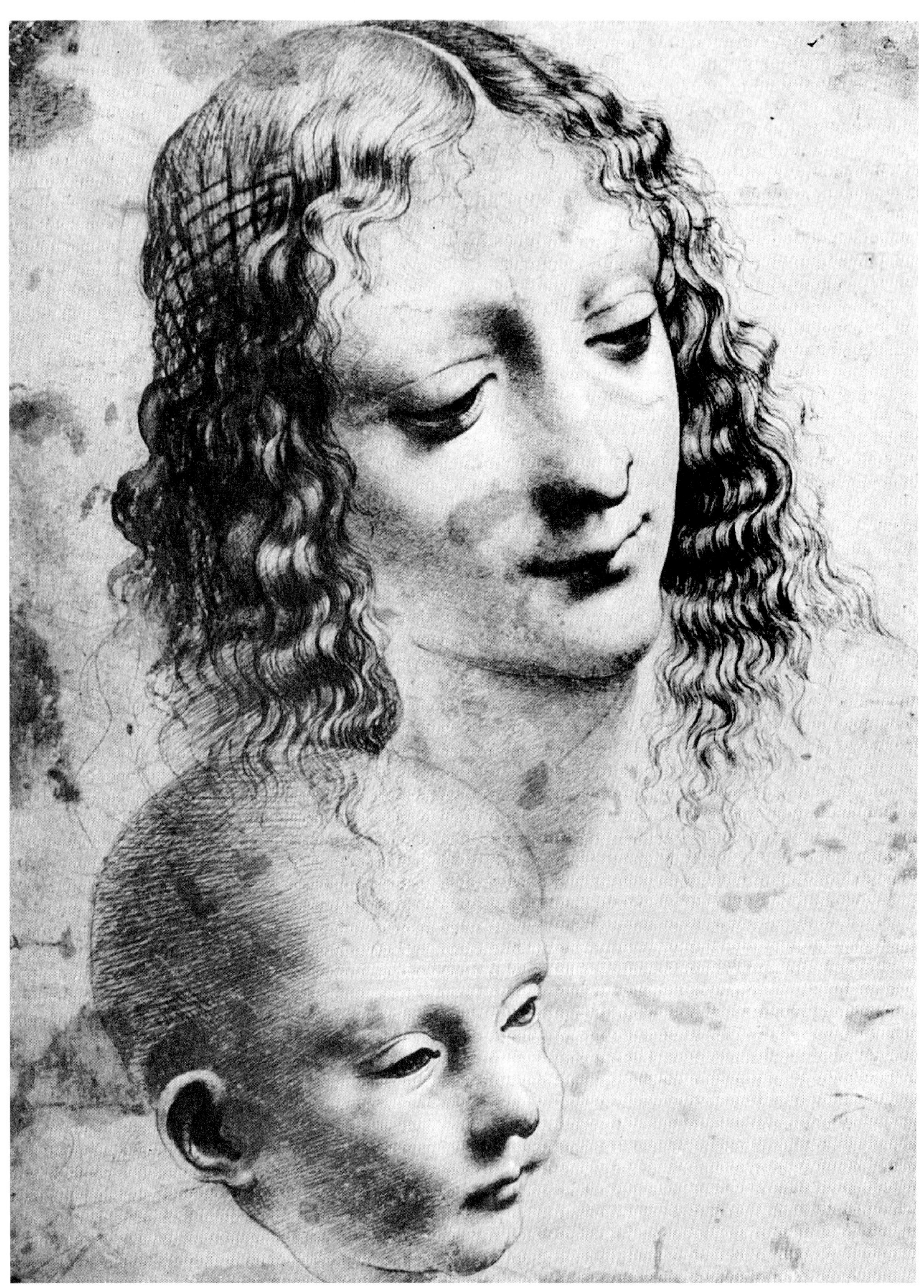

Giovanni Antonio Boltraffio

Great Portrait Drawings and Prints

Selected by
Carol Belanger Grafton

DOVER PUBLICATIONS, INC.
Mineola, New York

Library of Congress Cataloging-in-Publication Data

Great portrait drawings and prints / selected by Carol Belanger Grafton.
     p. cm. — (Dover pictorial archive series)
  ISBN 0-486-43402-8 (pbk.)
    1. Portraits, European—Catalogs. I. Grafton, Carol Belanger. II. Series.

N7597.5.G74 2004
743'.2—dc22

             2004045544

Book design by Carol Belanger Grafton

Manufactured in the United States of America
Dover Publications, Inc., 31 East 2nd Street, Mineola, N.Y. 11501

LIST OF PLATES

Frontispiece: GIOVANNI ANTONIO BOLTRAFFIO (1467–1516)
Study for the *Heads of the Virgin and Child.* Silverpoint shaded with brush and ink. 297 x 220mm.

1   HANS VON AACHEN (1552–1615)
Portrait of Giovanni da Bologna. Black and red chalk. 148 x 128mm.

2   BARTHEL BEHAM (1502–1540)
Portrait of a Bearded Man in a Flat Cap (J. Jost?) Black and red chalk. 352 x 281mm.

3   GIOVANNI BELLINI (1430?–1516)
Head of an Old Man. Point of the brush on blue paper, heightened with white. 260 x 190mm.

4   GEORGE BELLOWS (1882–1925)
Jean (c. 1920). Crayon. 457 x 292mm.

5   GIAN LORENZO BERNINI (1598–1680)
Portrait of a Man. Black and red chalk, with touches of white chalk, on light brown paper. 188 x 148mm.

6   FELIX BRACQUEMOND (1833–1914)
Portrait of M. Ed. de Goncourt. Charcoal on canvas. 550 x 379mm.

7   HANS BURGKMAIR THE ELDER (1473–1531)
Portrait of Wolfgang von Maen. Black chalk, retouched with brush in bistre. 351 x 272mm.

8   CARLETTO CALIARI (1570–1596)
Head of an Ecclesiastic. Black, brown, red and white chalks on blue laid paper. 305 x 215mm.

9   ROSALBA CARRIERA (1675–1757)
Head of a Child. Pastels on light gray paper. 340 x 280mm.

10   ANTONIO DEL CASTILLO (1616–1668)
Portrait of a Gentleman. Black and red chalk. 290 x 210mm.

11   THÉODORE CHASSÉRIAU (1819–1856)
Portrait of Madame Borg de Balsam. Pencil on white paper. 340 x 270 mm.

12   *After* PETRUS CHRISTUS (c. 1410–1472/73)
Portrait of a Young Man with a Falcon. Silverpoint on ivory prepared paper. 189 x 143mm.

13   JEAN-BAPTISTE-CAMILLE COROT (1796–1875)
My Agar. Pencil. 178 x 143mm.

14   ANTOINE COYPEL (1661–1722)
Young Woman Looking Over Her Shoulder. Black, red and white chalk, pink pastel, on brown paper. 350 x 268mm.

33 WILLIAM M. HARNETT (1848–1892)
Head of a Woman. Black crayon and brown wash with touches of white.
495 x 413mm.

34 HANS HOLBEIN THE ELDER (1460/70–1524)
Seated Woman with Long Loose Hair. Silverpoint on prepared paper with some
heightenings in red and white chalk, reinforced in pen. 140 x 103mm.

35 WOLF HUBER (c. 1485–1553)
Head of a Young Man. Black and white chalk on red prepared paper. 294 x 198mm.

36 JEAN-AUGUSTE-DOMINIQUE INGRES (1780–1867)
Portrait of Paganini. Pencil. 295 x 215mm.

37 AUGUSTUS JOHN (1879–1961)
Portrait of Mrs. Derwent Lees. Pencil. 394 x 245mm.

38 EASTMAN JOHNSON (1824–1906)
Head of a Young Girl. Charcoal and chalk. 483 x 381mm.

39 JACOB JORDAENS (1593–1678)
Head of an Old Man Drinking (Portrait of Adam van Noort). Black and red chalk,
heightened with white. 187 x 136mm.

40 OSCAR KOKOSCHKA (1886–1980)
Portrait of a Lady. Charcoal on ivory-colored paper. 604 x 445mm.

41 KAETHE KOLLWITZ (1867–1945)
Self-Portrait with a Pencil. Charcoal. 476 x 635mm.

42 SIR PETER LELY (1618–1680)
A Young Girl (The Lady Islington). Black chalk heightened with white. 280 x 170mm.

43 LEONARDO DA VINCI (1452–1519)
Head of a Warrior—The "Red Head". Red chalk on pale brownish-pink-grounded
paper. 226 x 201mm.

44 LUCAS VAN LEYDEN (1494–1533)
Portrait of a Young Woman. Black chalk, the face lightly worked over with red chalk.
363 x 330mm.

45 EGRON SILLIF LUNDGREN (1815–1875)
A Young Woman with a Fan. Red chalk, with blue and red washes. 354 x 243mm.

46 SEBASTIANO MAINARDI (d. 1513)
Angels' Heads. Silverpoint, heightened with white, on orange-red ground.
170 x 255mm.

47 HENRI MATISSE (1869–1954)
The Plumed Hat. Pencil. 350 x 476mm.

48 MICHELANGELO BUONARROTI (1475–1564)
Portrait of Andrea Quaratesi. Black chalk, partly stippled. 411 x 292mm.

49 CHARLES-JOSEPH NATOIRE (1700–1777)
Profile of a Young Lady in Low-cut Bodice. Red chalk, heightened with white, on
brownish gray paper. 203 x 133mm.

50 REMBRANDT PEALE (1778–1860)
John Amory, Jr. Red and black chalk, and wash, on white paper. 171 x 143mm.

68 PETER PAUL RUBENS (1577–1640)
Young Woman with Crossed Hands. Black and red chalk, heightened with white.
473 x 354mm.

69 GIOVANNI BATTISTA TIEPOLO (1696–1770)
Head of a Man. Red and white chalk on blue paper. 323 x 252mm.

70 *Attributed to* JOHN-BAPTISTE VAN LOO (1684–1745)
The Head of a Girl. Black, brown, red and white chalk on buff paper. 396 x 320mm.

---

71 CAMILLE PISSARRO (1831–1903)
Portrait of Cézanne (full-face). Pencil on page from sketchbook. 190 x 111mm.

72 JACOPO DA PONTORMO (1494–1557)
Half-Length Portrait of a Seated Man in Artisan's Costume. Charcoal. 385 x 255mm.

73 PIERRE PUVIS DE CHAVANNES (1824–1898)
Portrait of Madame Montrosier. Pencil on buff-colored wove paper. 495 x 333mm.

74 FRANÇOIS QUESNEL (1543–1617)
Portrait said to be Christine of Lorraine, Grand Duchess of Tuscany. Black and red chalk.
300 x 210mm.

75 ODILON REDON (1840–1916)
Young Woman. Charcoal. 523 x 375mm.

76 REMBRANDT HARMENSZ VAN RIJN (1606–1669)
Portrait of Saskia in a Turban. Black chalk and brown wash, on grayish paper.
195 x 140mm.

77 GUIDO RENI (1575–1642)
Head of a Young Woman Looking Upwards. Black and red chalk, with touches of white
chalk, on pale brown paper. 377 x 270mm.

78 CHARLES BALTHAZAR JULIEN FAVRET DE SAINT-MÉMIN (1770–1852)
John Hughes. Black and white crayon on pink laid paper. 520 x 381mm.

79 JOHN SINGER SARGENT (1856–1925)
Nettie Huxley. Pencil. 233 x 149mm

80 ANDREA D'AGNOLO DEL SARTO (1486–1530)
Head of a Boy (study for John the Baptist in the Galleria Pitti). Charcoal. 270 x 200mm.

81 GOTTFRIED SCHADOW (1764–1850)
Portrait of of the Actress Unger. Black and colored chalk. 375 x 265mm.

82 EGON SCHIELE (1890–1918)
Portrait of Heinrich Rieger. Charcoal and gouache on paper. 448 x 292mm.

83 JAKOB MATHIAS SCHMUTZER (1733–1811)
Head of a Young Man Looking to the Left. Reddish-brown chalk. 472 x 368mm.

84 MARTIN SCHONGAUER (1445–1491)
Angel's Head. Pen and brown ink. 130 x 108mm.

85 GEORGES SEURAT (1859–1891)
A Girl with a Sketchbook. Conté pencil. 300 x 215mm.

86 JOHN SLOAN (1871–1951)
The Black Hat. Black crayon. 300 x 235mm.

87 ALBERT EDWARD STERNER (1863–1946)
    My Wife in October 1897. Sanguine. 356 x 254mm.

88 GEORG STRAUCH (1613–1675)
    Man Seated Before a Small Picture. Bistre drawing with gray india ink. 293 x 204mm.

89 JACOPO TINTORETTO (1518–1594)
    Study After an Antique Head. Black chalk, heightened with white, on faded blue
    paper. 340 x 230mm.

90 JAMES TISSOT (1836–1902)
    The Convalescent. Drypoint and etching. 225 x 162mm.

91 TITIAN (TIZIANO VECELLIO) (c. 1485–1576)
    Portrait of a Young Woman. Black and white chalk on brown paper. 419 x 265mm.

92 HENRI DE TOULOUSE-LAUTREC (1864–1901)
    Portrait of Jane Avril. Sanguine drawing on blue paper. 478 x 326mm.

93 *Attributed to* EUGÉNIE TRIPIER-LE FRANC (1805–1872)
    Portrait. Pencil, sepia and gouache on paper. 170 x 127mm.

94 ANTHONY VAN DYCK (1599–1641)
    Portrait of Hendrik van Balen. Black chalk. 243 x 198mm.

95 DIEGO VELÁZQUEZ (1599–1660)
    Portrait of a Girl. Black chalk on blue-gray paper, heightened with white.
    276 x 187mm.

96 BARTOLOMMEO VENETO (1502–1530)
    Head and Shoulders of a Youth Wearing a Cap. Chalk heightened with white.
    380 x 286mm.

97 VERONESE (PAOLO CALIARI) (1528–1588)
    Head of a Young Woman. Black chalk, heightened with white on blue-gray paper.
    347 x 231mm.

98 ANDREA DEL VERROCCHIO (1435–1488)
    Head of a Woman with Elaborate Coiffure. Black chalk heightened with white.
    325 x 273mm.

99 ANTOINE WATTEAU (1684–1721)
    Half-Length Figure of a Woman with Hands Folded. Red and black chalk on tan paper.
    200 x 140mm.

100 ROGIER VAN DER WEYDEN (1399/1400–1464)
    St. Mary Magdalen. Silverpoint on ivory prepared paper. 176 x 130mm.

101 DAVID WILKIE (1785–1841)
    Mrs. Grant, Knitting. Pencil and watercolor, heightened with white chalk.
    337 x 273mm.

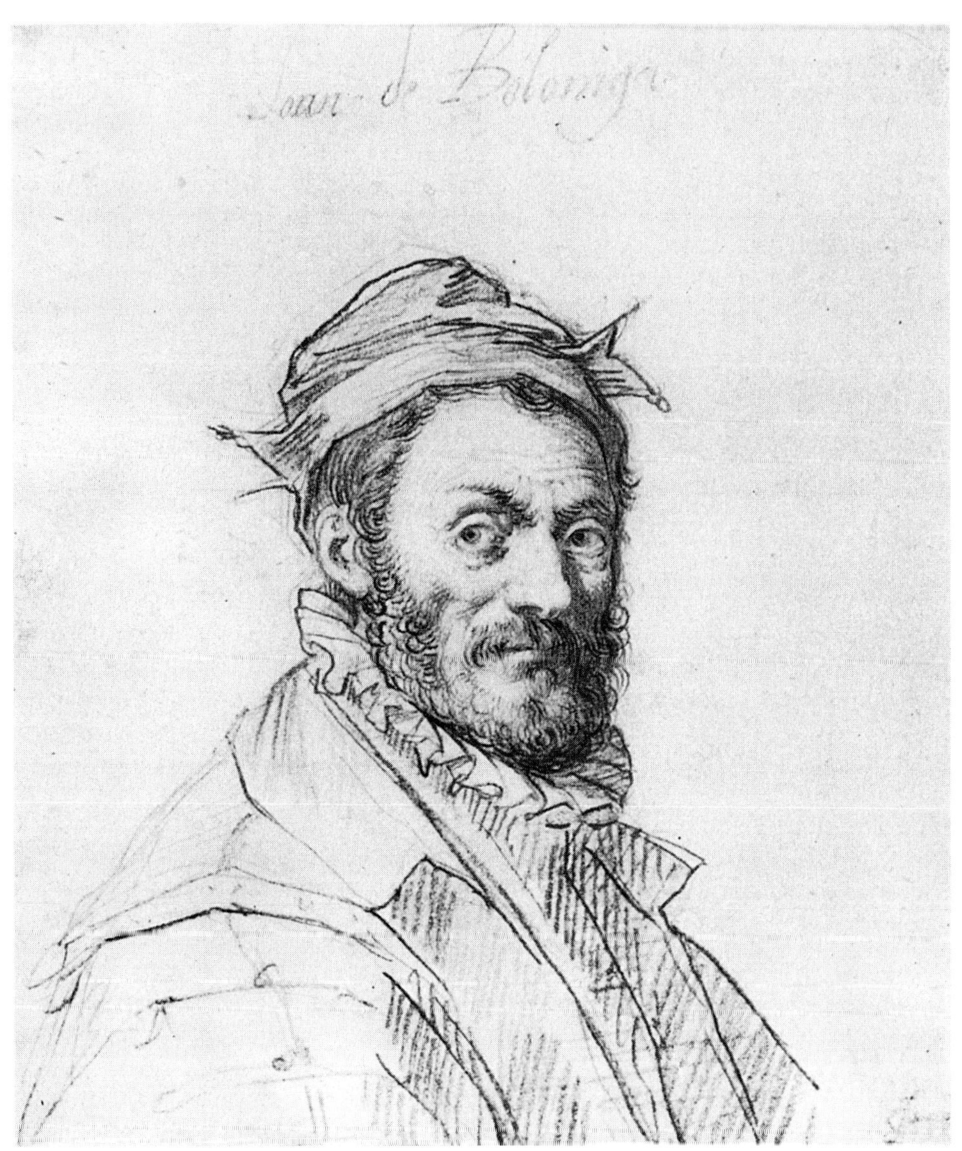

Plate 1. HANS VON AACHEN

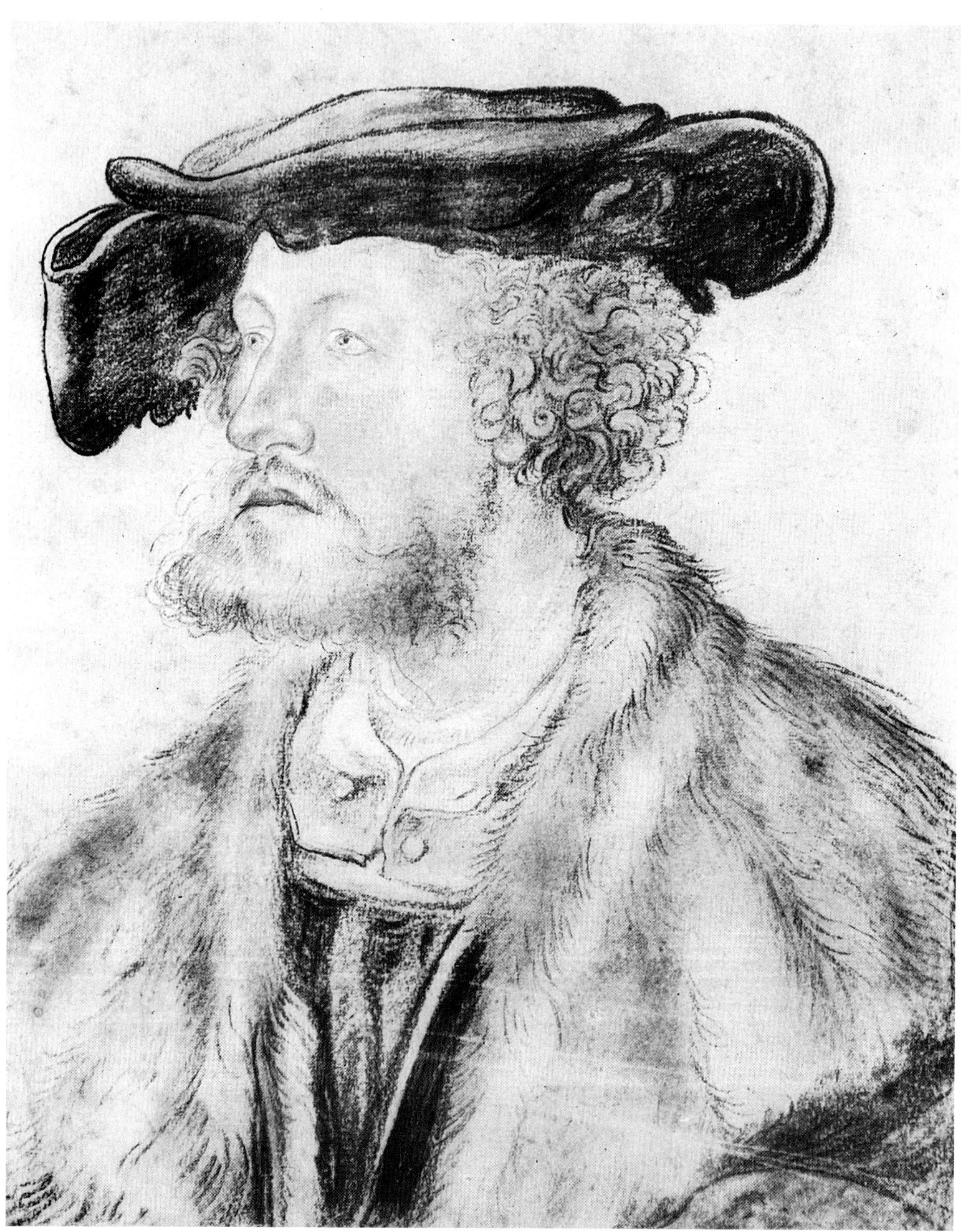

Plate 2. Barthel Beham

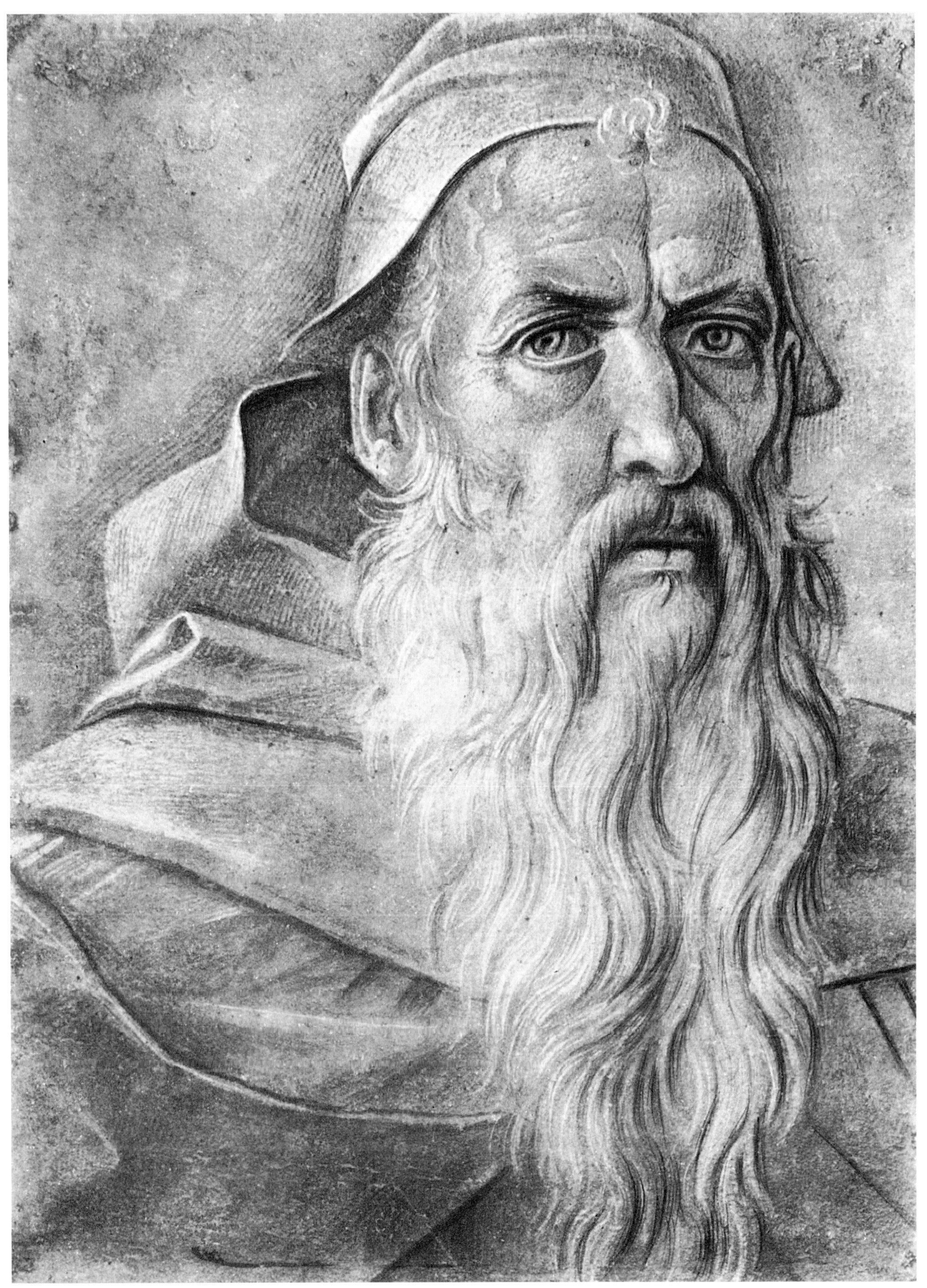

Plate 3. Giovanni Bellini

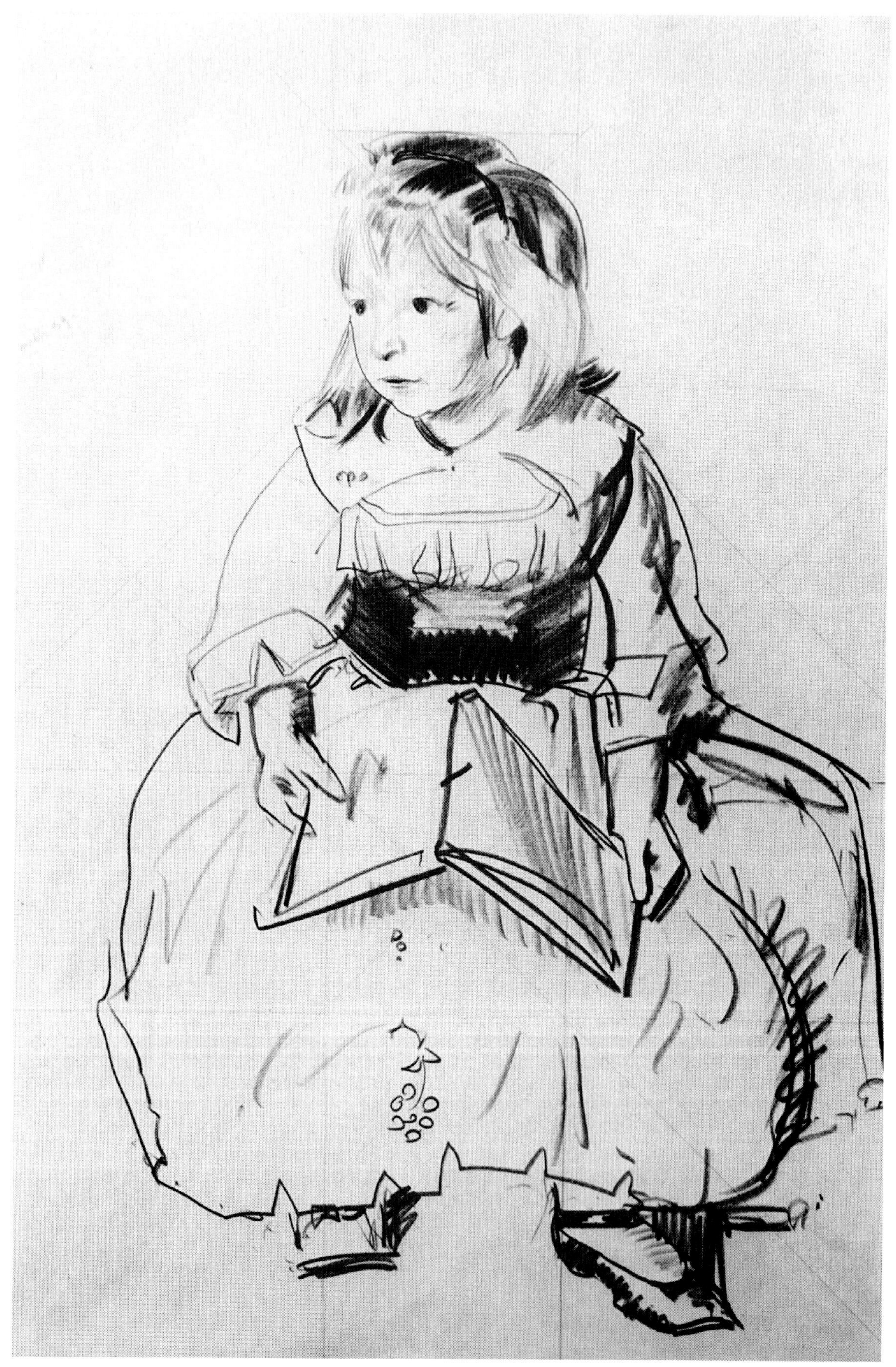

Plate 4. GEORGE BELLOWS

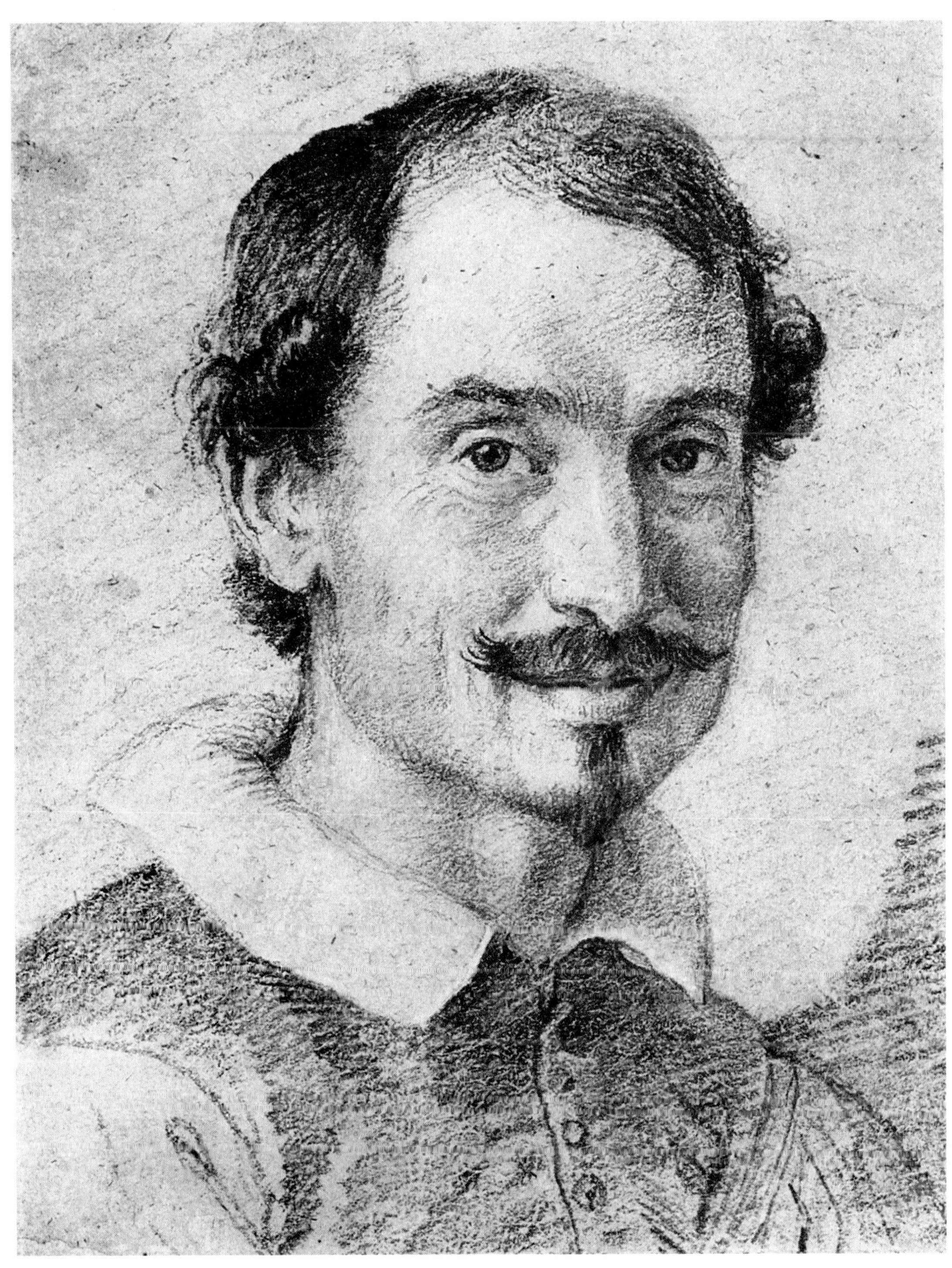

Plate 5. Gian Lorenzo Bernini

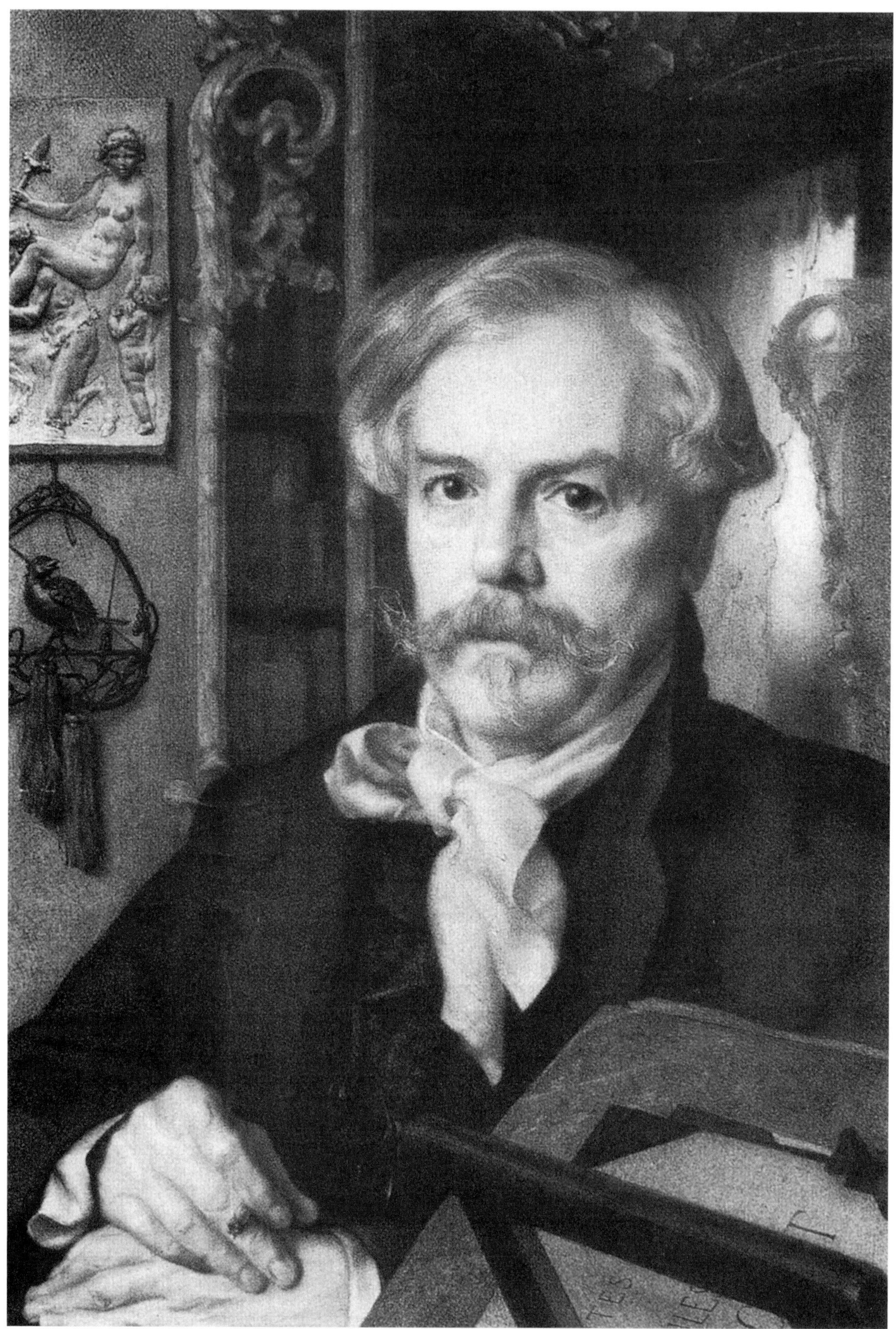

Plate 6. Félix Bracquemond

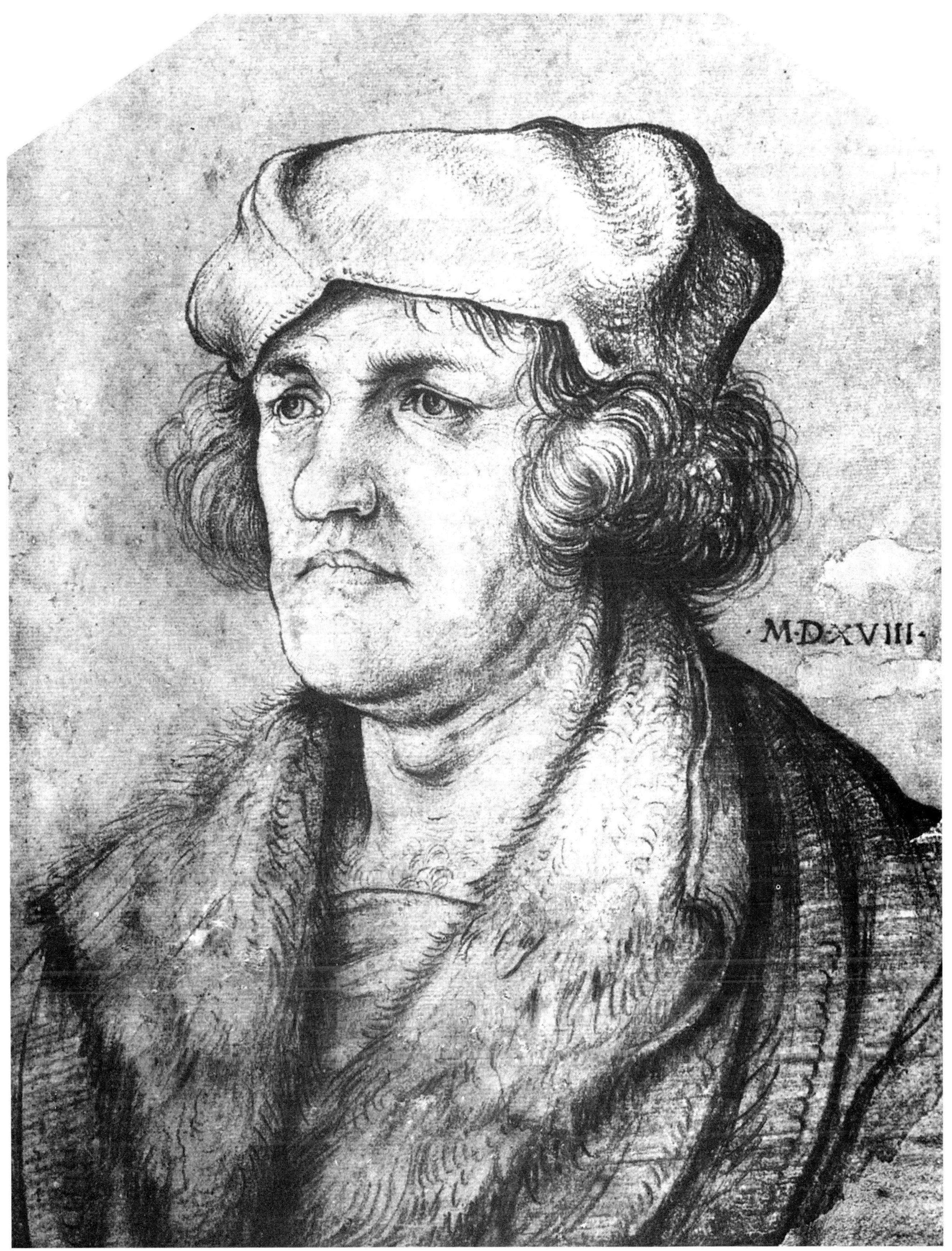

Plate 7. HANS BURGKMAIR THE ELDER

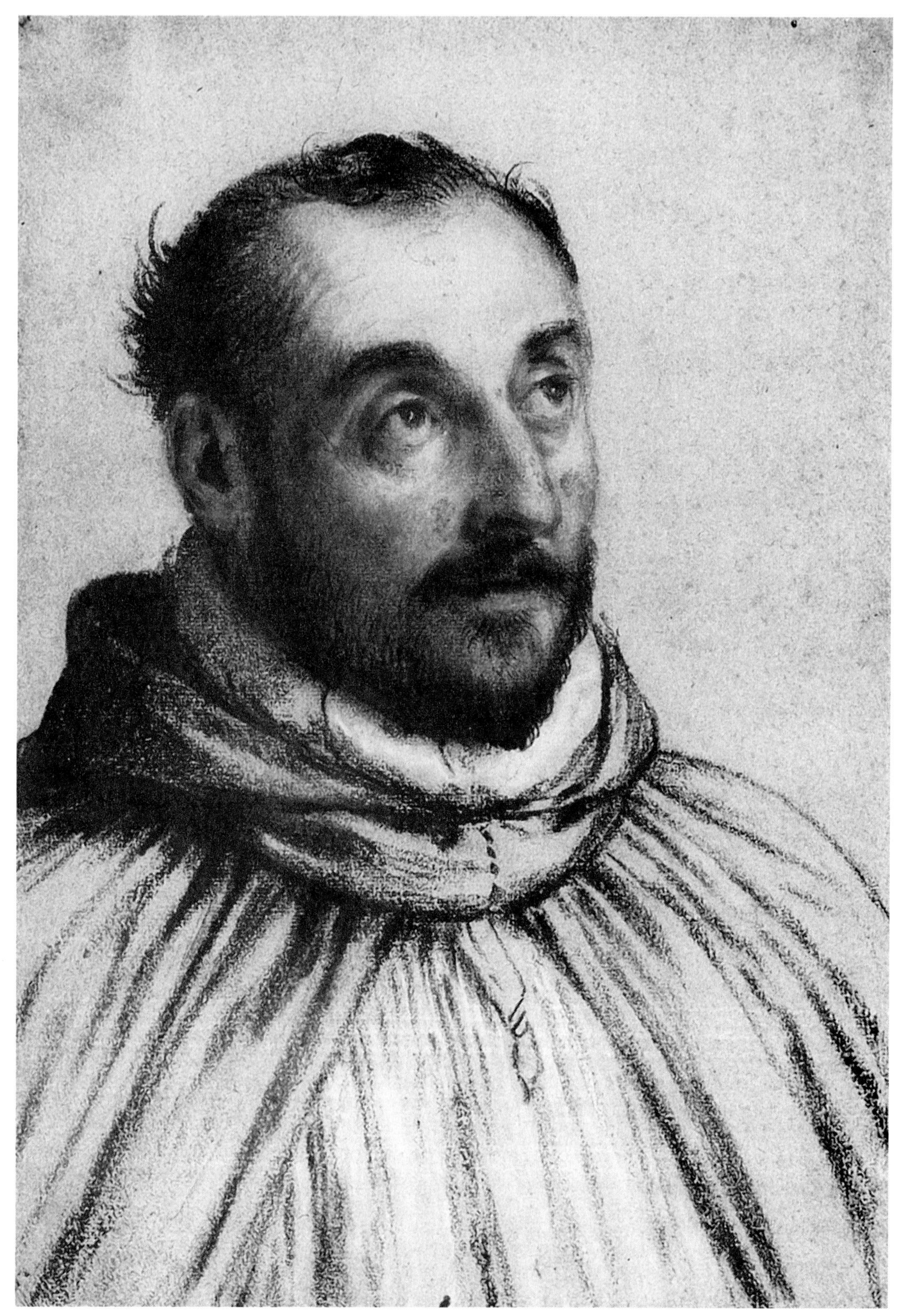

Plate 8. Carletto Caliari

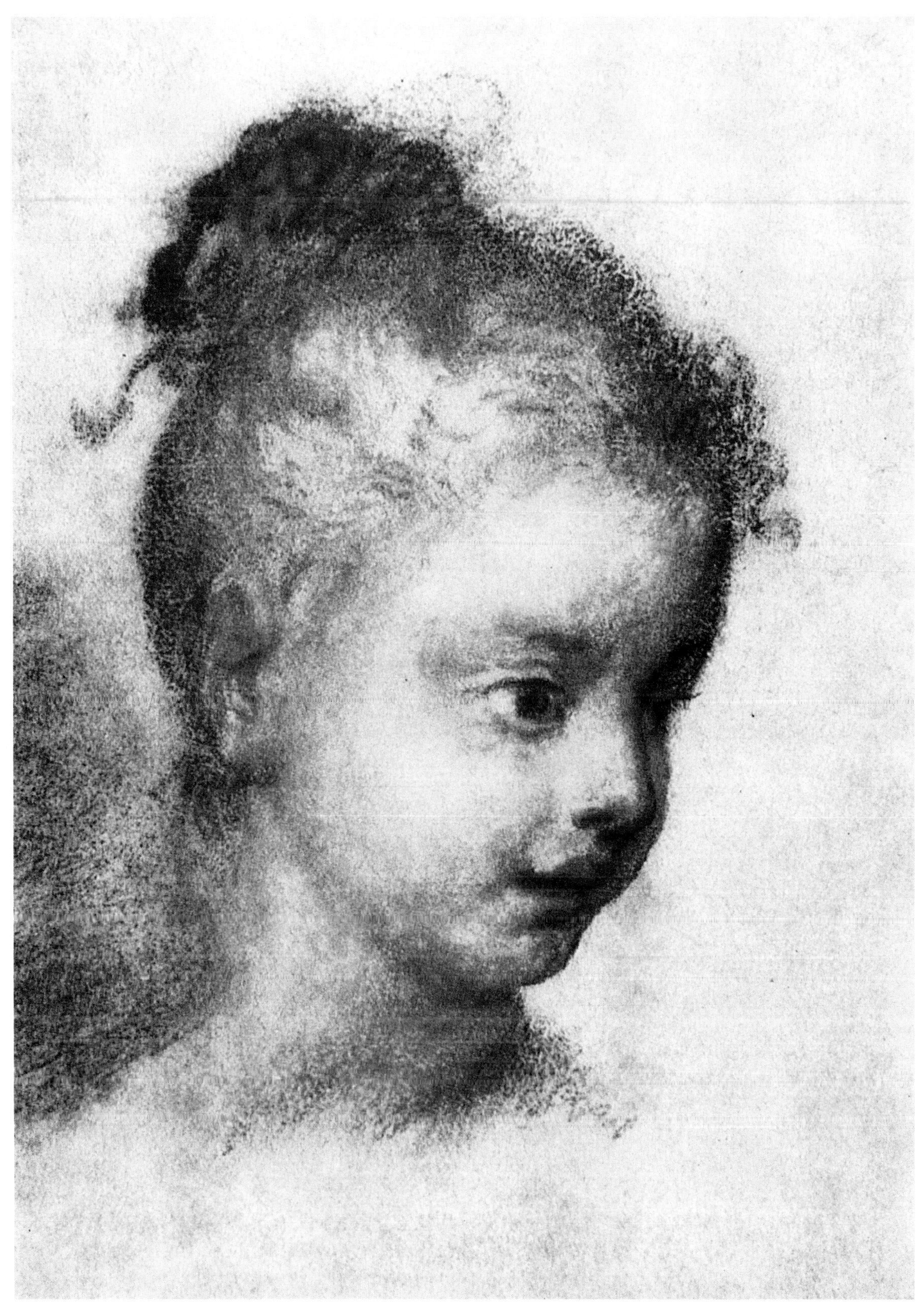

Plate 9. Rosalba Carriera

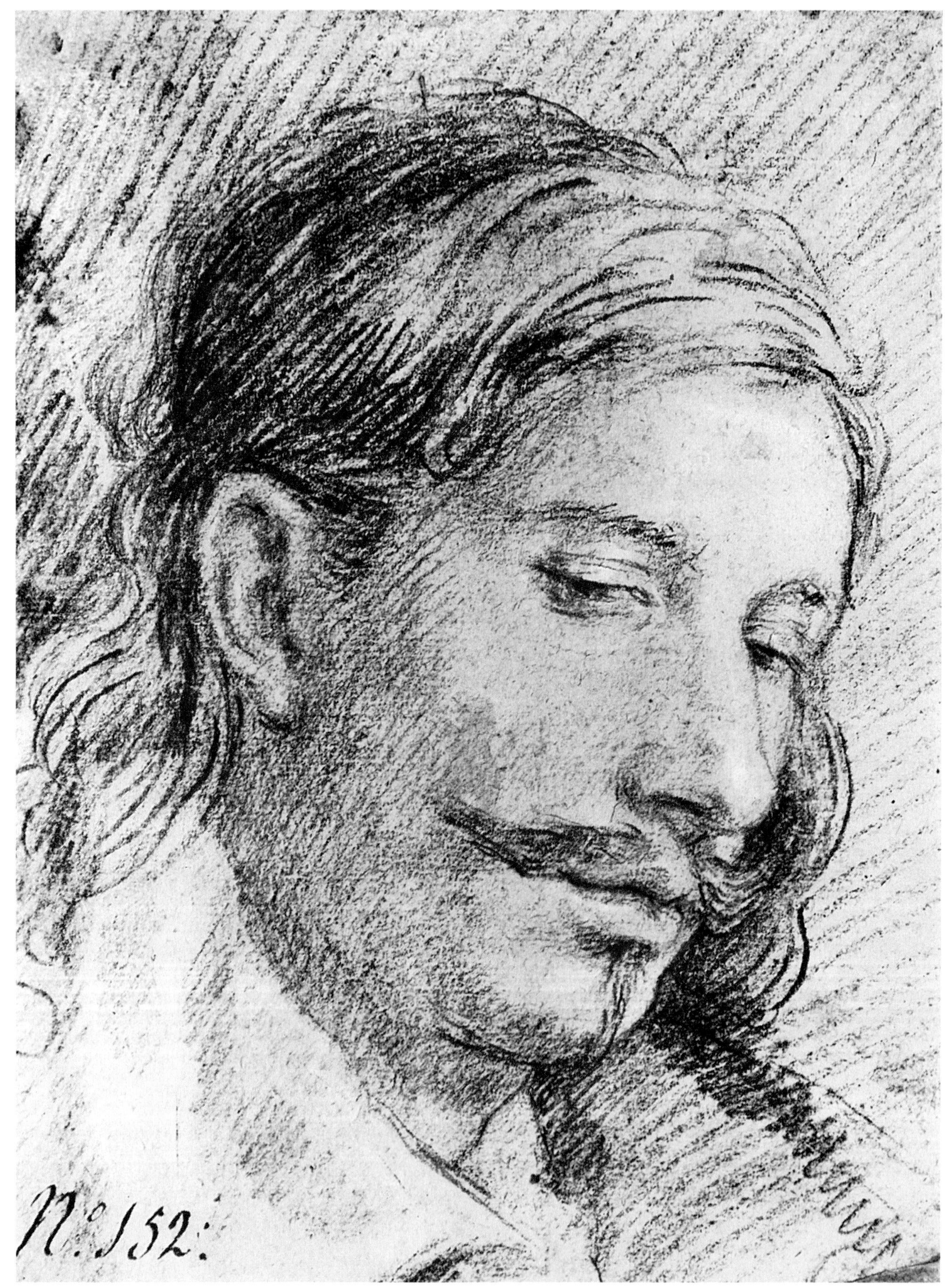

Plate 10. ANTONIO DEL CASTILLO

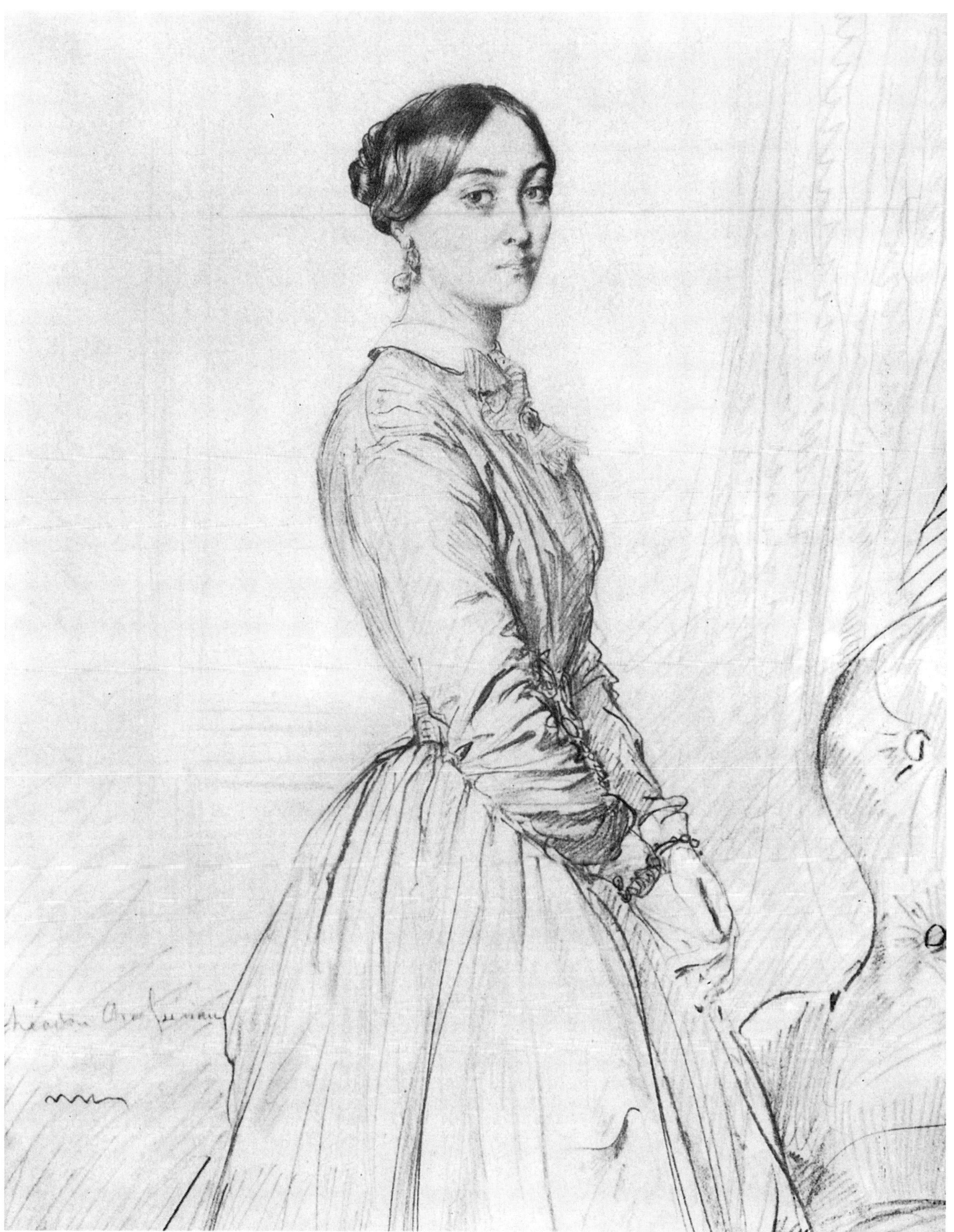

Plate 11. THÉODORE CHASSÉRIAU

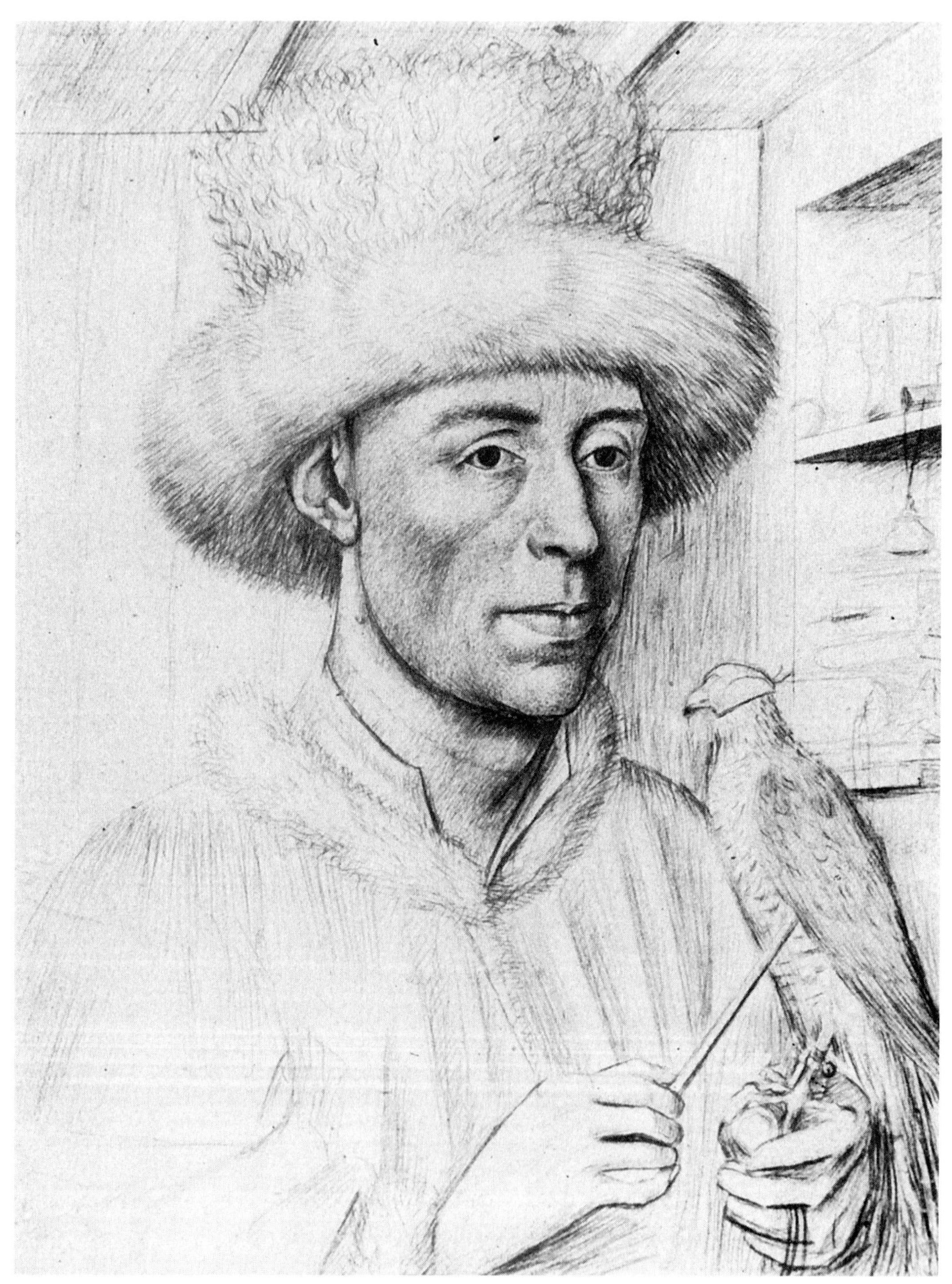

Plate 12. After Petrus Christus

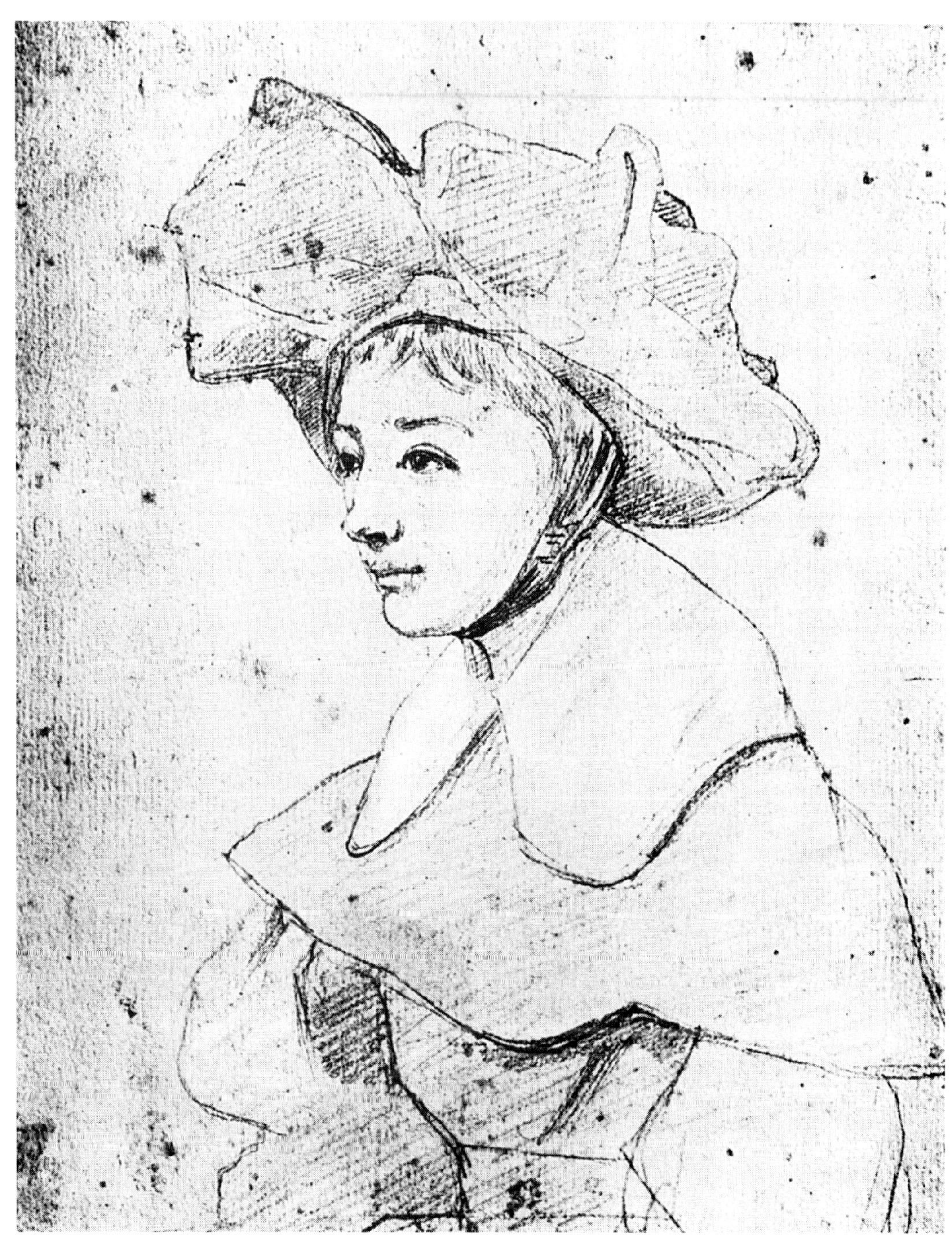

Plate 13. Jean-Baptiste-Camille Corot

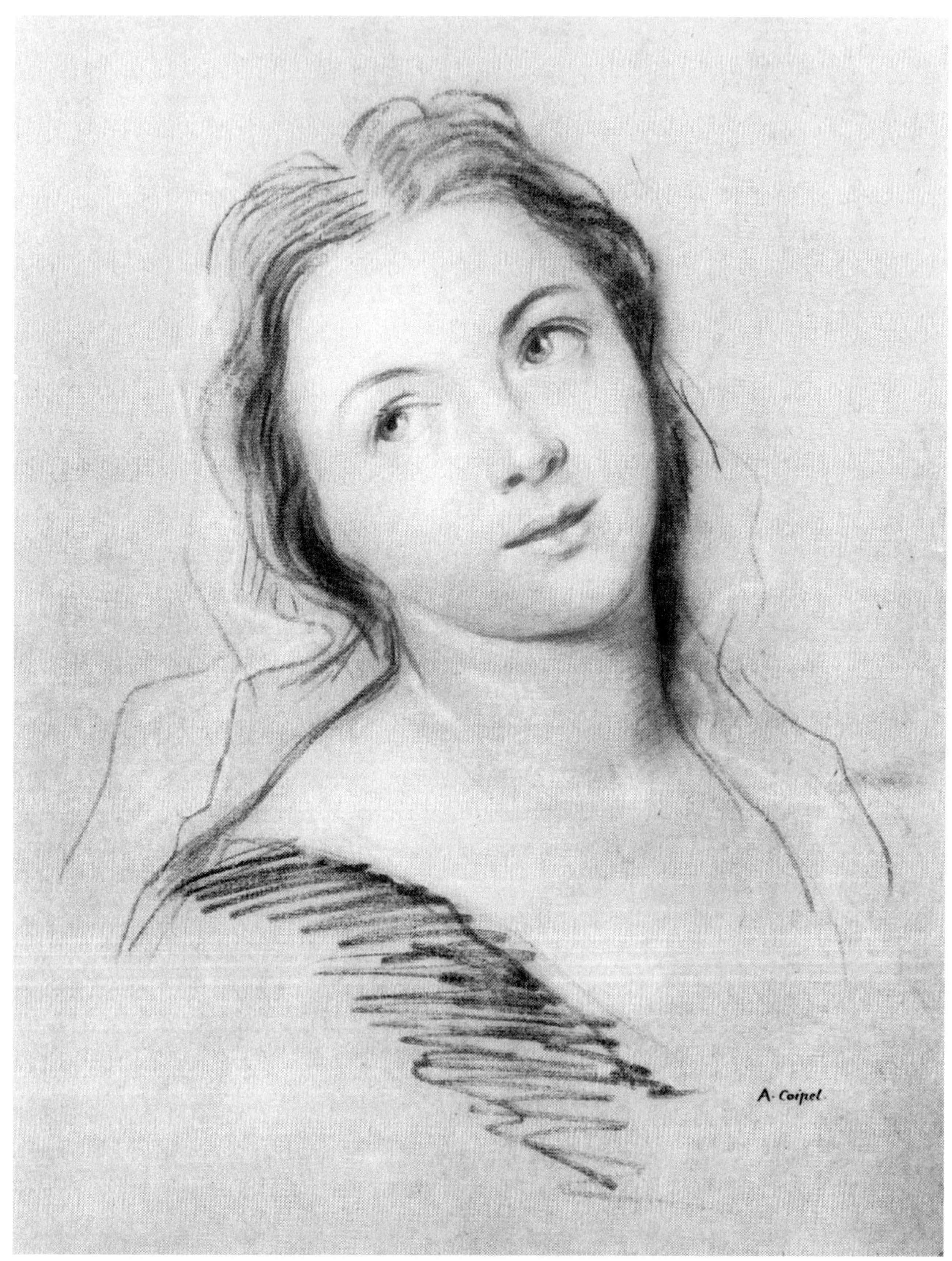

Plate 14. ANTOINE COYPEL

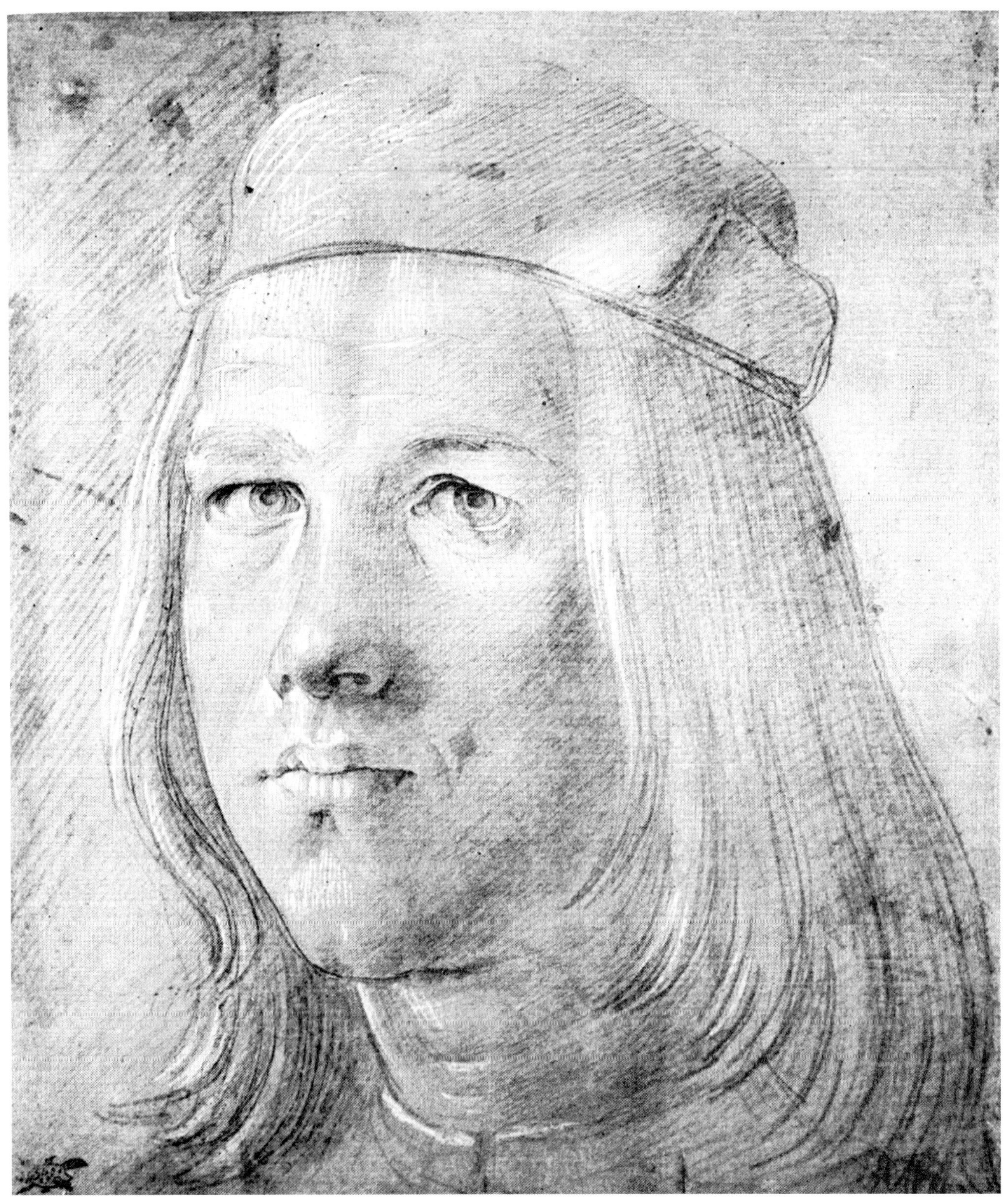

Plate 15. Lorenzo di Credi

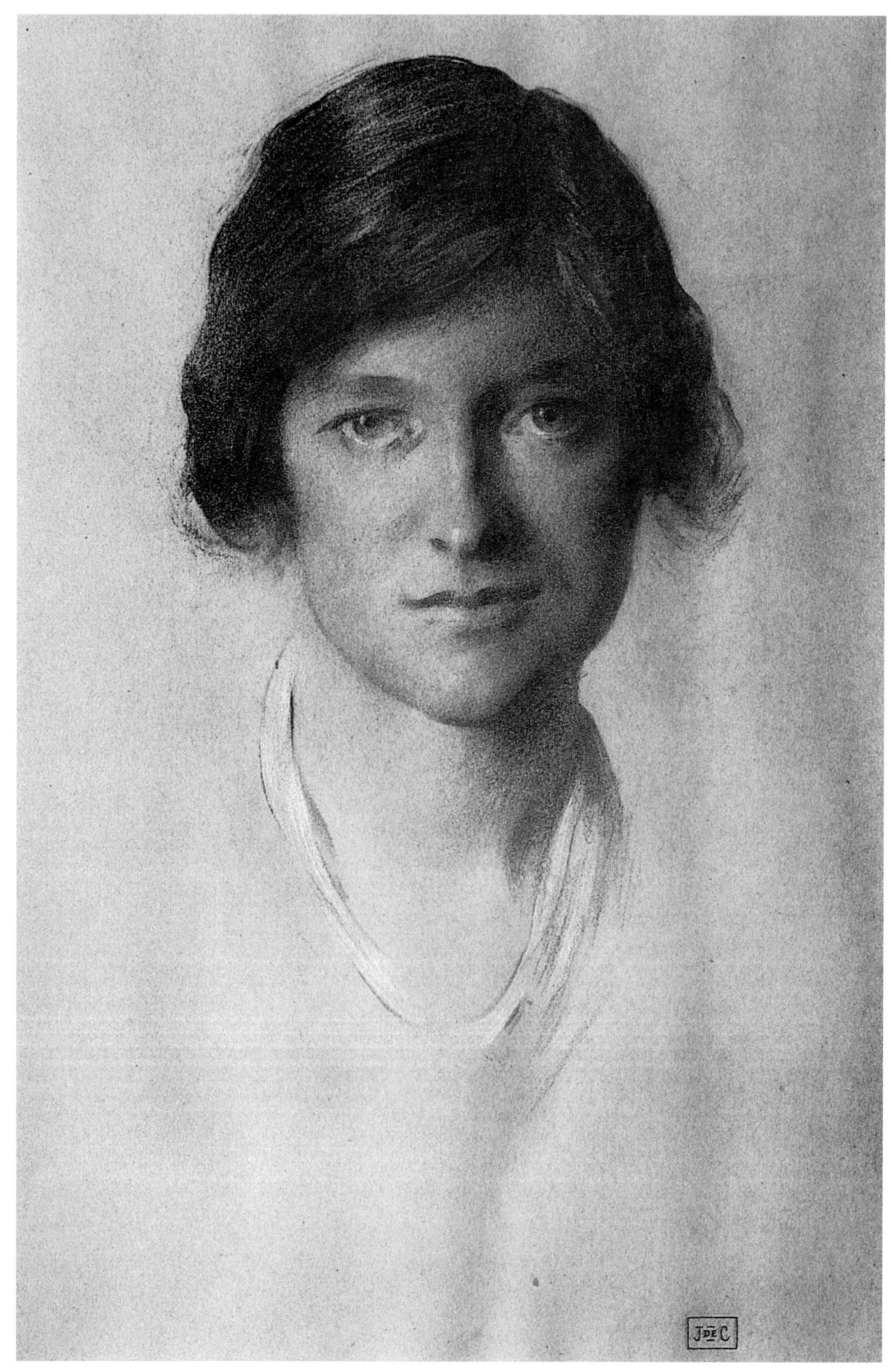

Plate 16. JOSEPH R. DE CAMP

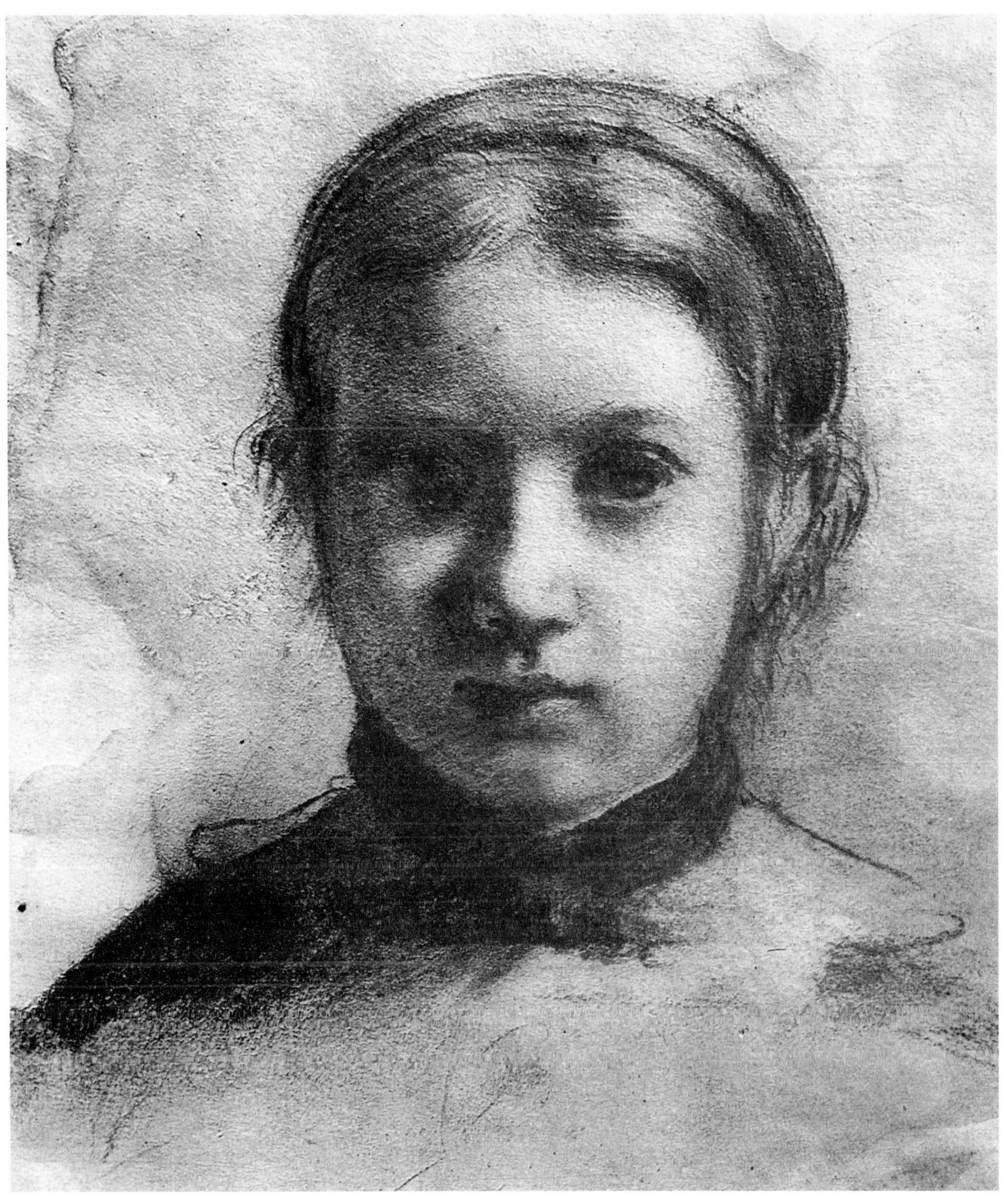

Plate 17. EDGAR DEGAS

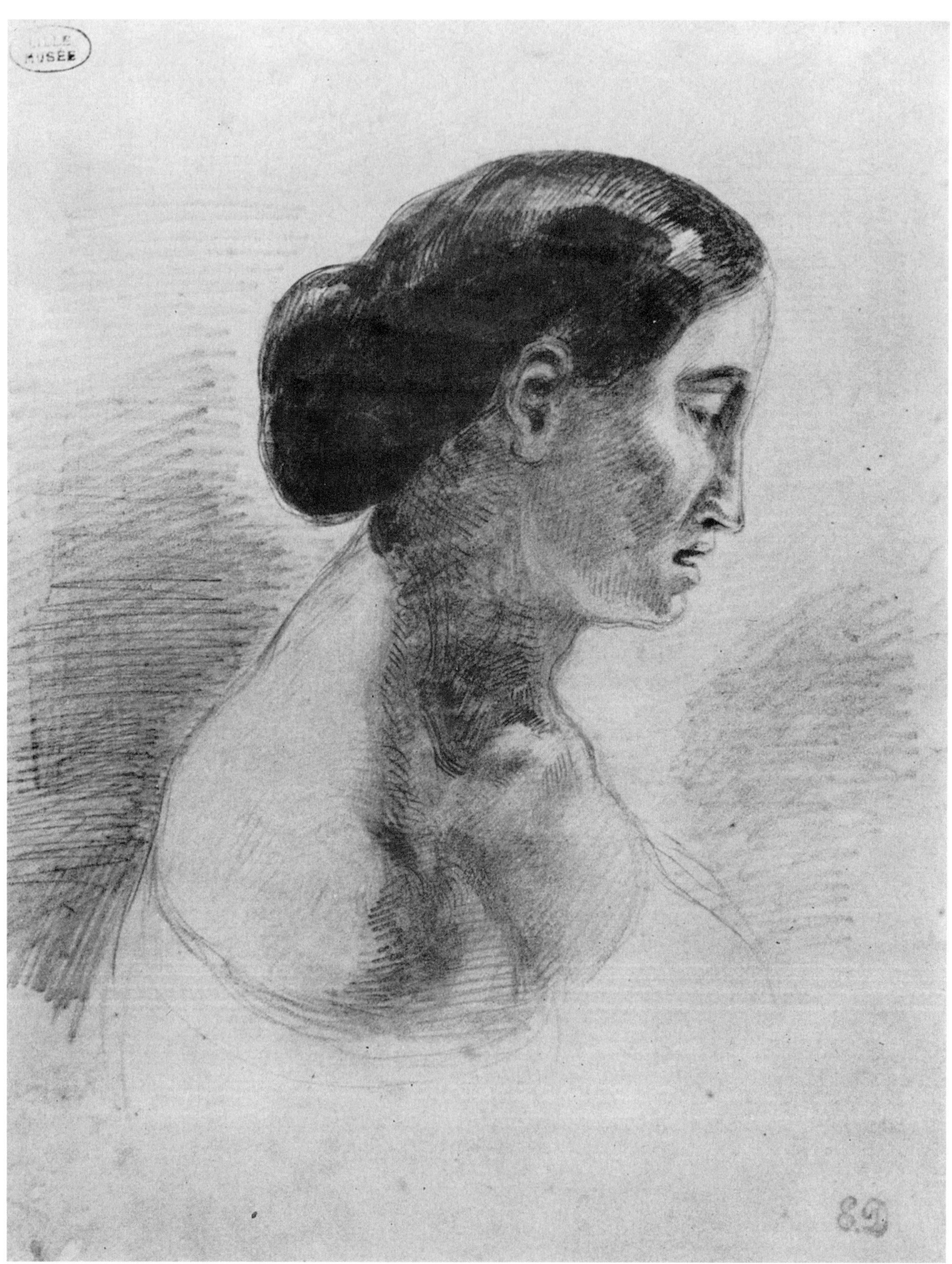

Plate 18. Eugène Delacroix

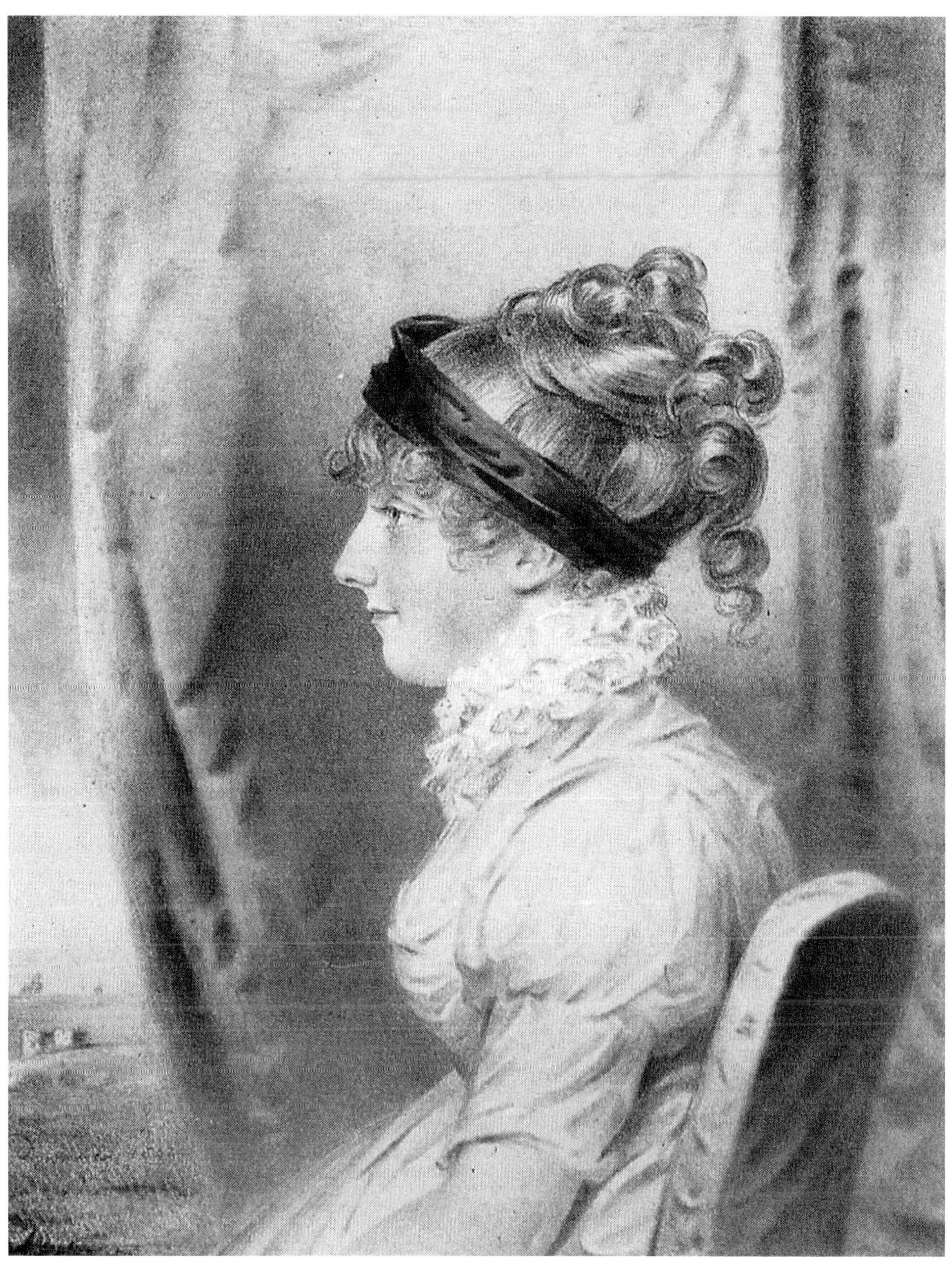

Plate 19. JOHN DOWNMAN

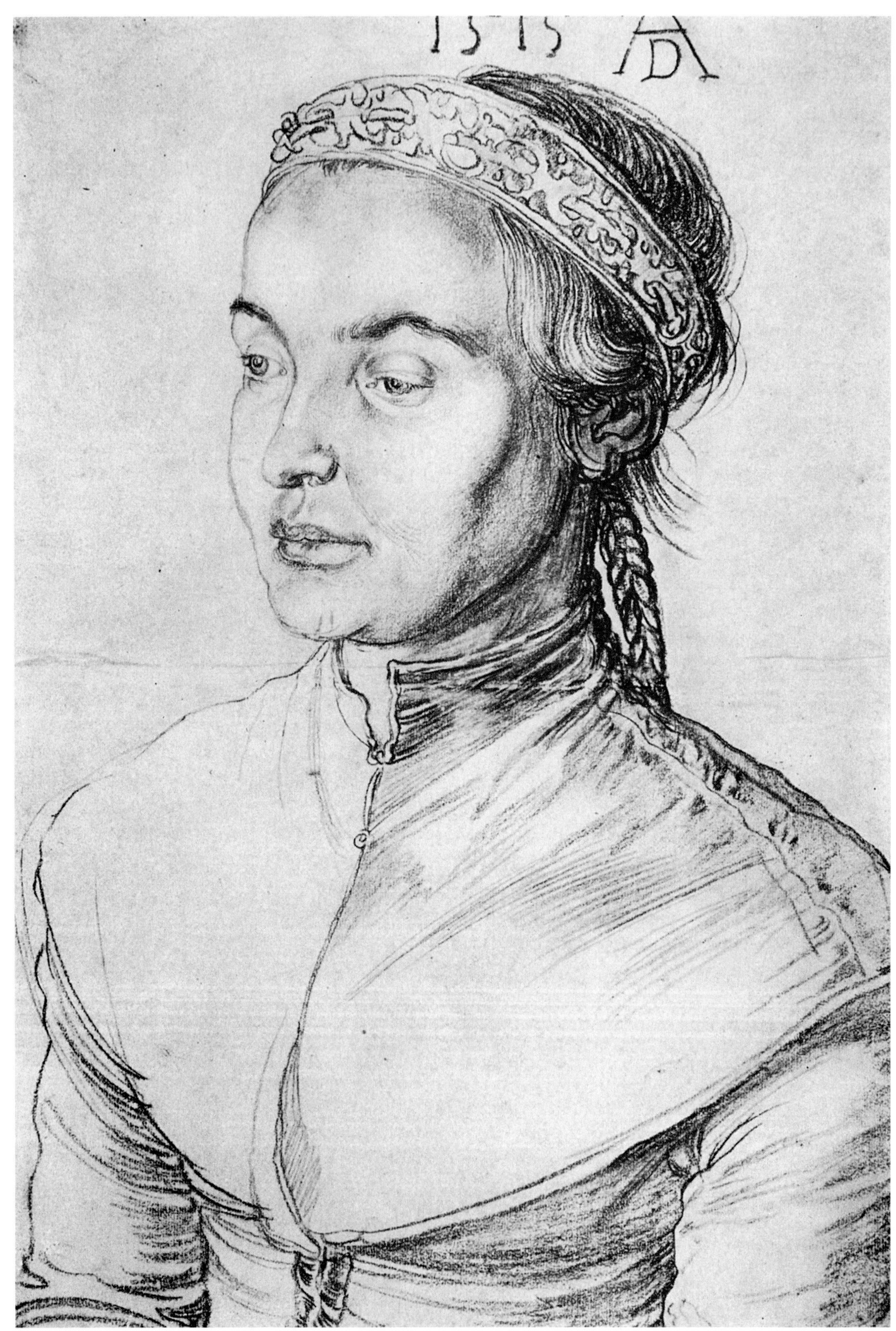

Plate 20. ALBRECHT DÜRER

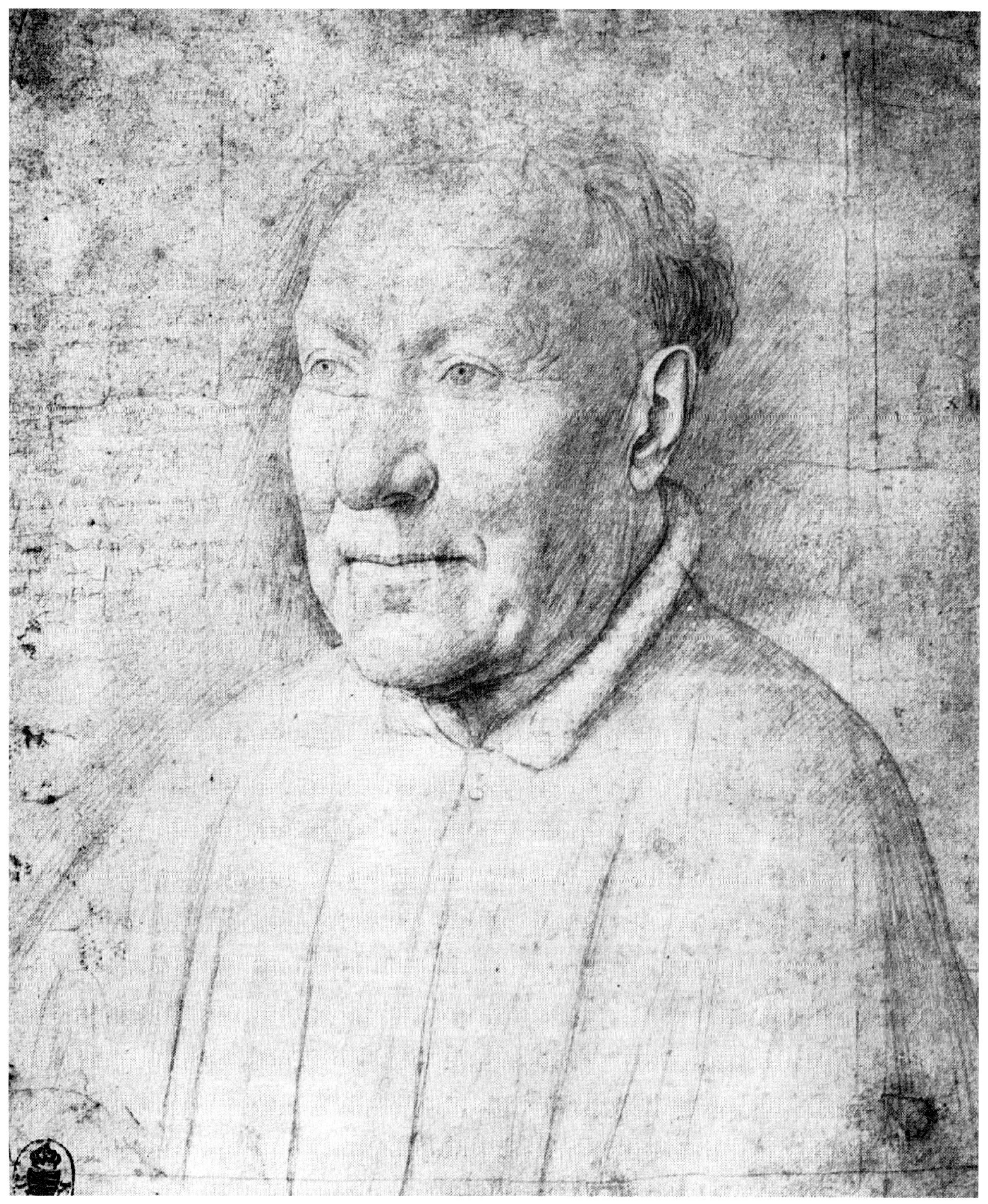

Plate 21. Jan van Eyck

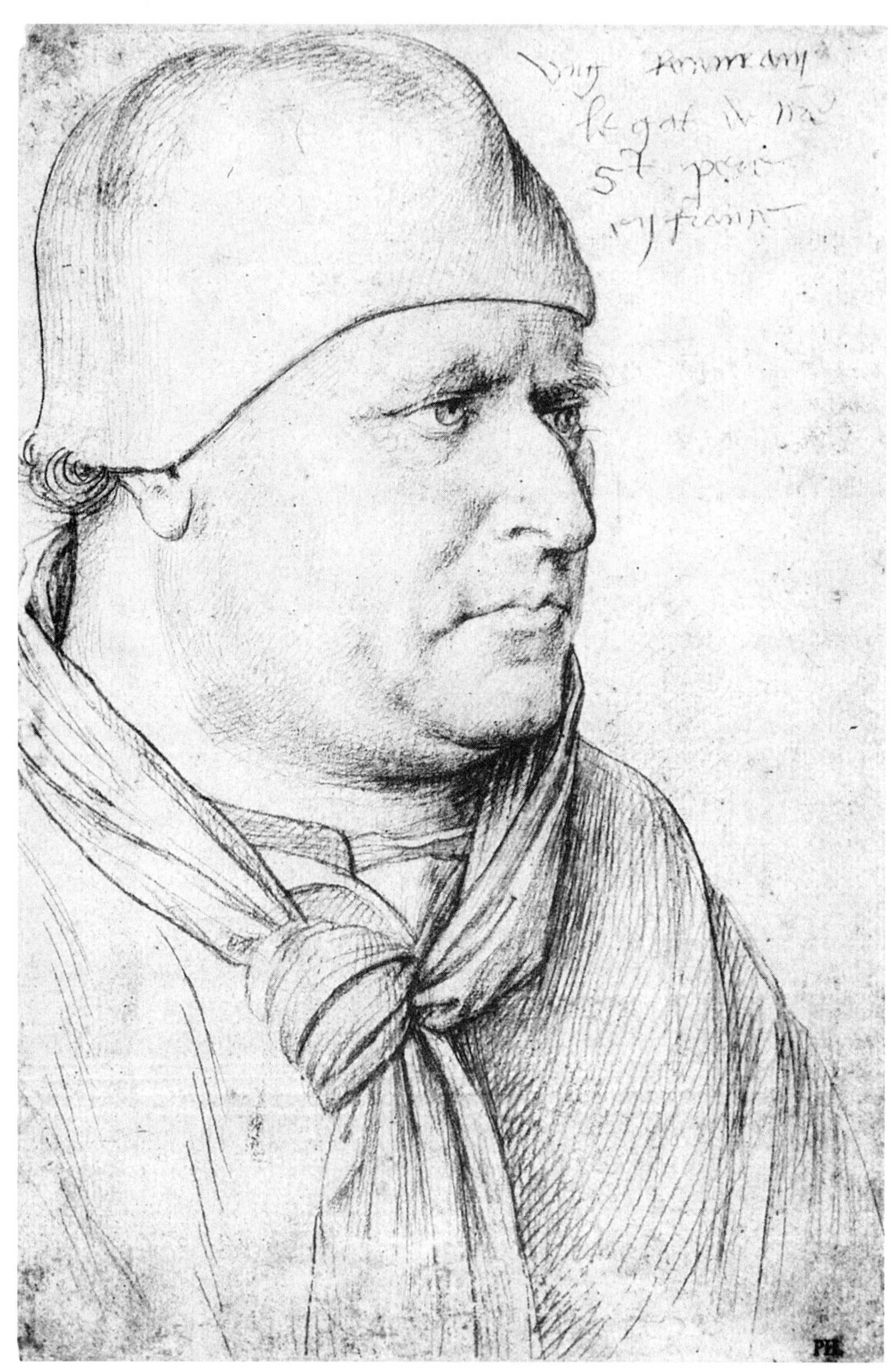

Plate 22. JEAN FOUQUET

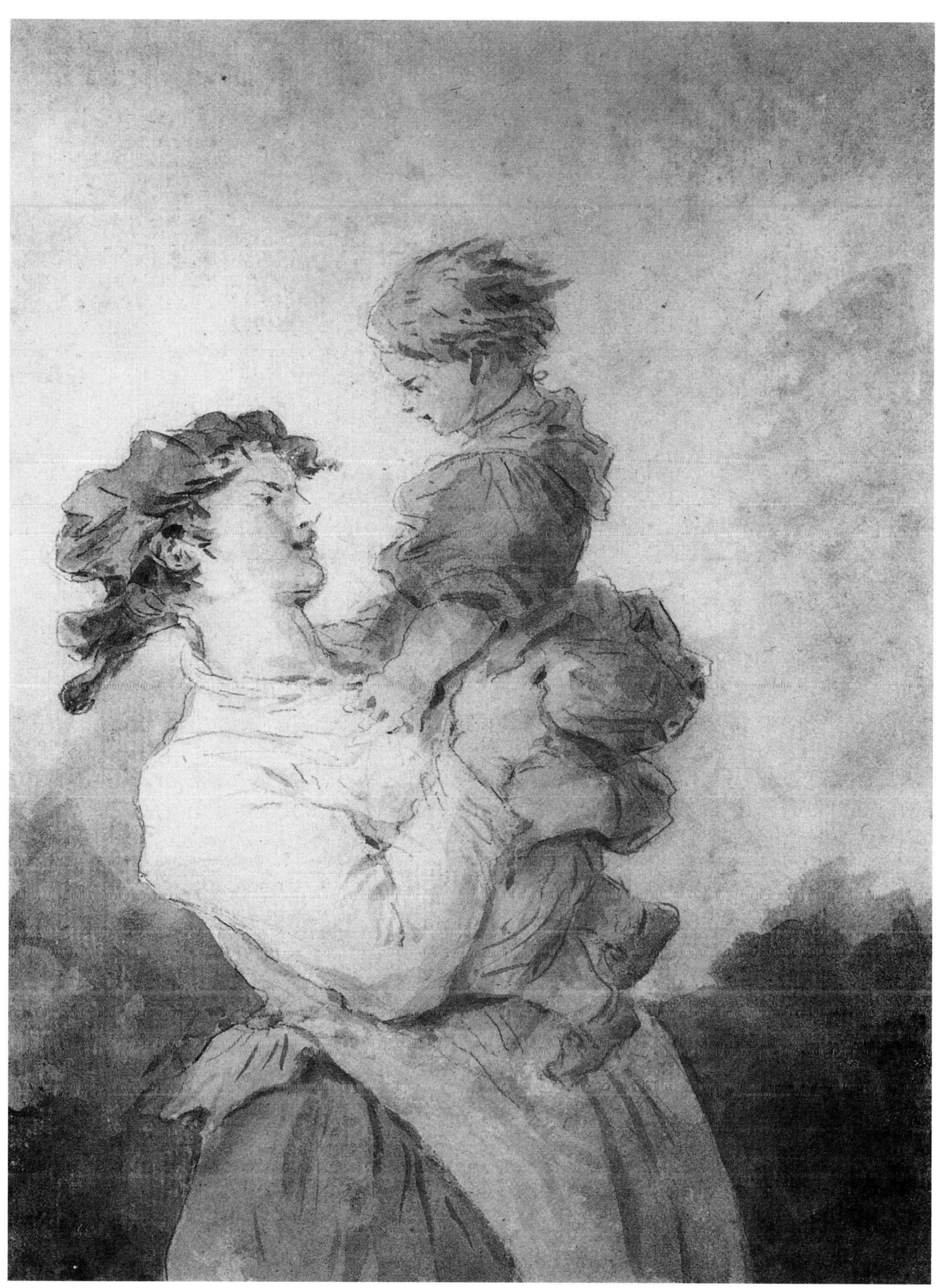

Plate 23. JEAN-HONORÉ FRAGONARD

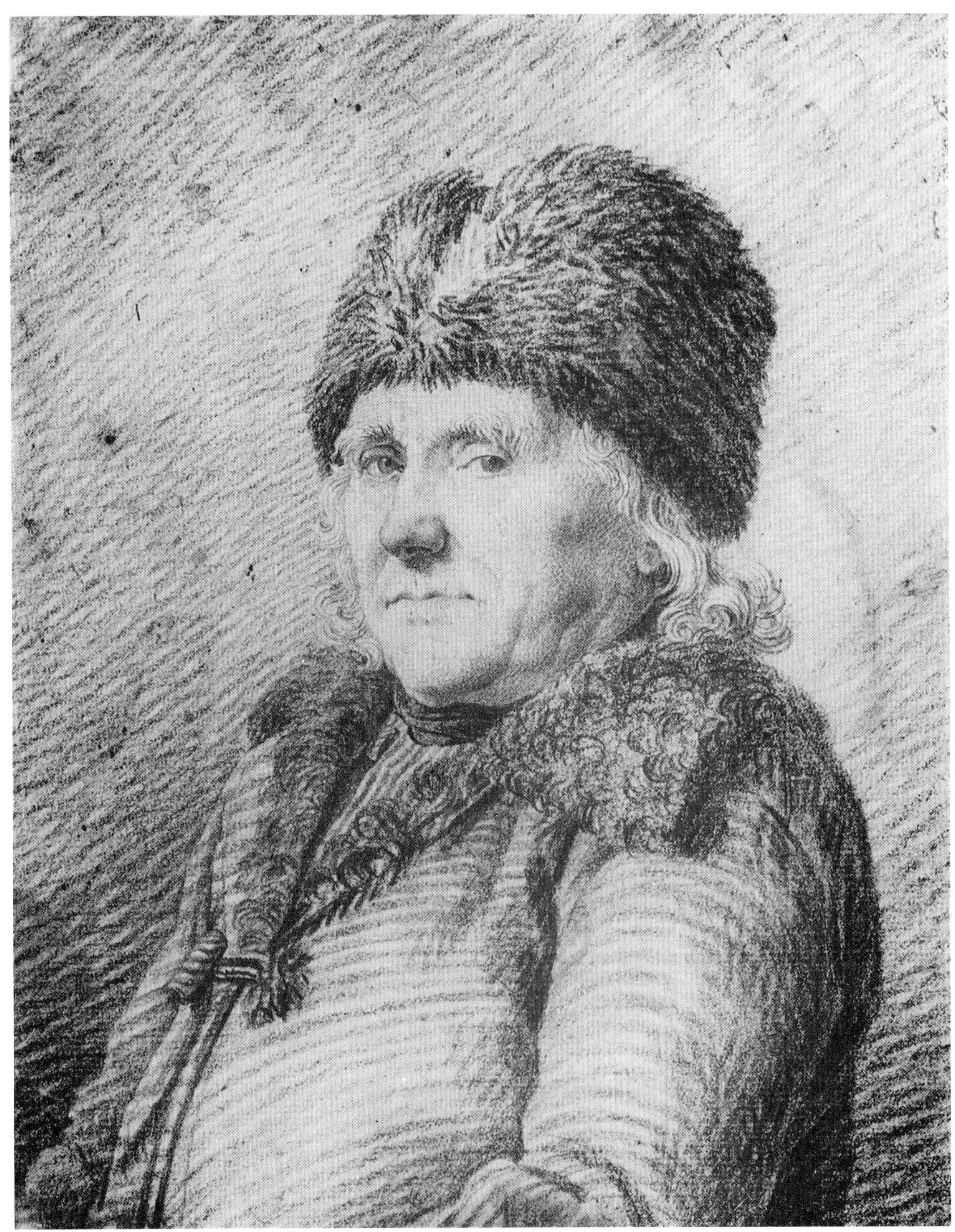

Plate 24. CASPAR DAVID FRIEDRICH

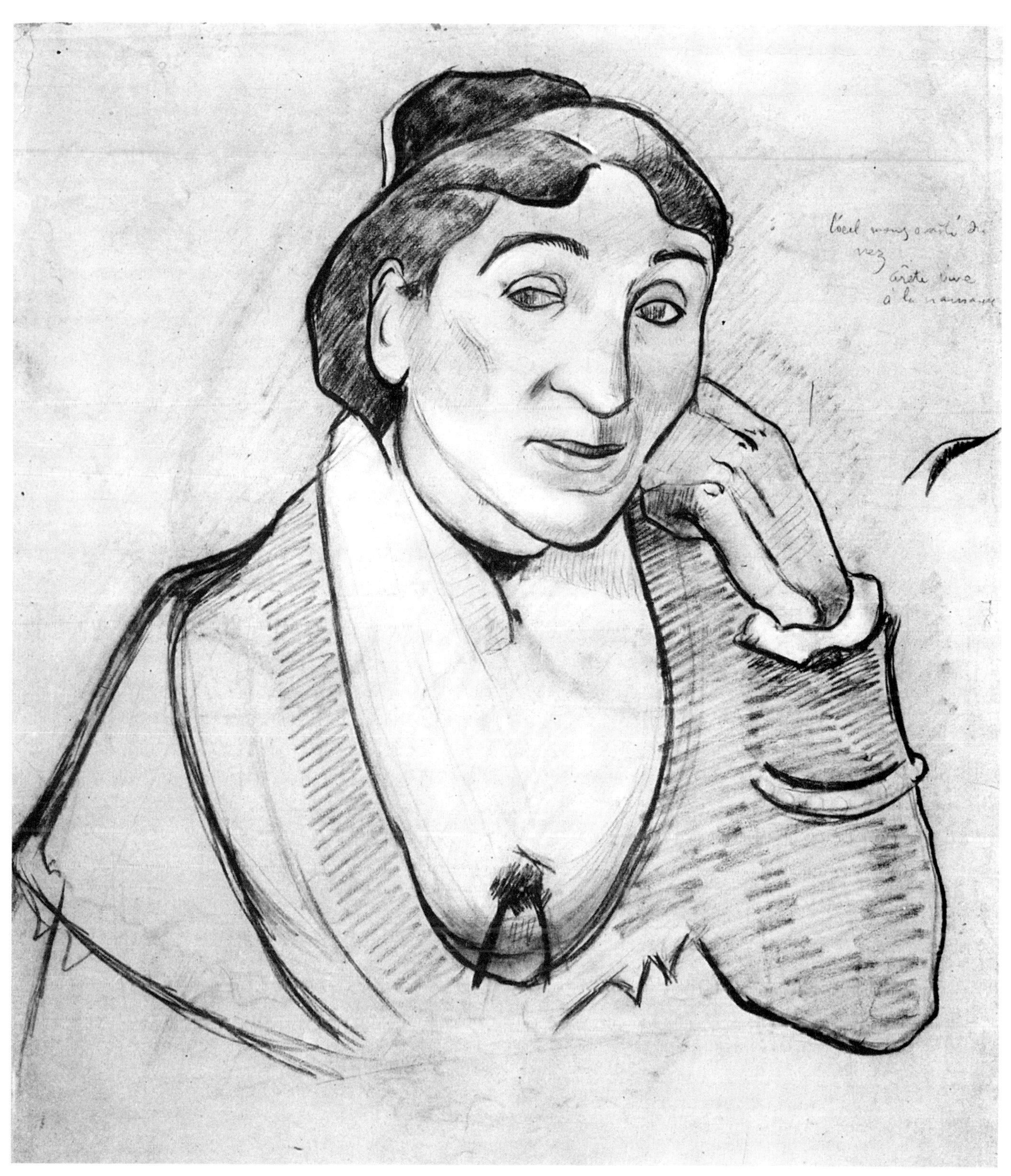

Plate 25. Paul Gauguin

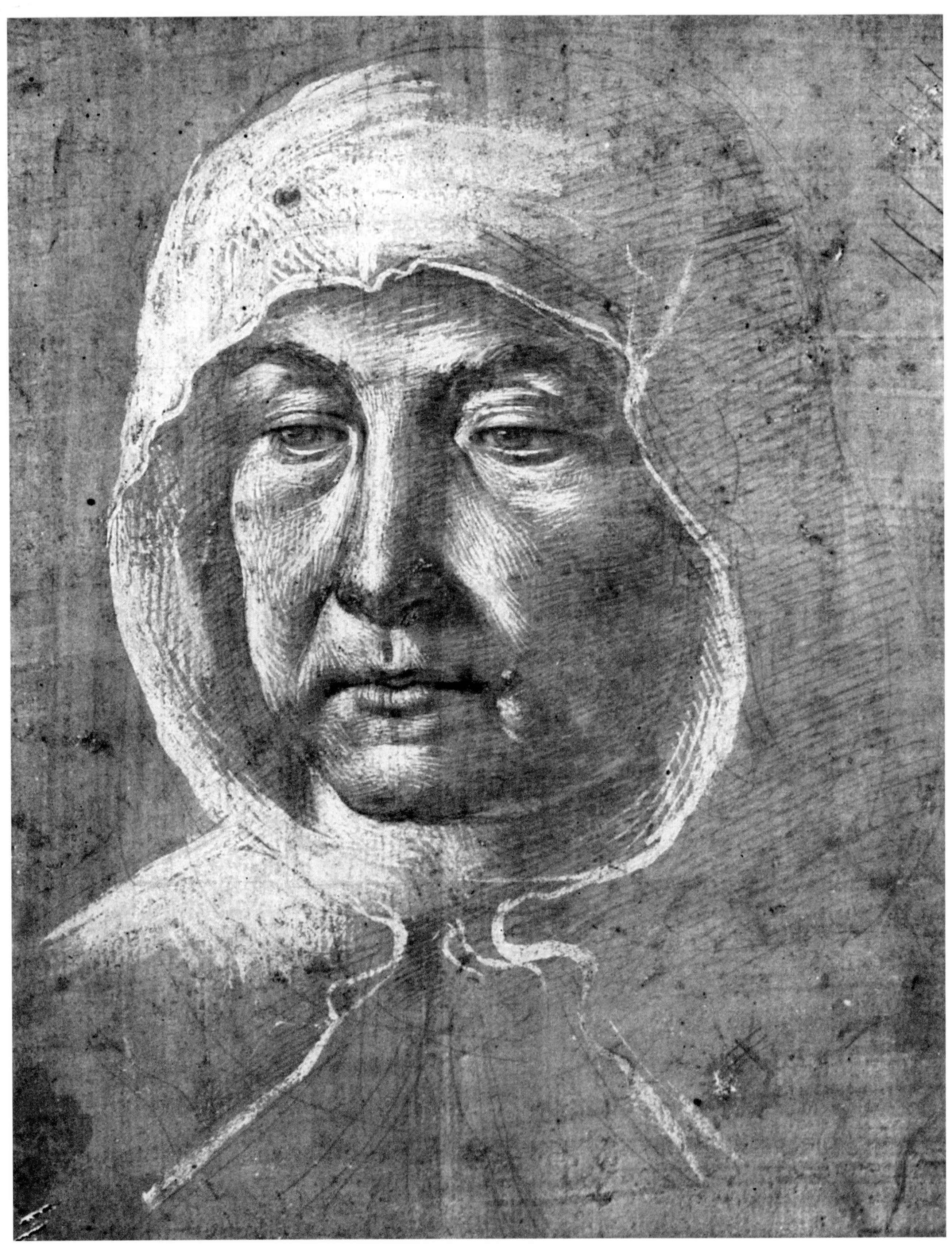

Plate 26. GHIRLANDAIO (DOMENICO DI TOMMASO BIGORDI)

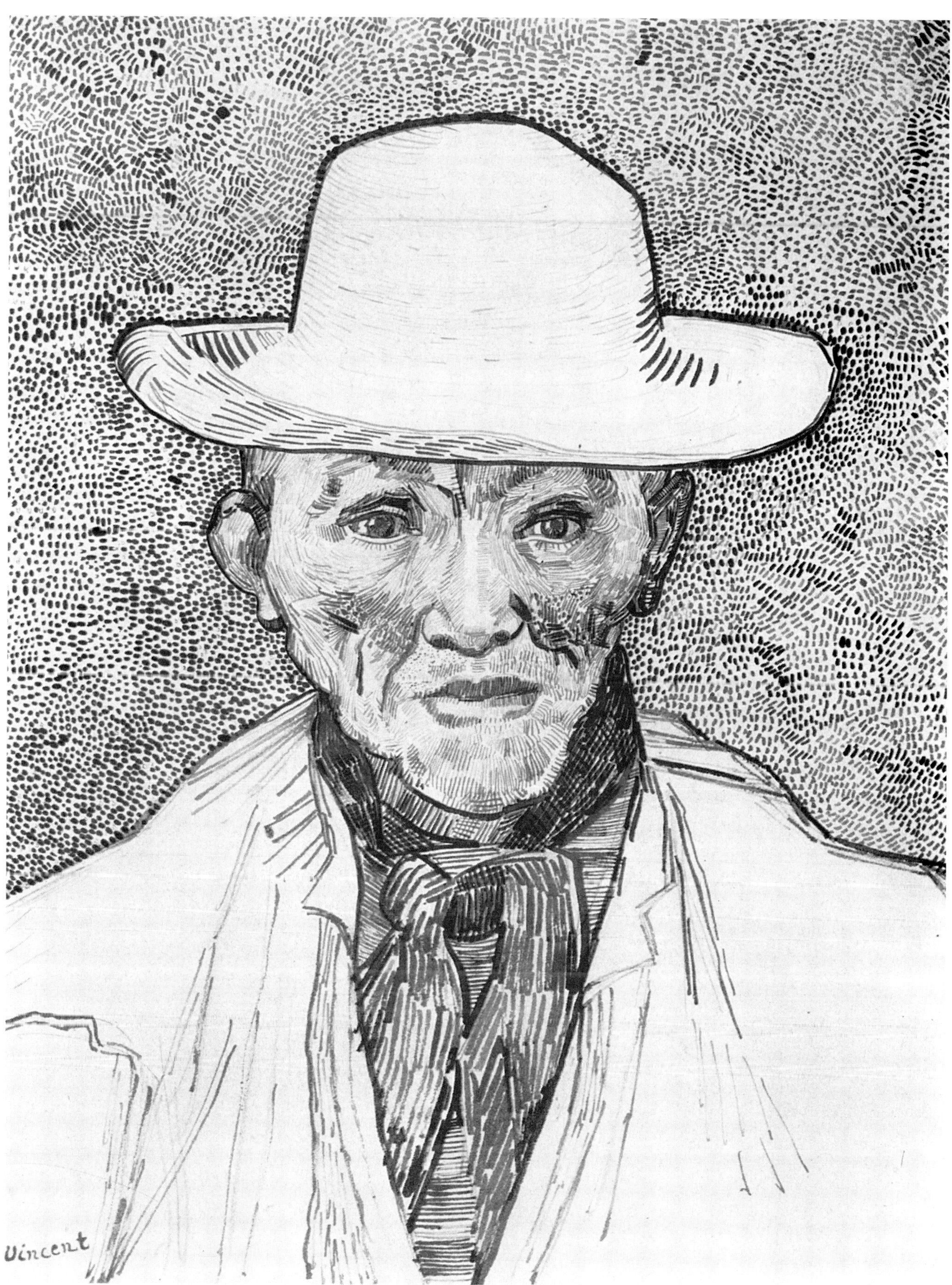

Plate 27. Vincent van Gogh

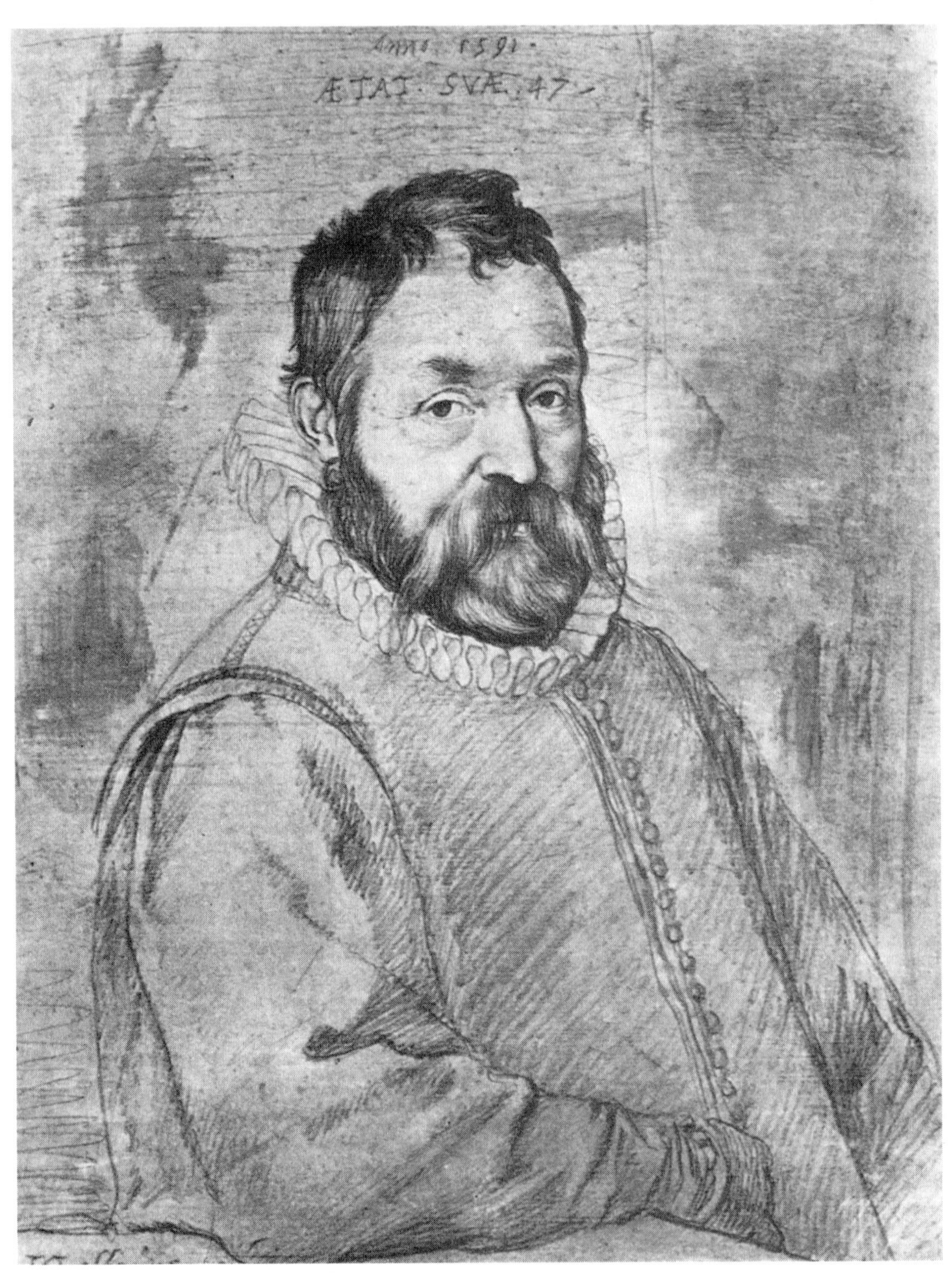

Plate 28. HENDRICK GOLTZIUS

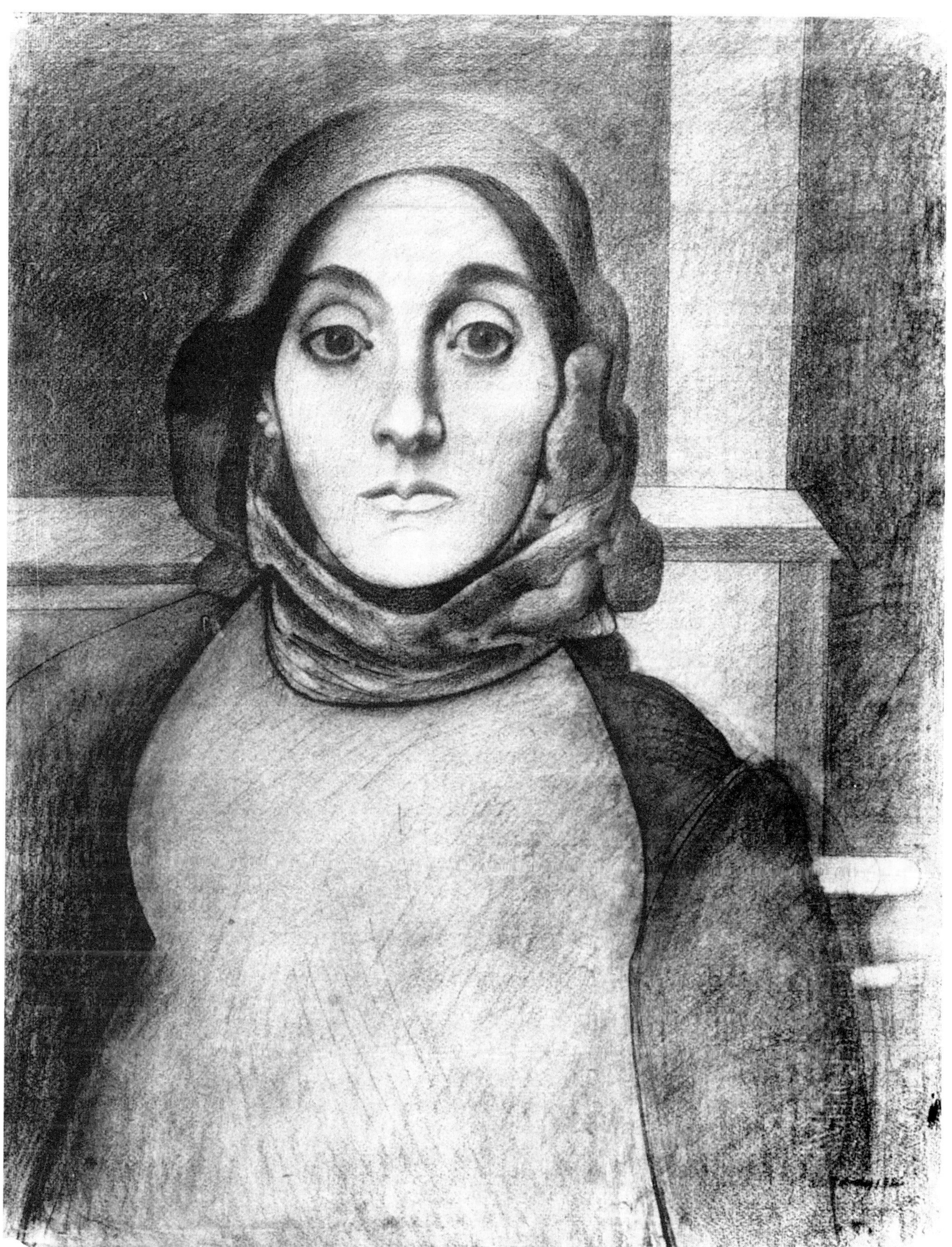

Plate 29. ARSHILE GORKY

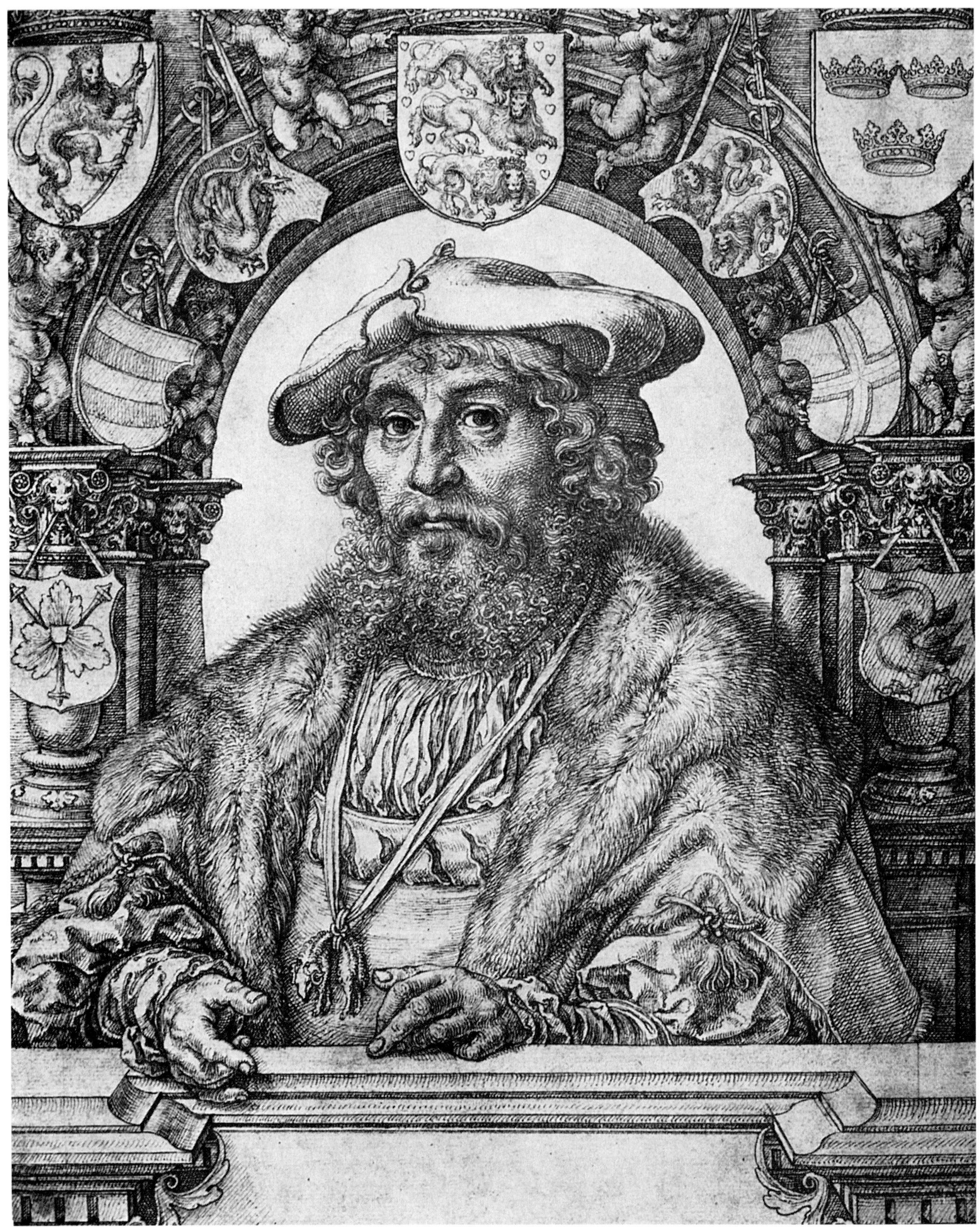

Plate 30. JAN GOSSAERT VAN MABUSE

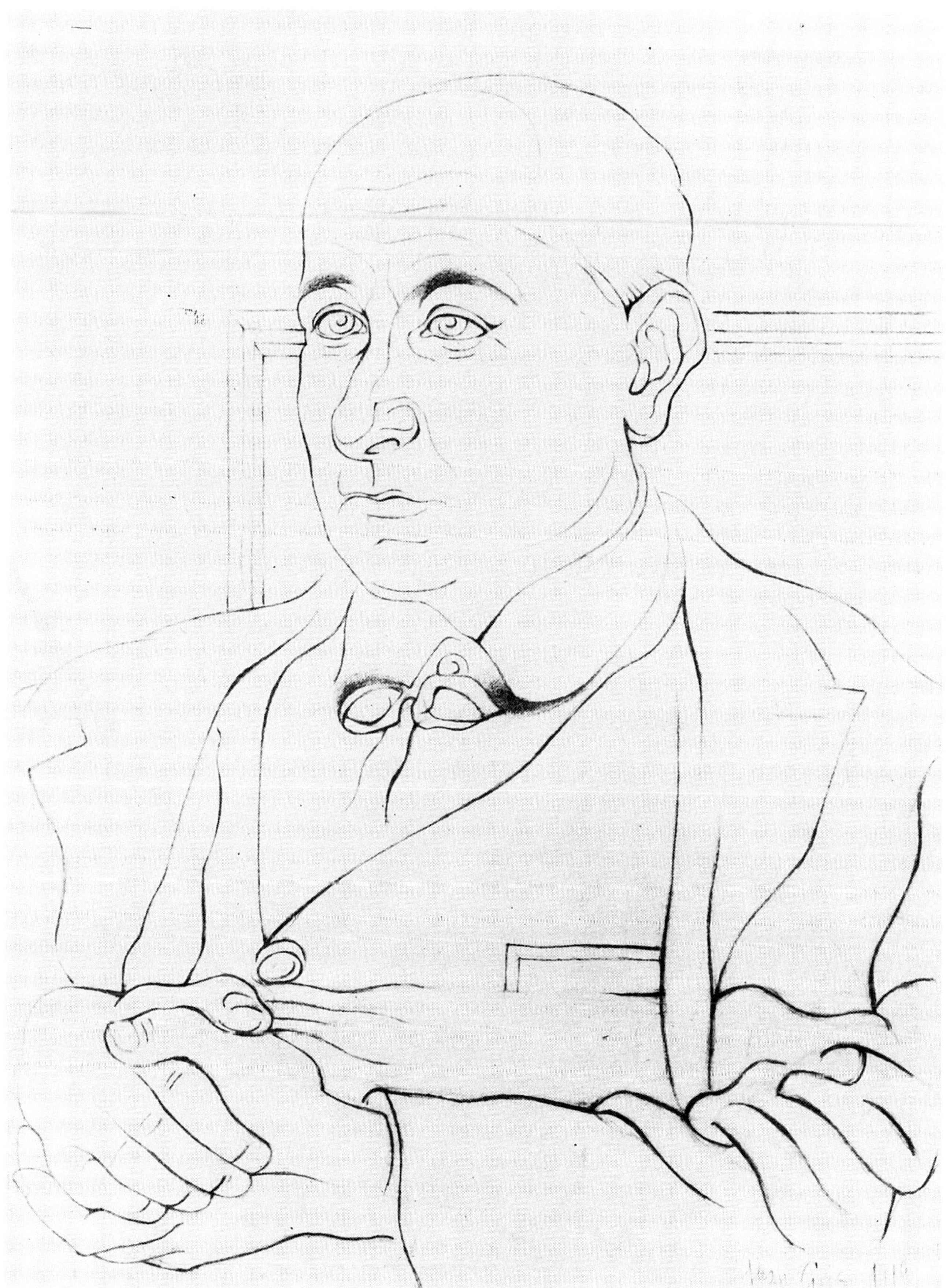

Plate 31. JUAN GRIS

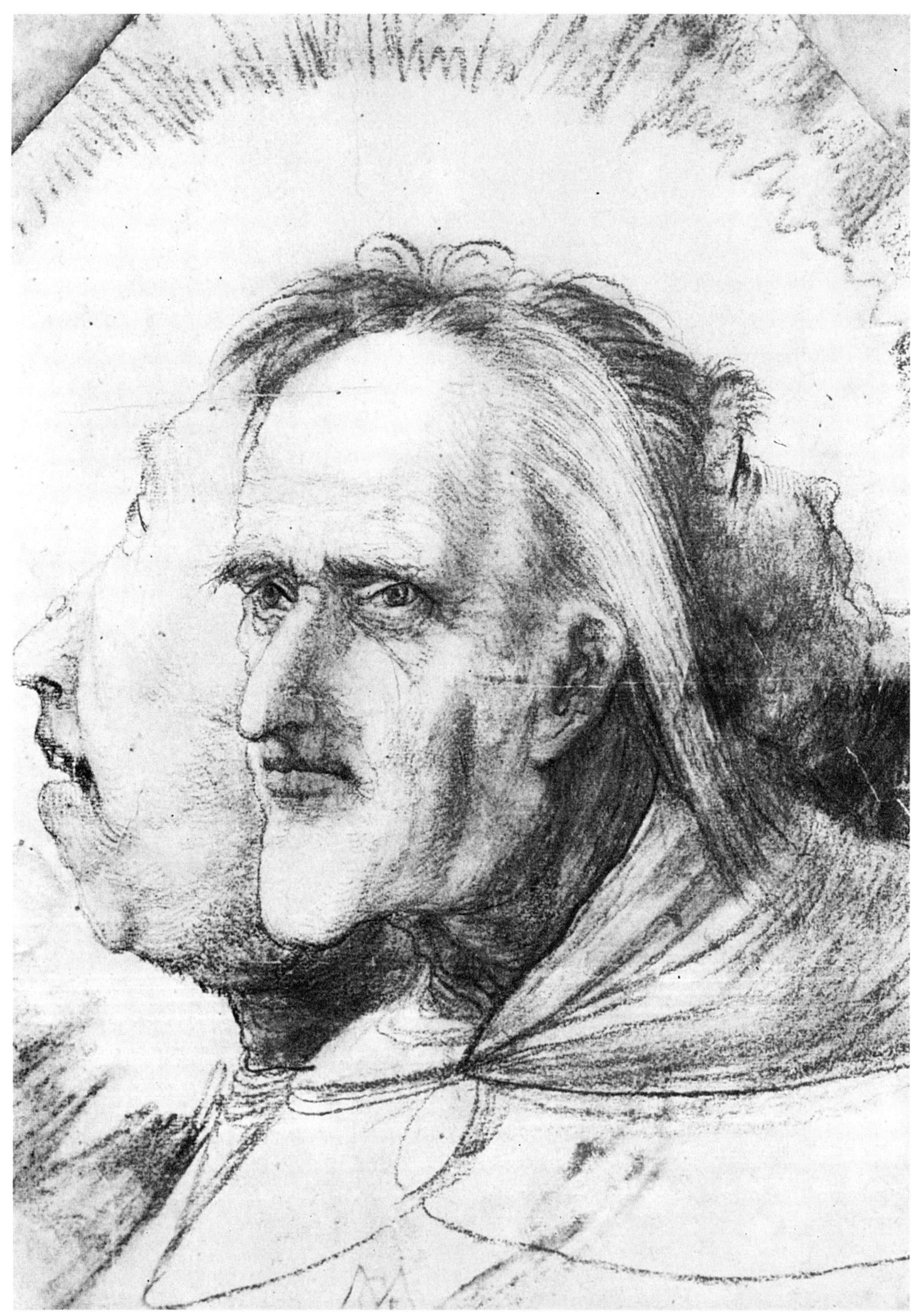

Plate 32. Matthias Grünewald

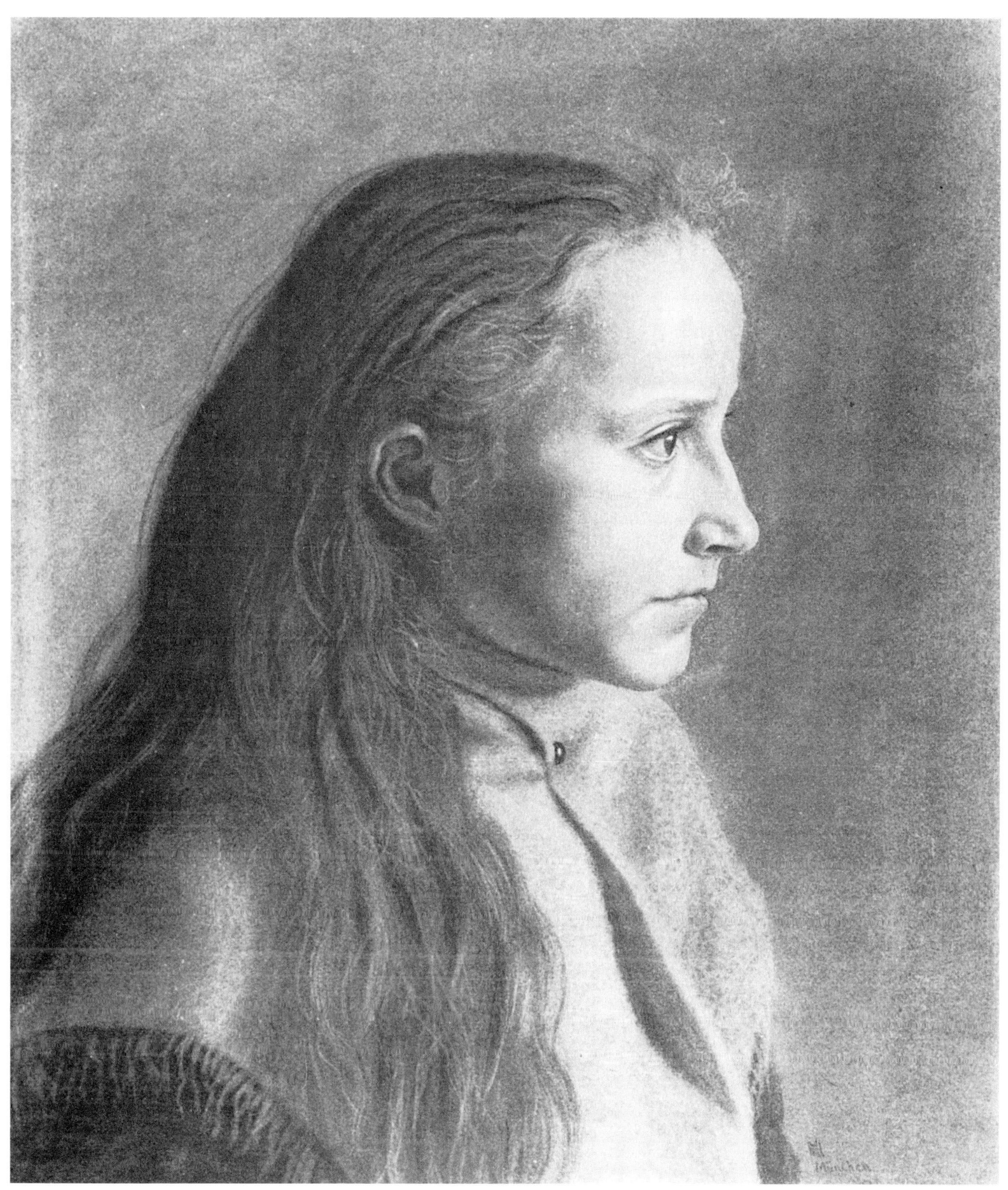

Plate 33. William M. Harnett

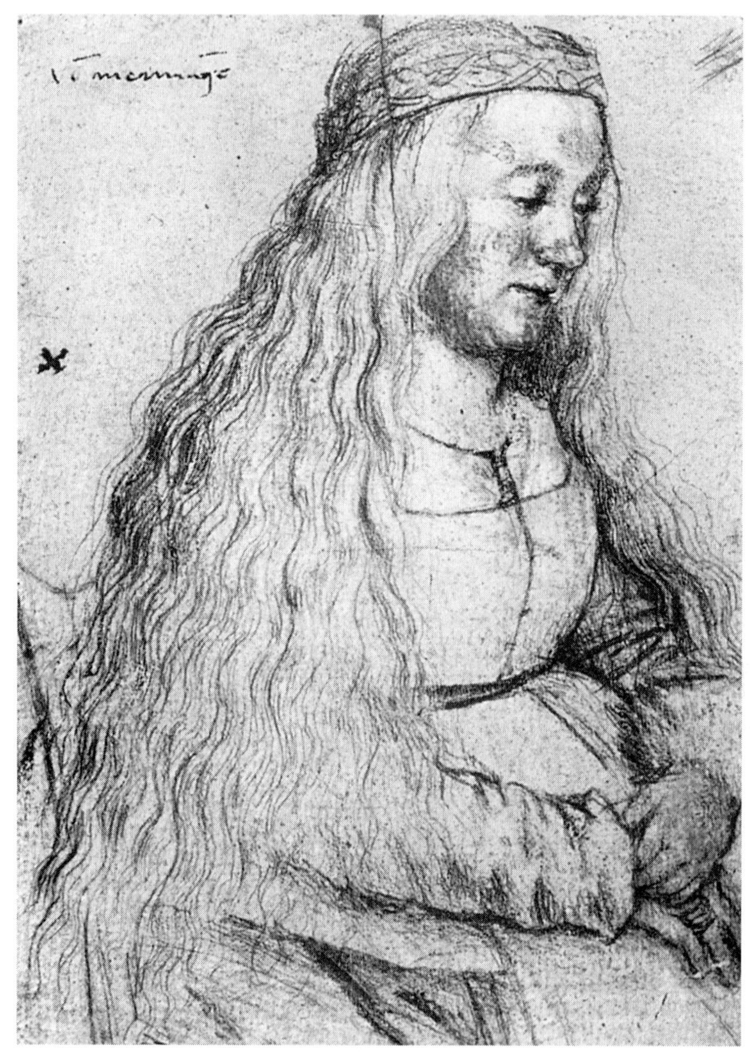

Plate 34. HANS HOLBEIN THE ELDER

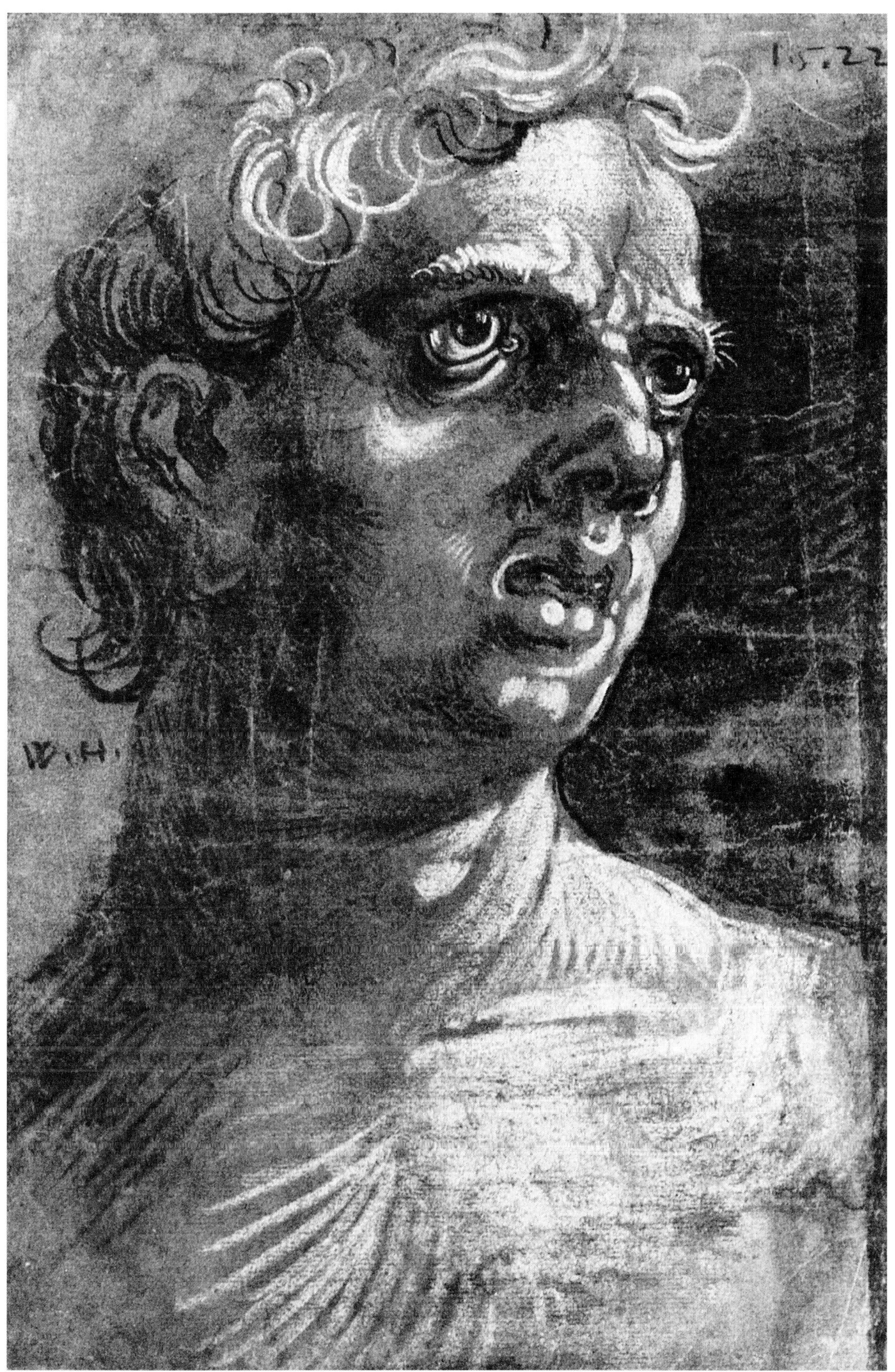

Plate 35. WOLF HUBER

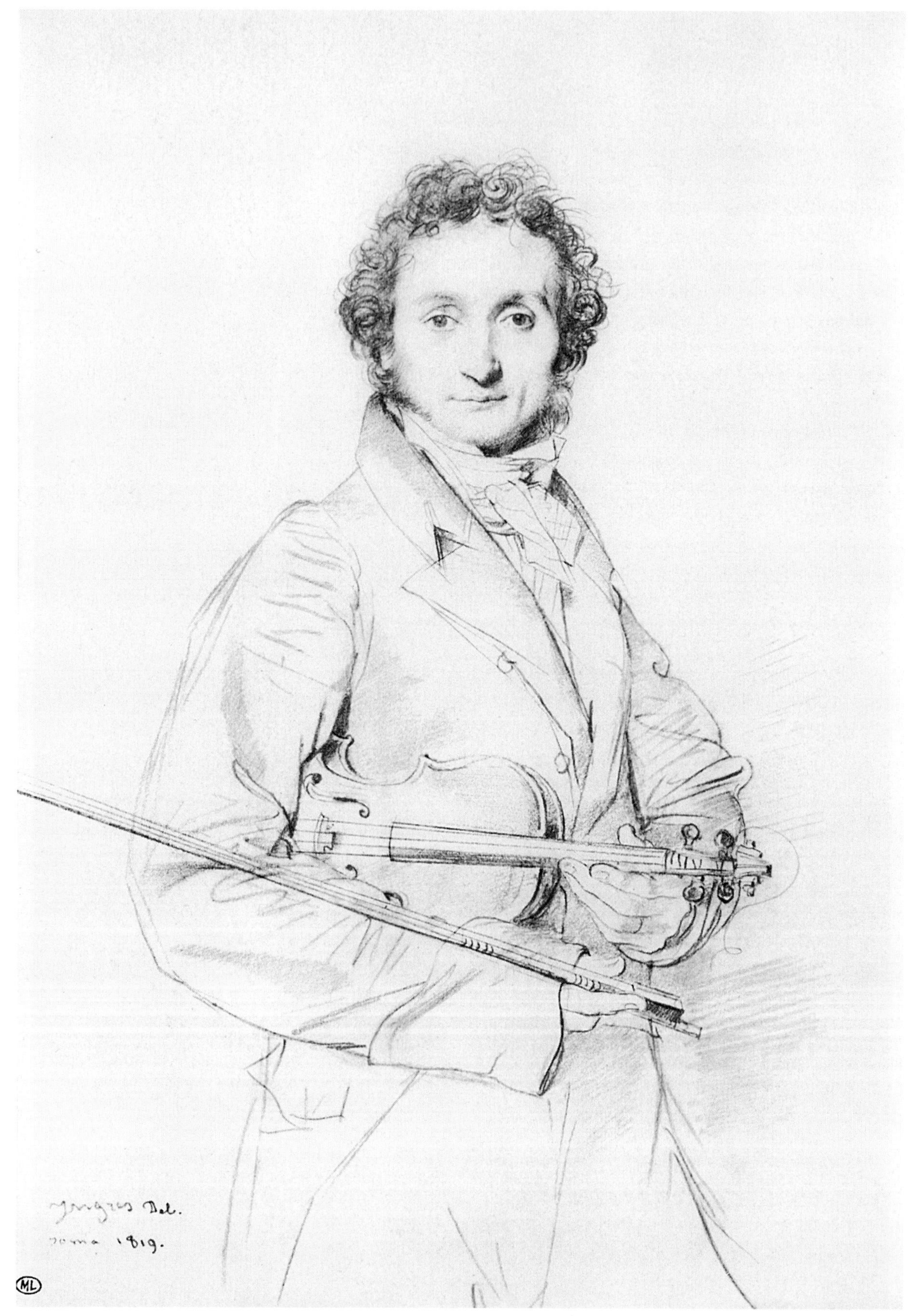

Plate 36. Jean-Auguste-Dominique Ingres

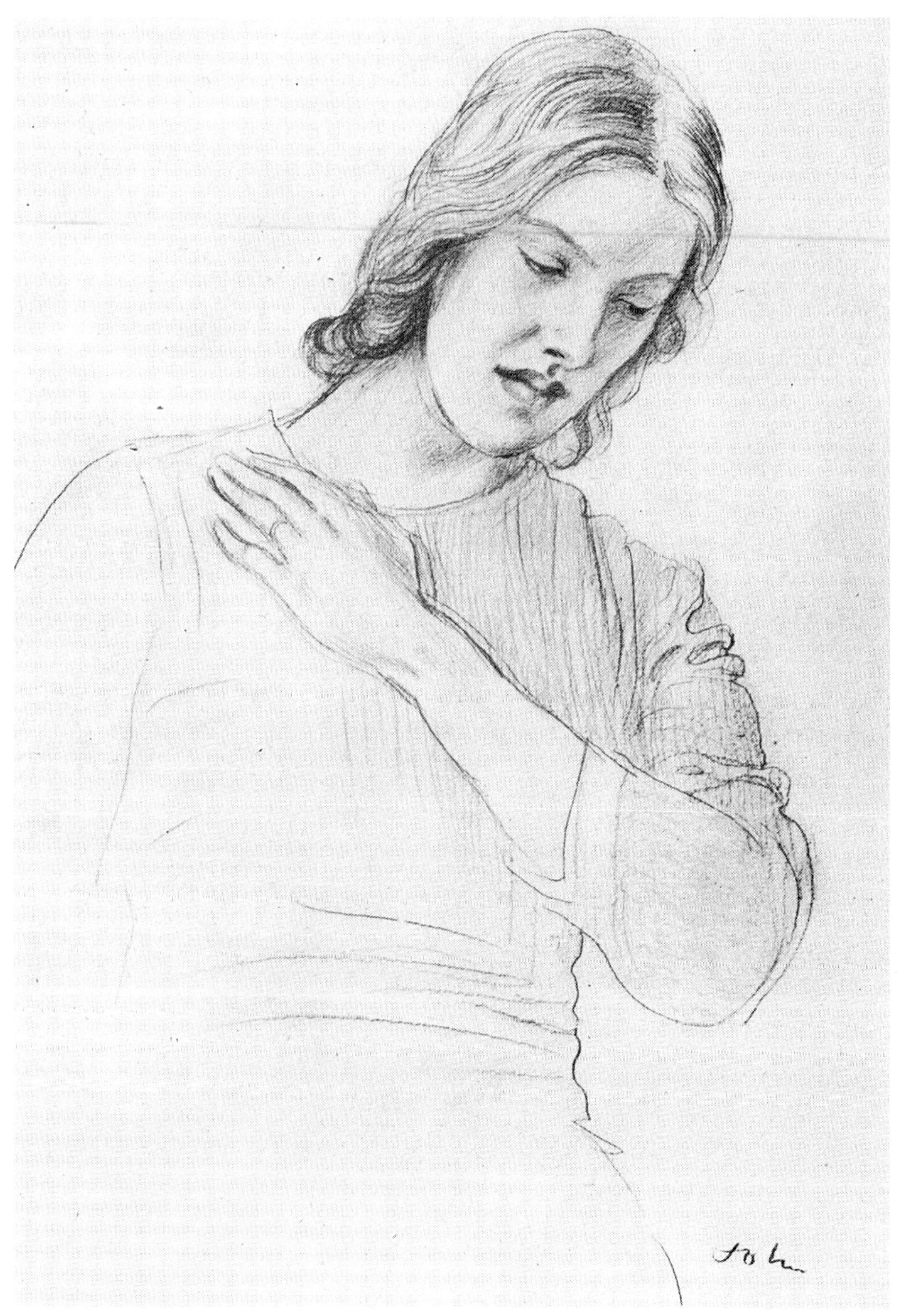

Plate 37. Augustus John

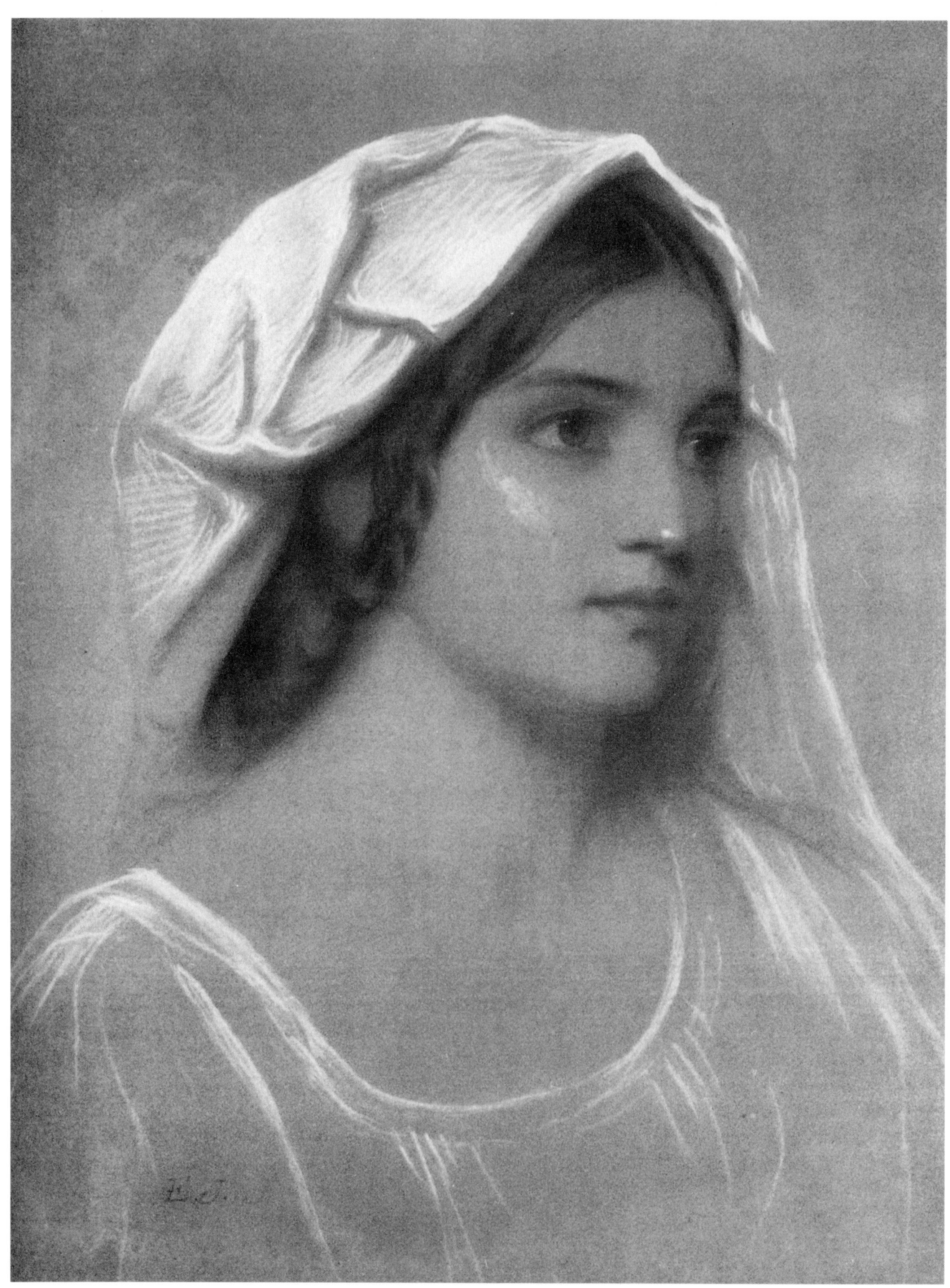

Plate 38. Eastman Johnson

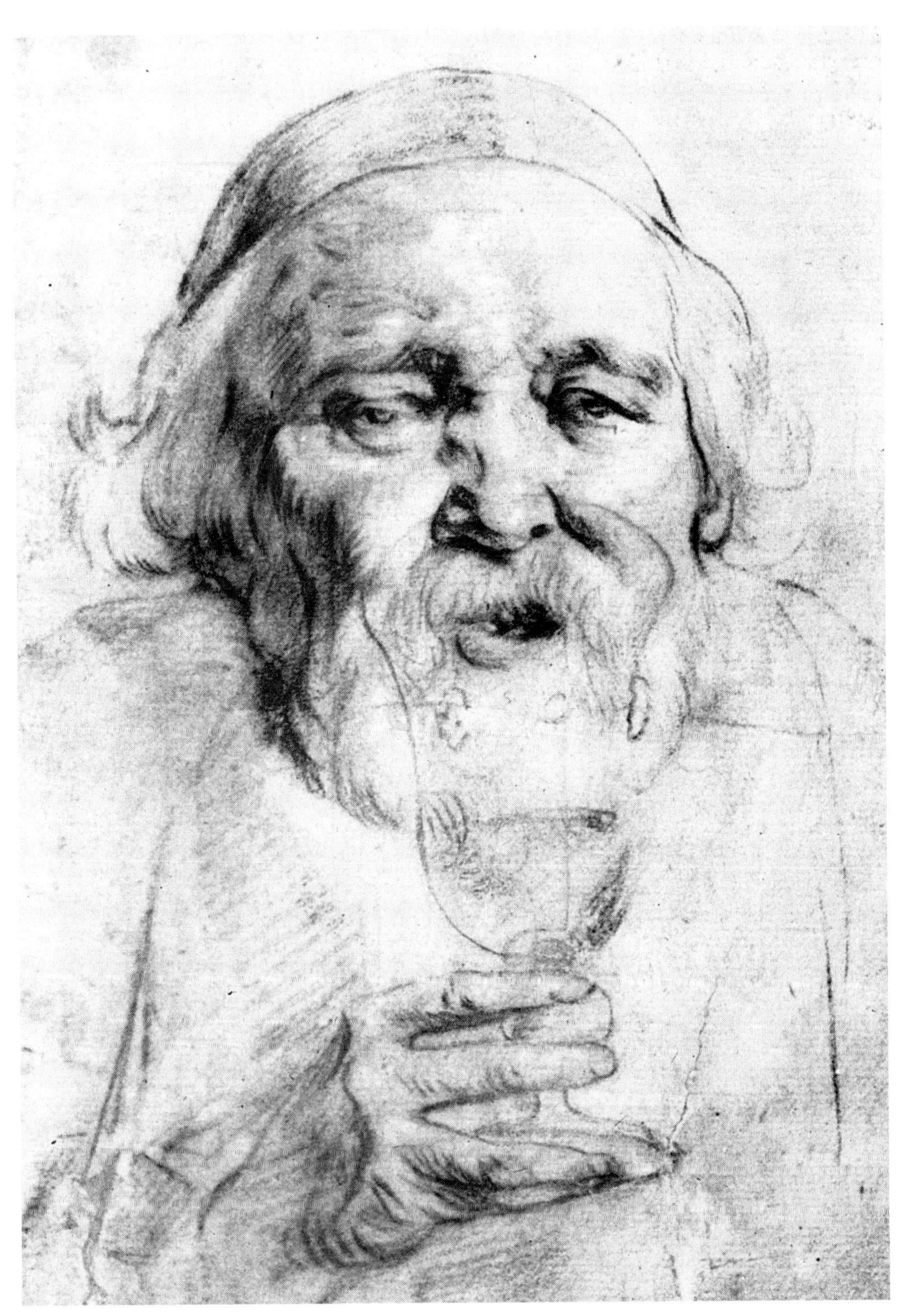

Plate 39. Jacob Jordaens

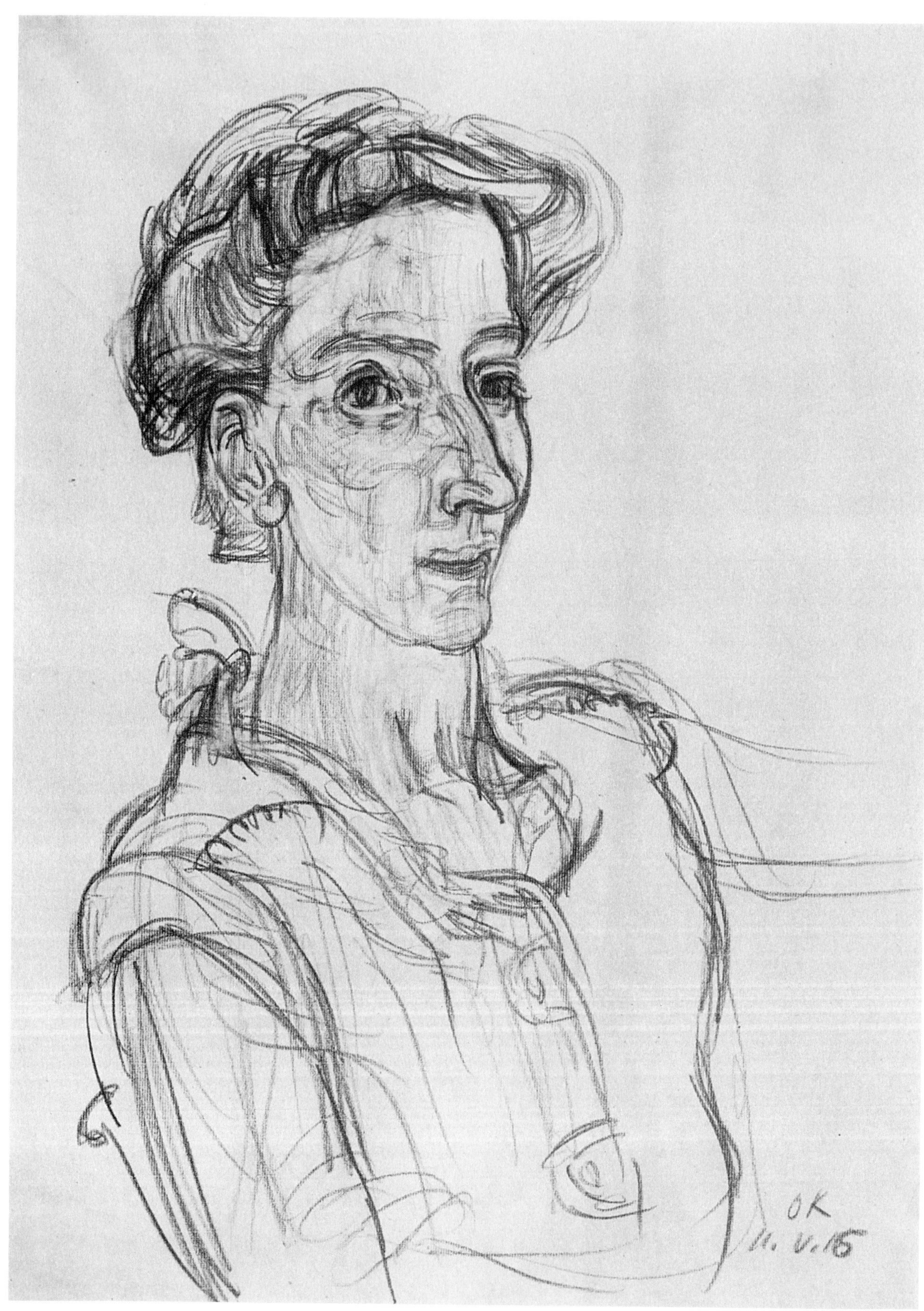

Plate 40. OSCAR KOKOSCHKA

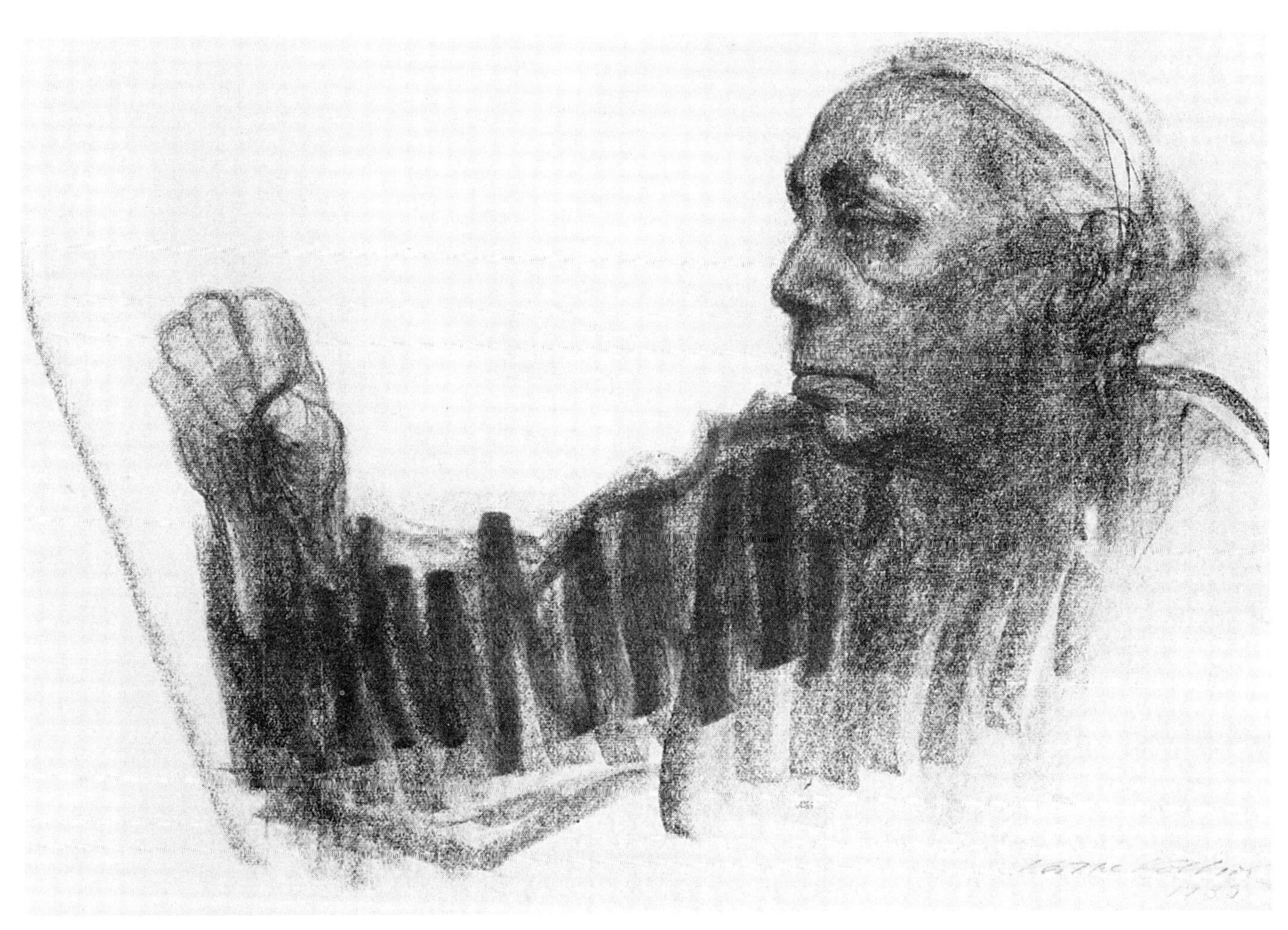

Plate 41. KAETHE KOLLWITZ

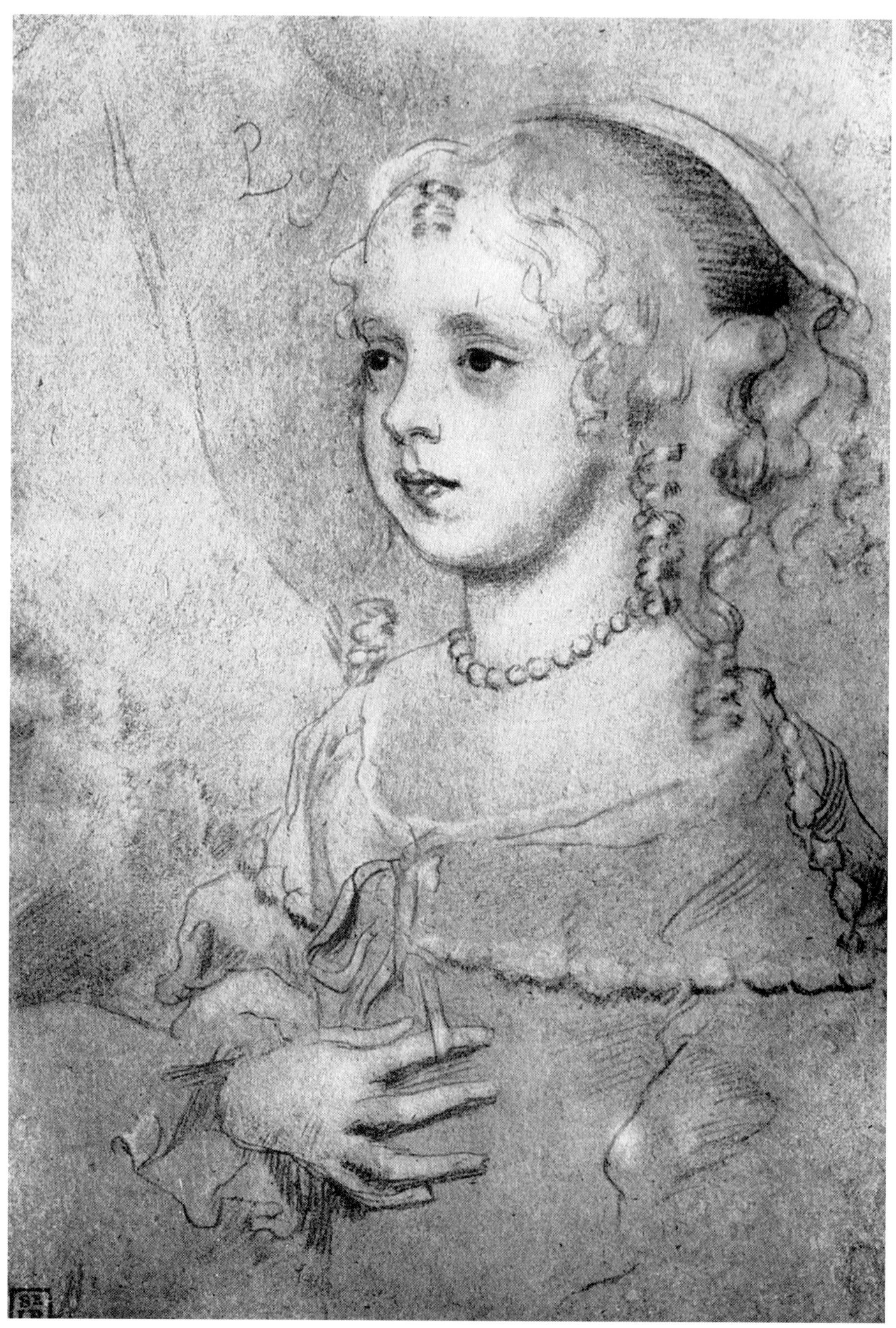

Plate 42. SIR PETER LELY

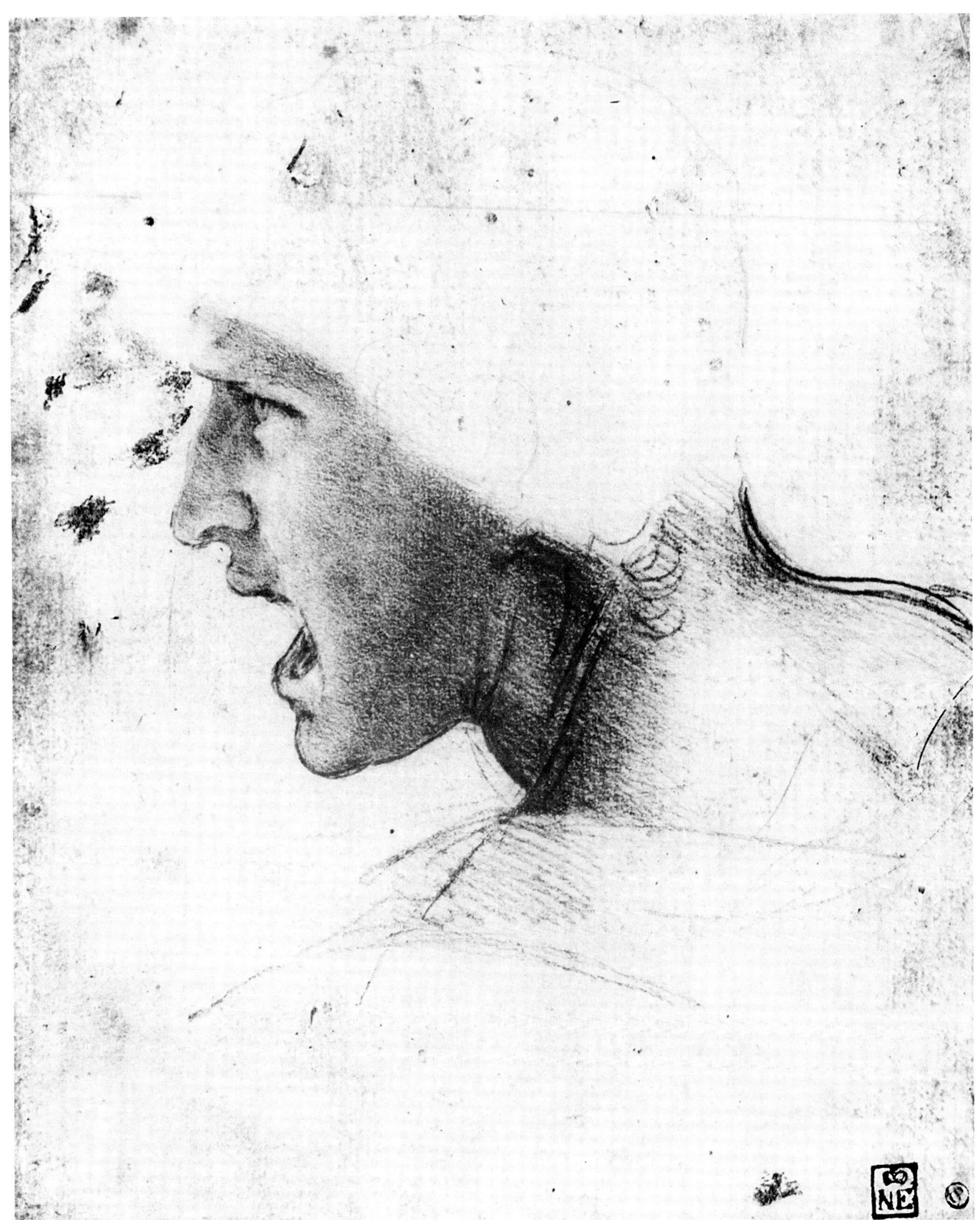

Plate 43. Leonardo da Vinci

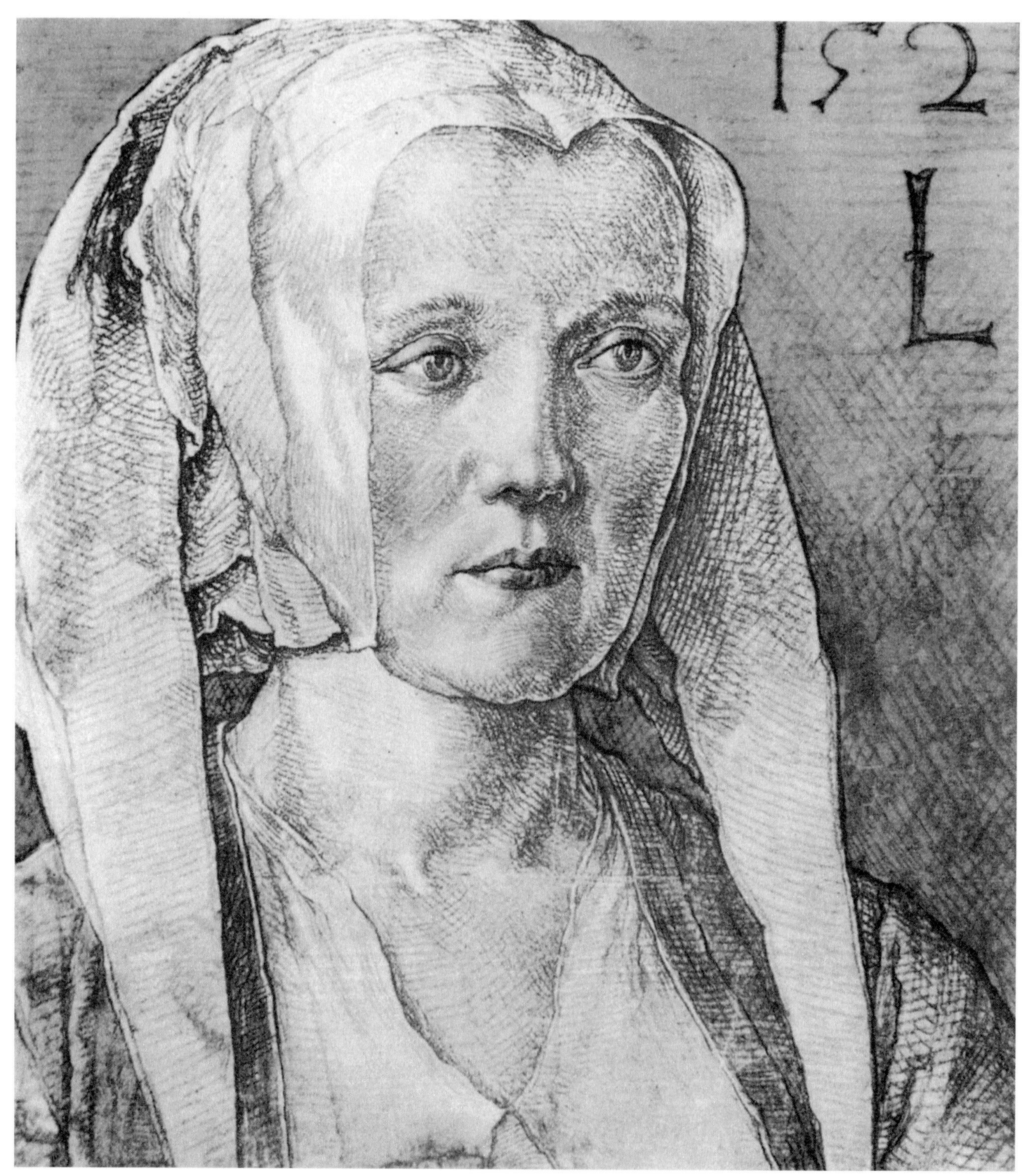

Plate 44. Lucas van Leyden

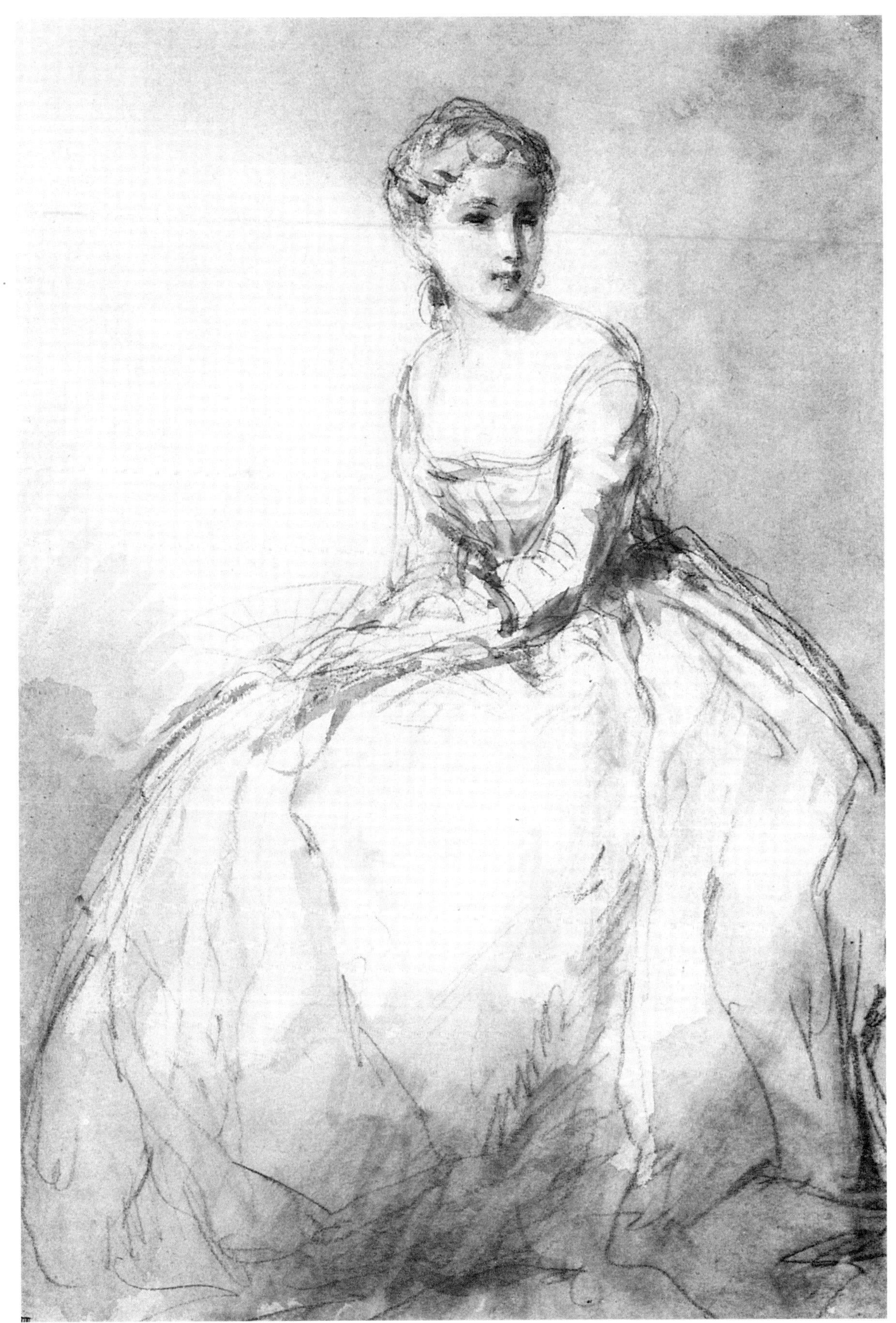

Plate 45. EGRON SILLIF LUNDGREN

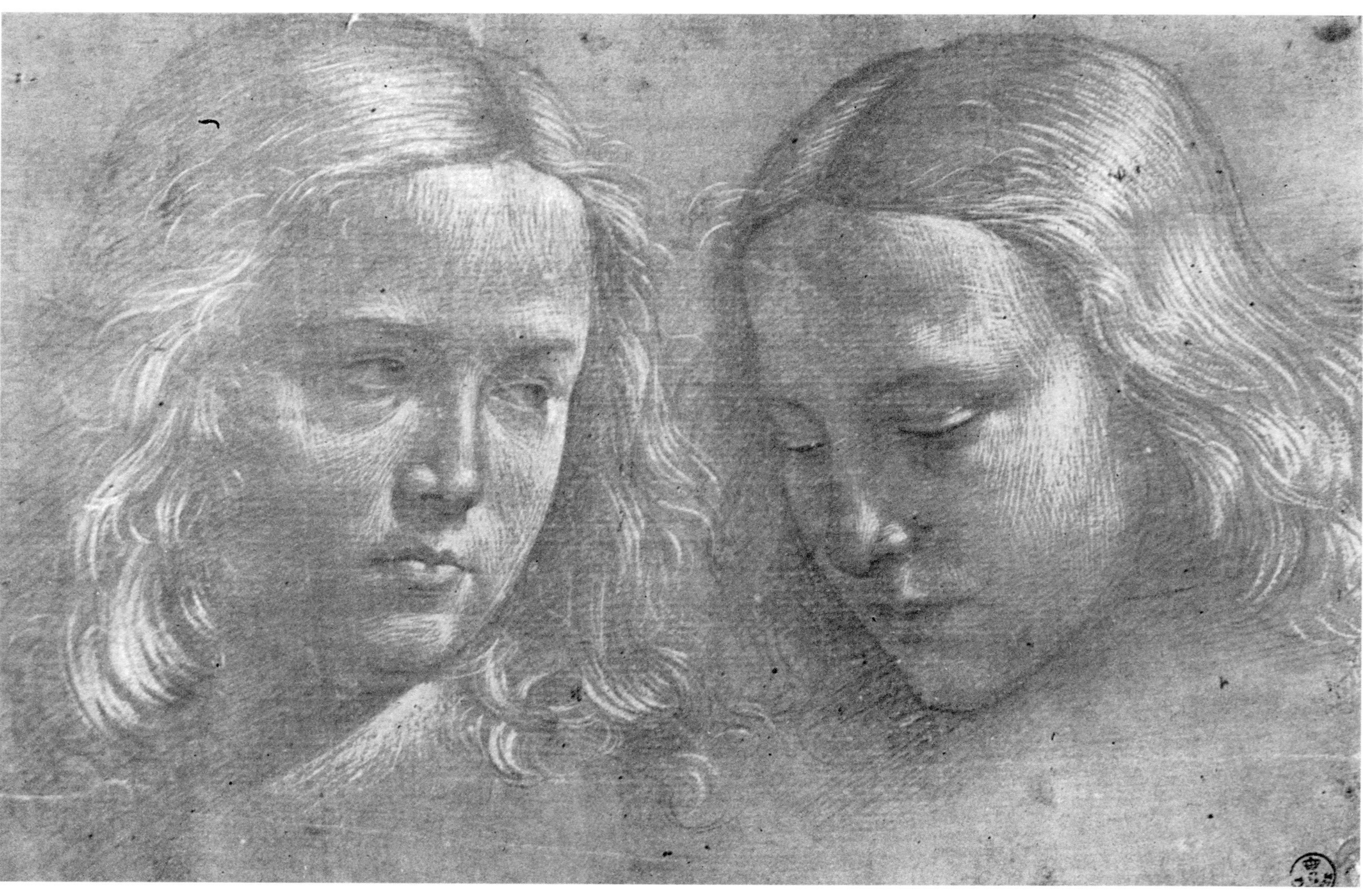

Plate 46. Sebastiano Mainardi

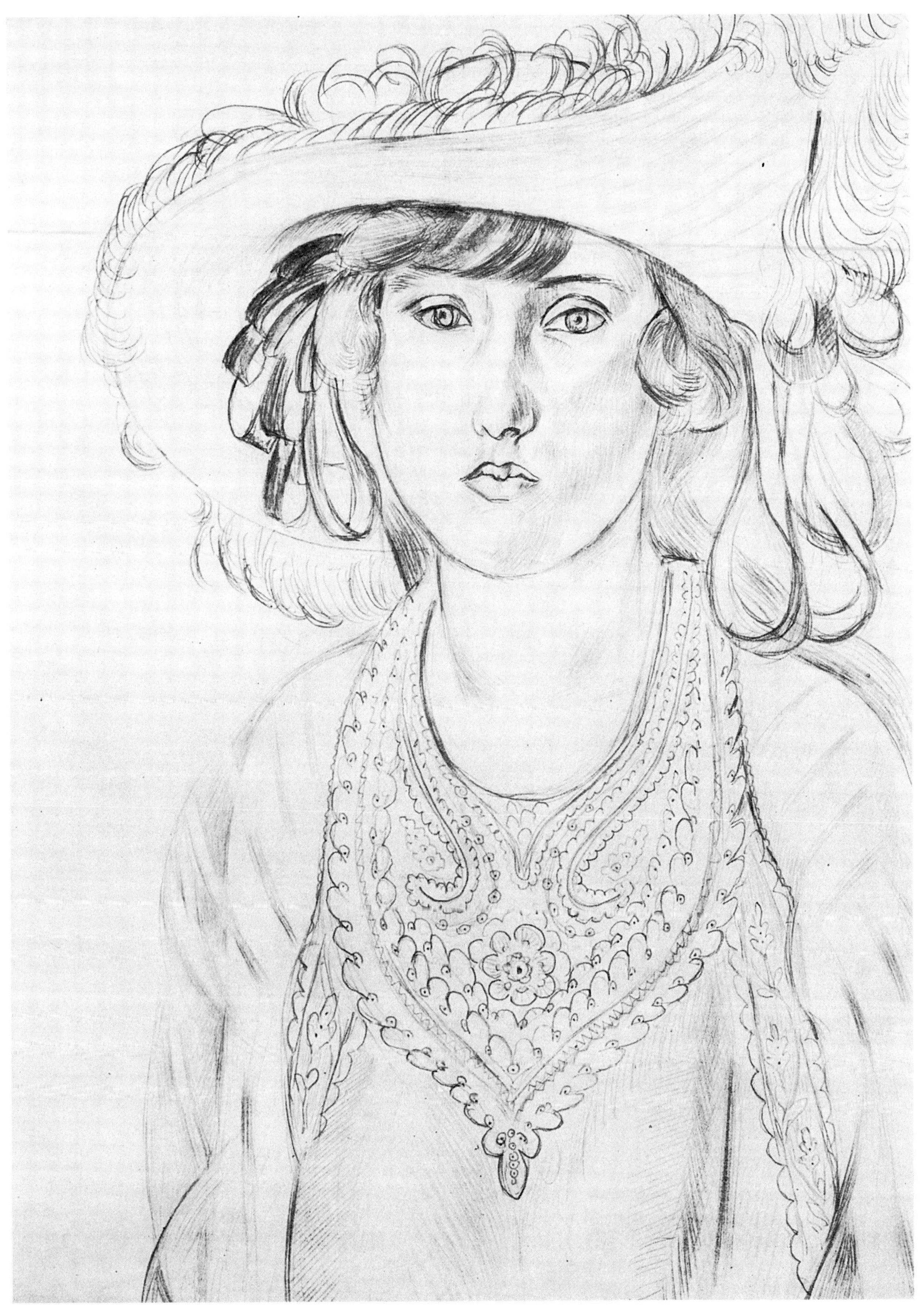

Plate 47. HENRI MATISSE

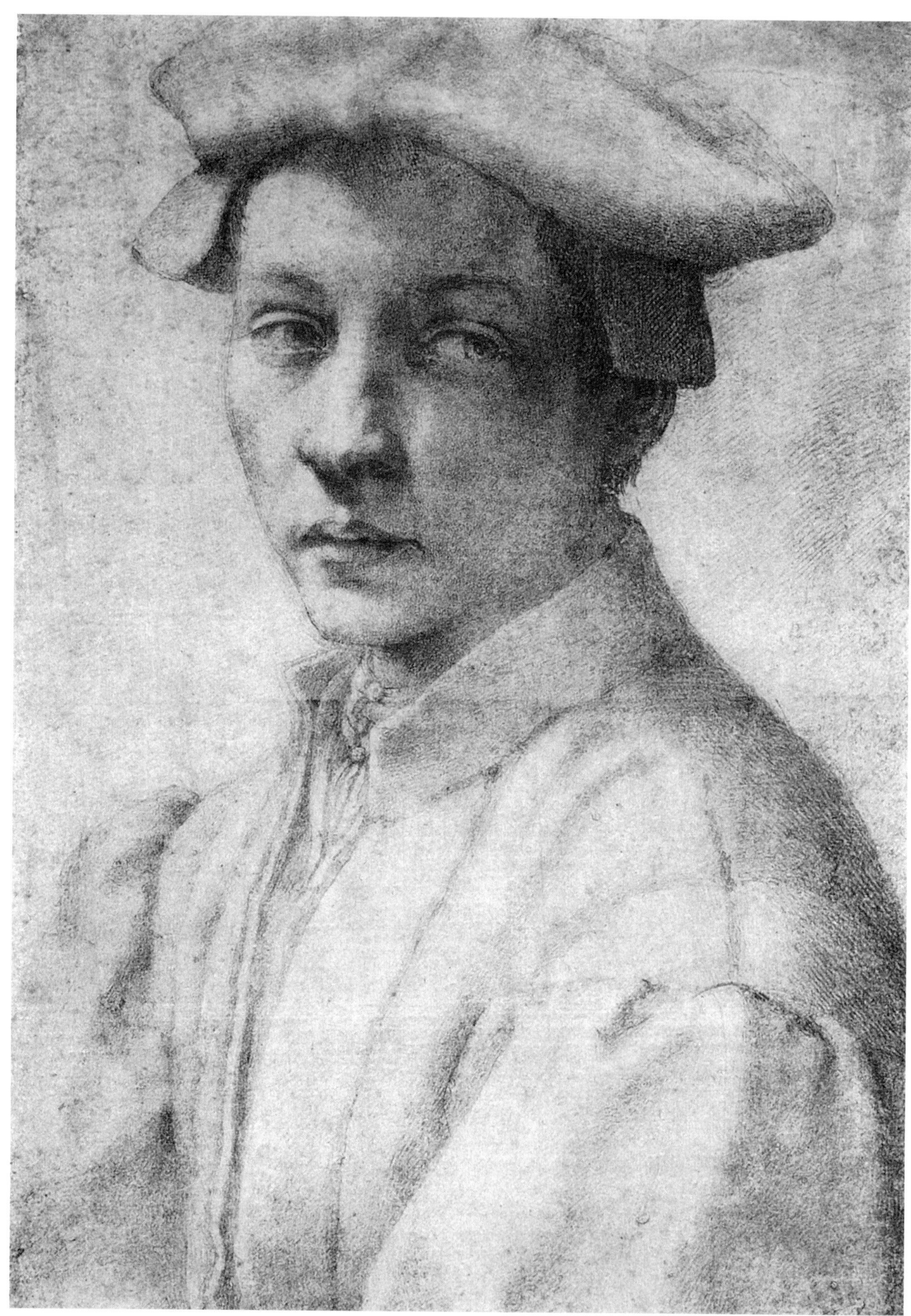

Plate 48. Michelangelo Buonarroti

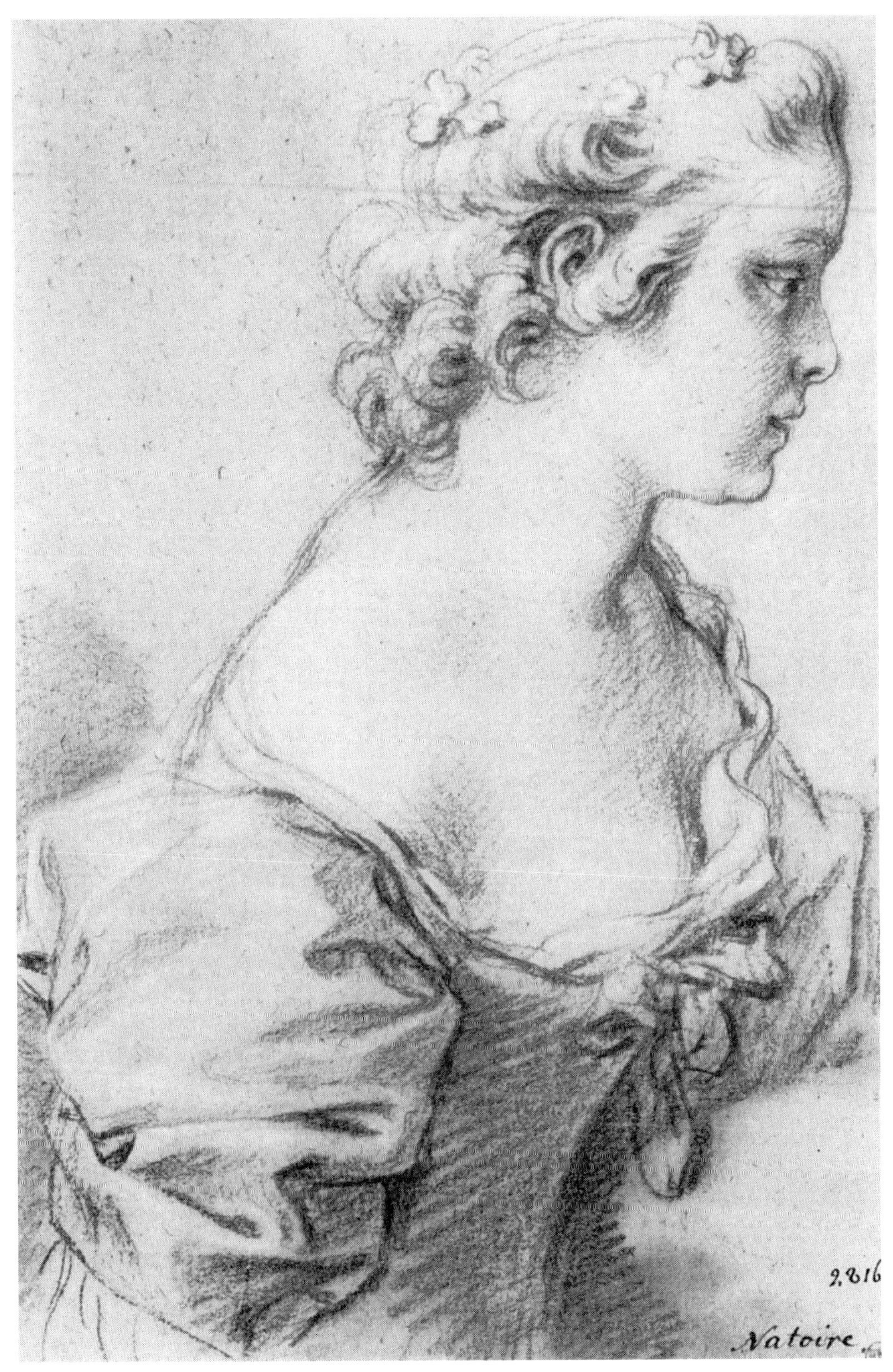

Plate 49. CHARLES-JOSEPH NATOIRE

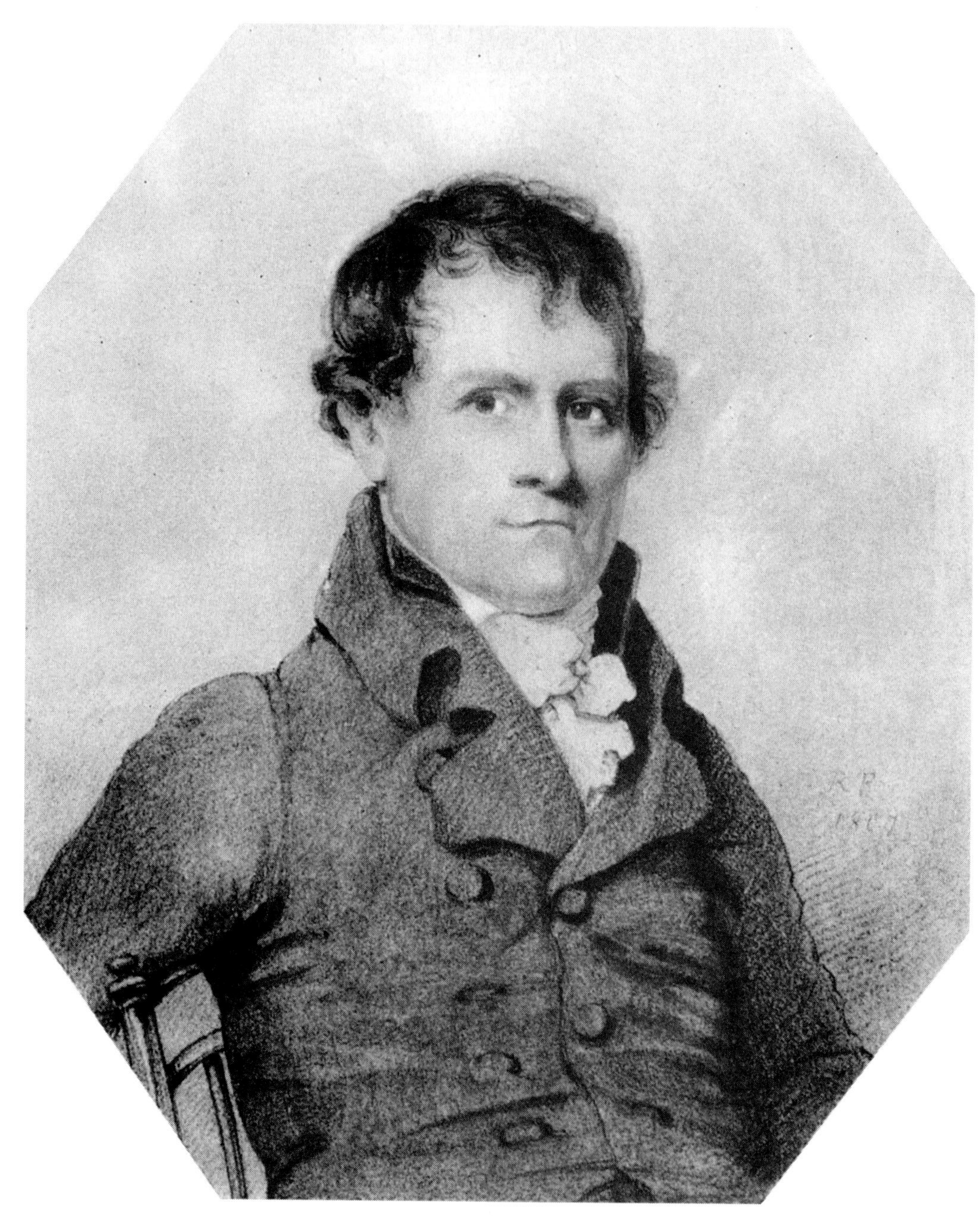

Plate 50. Rembrandt Peale

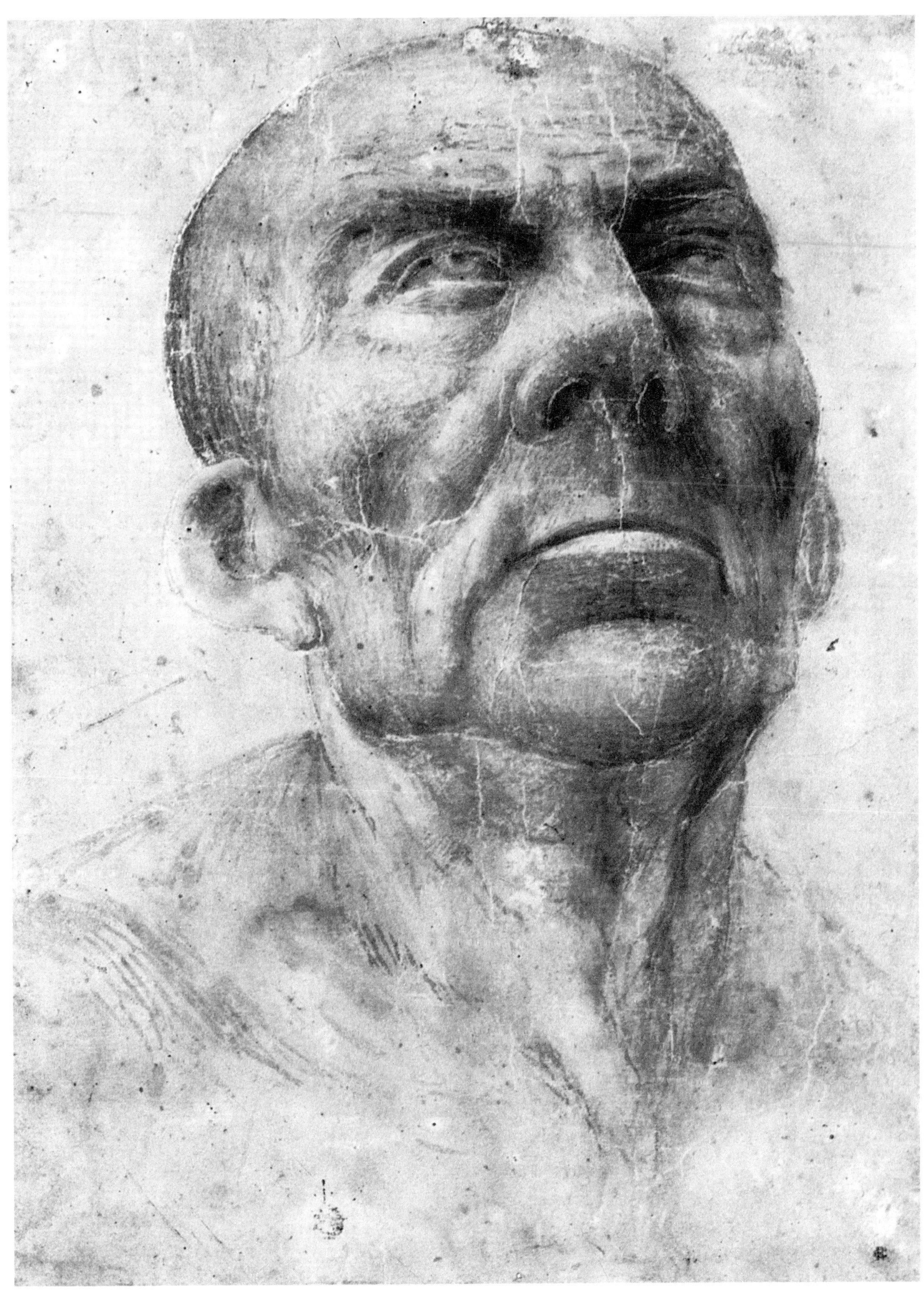

Plate 51. PELLEGRINO DA SAN DANIELE

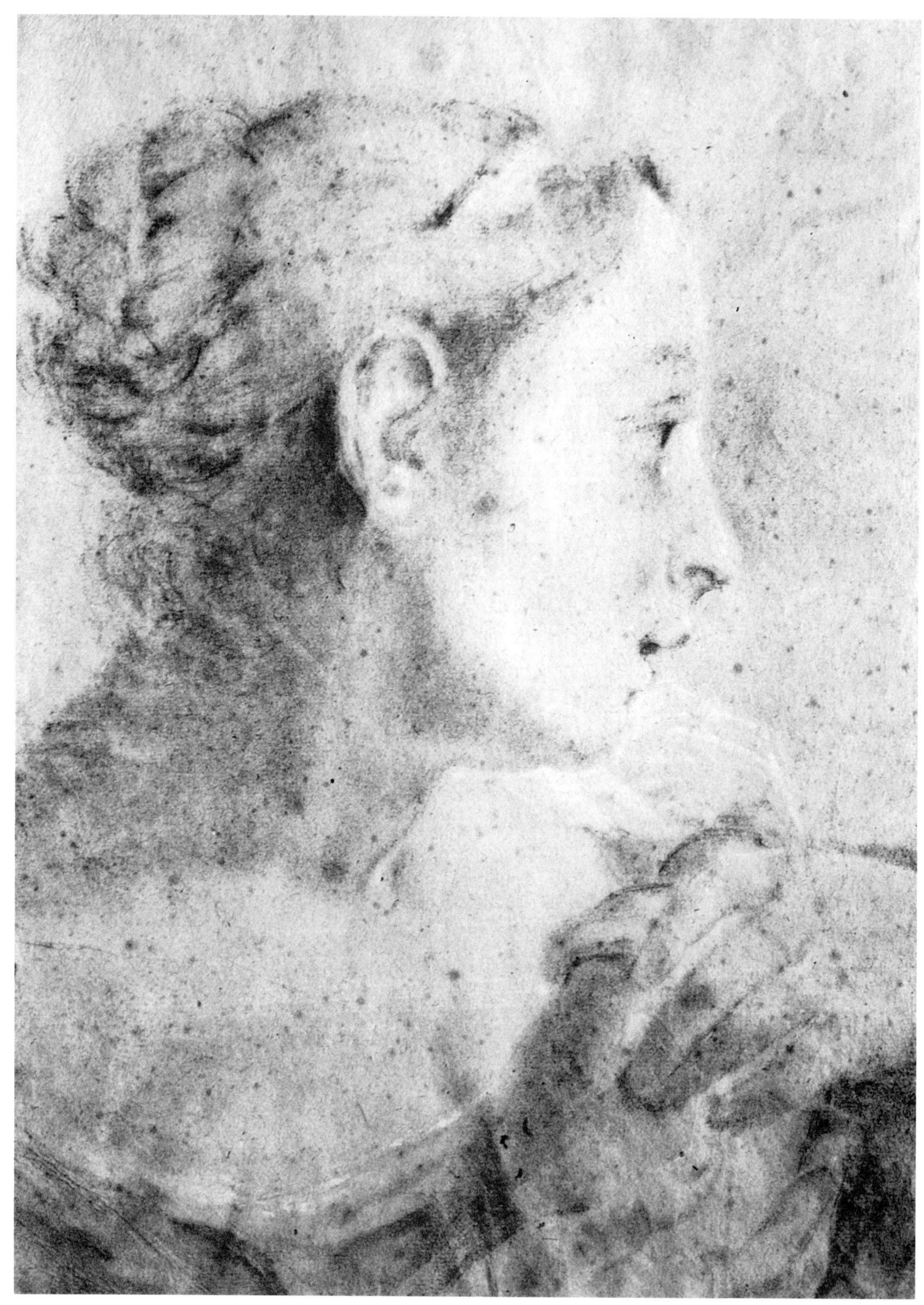

Plate 52. GIOVANNI BATTISTA PIAZZETTA

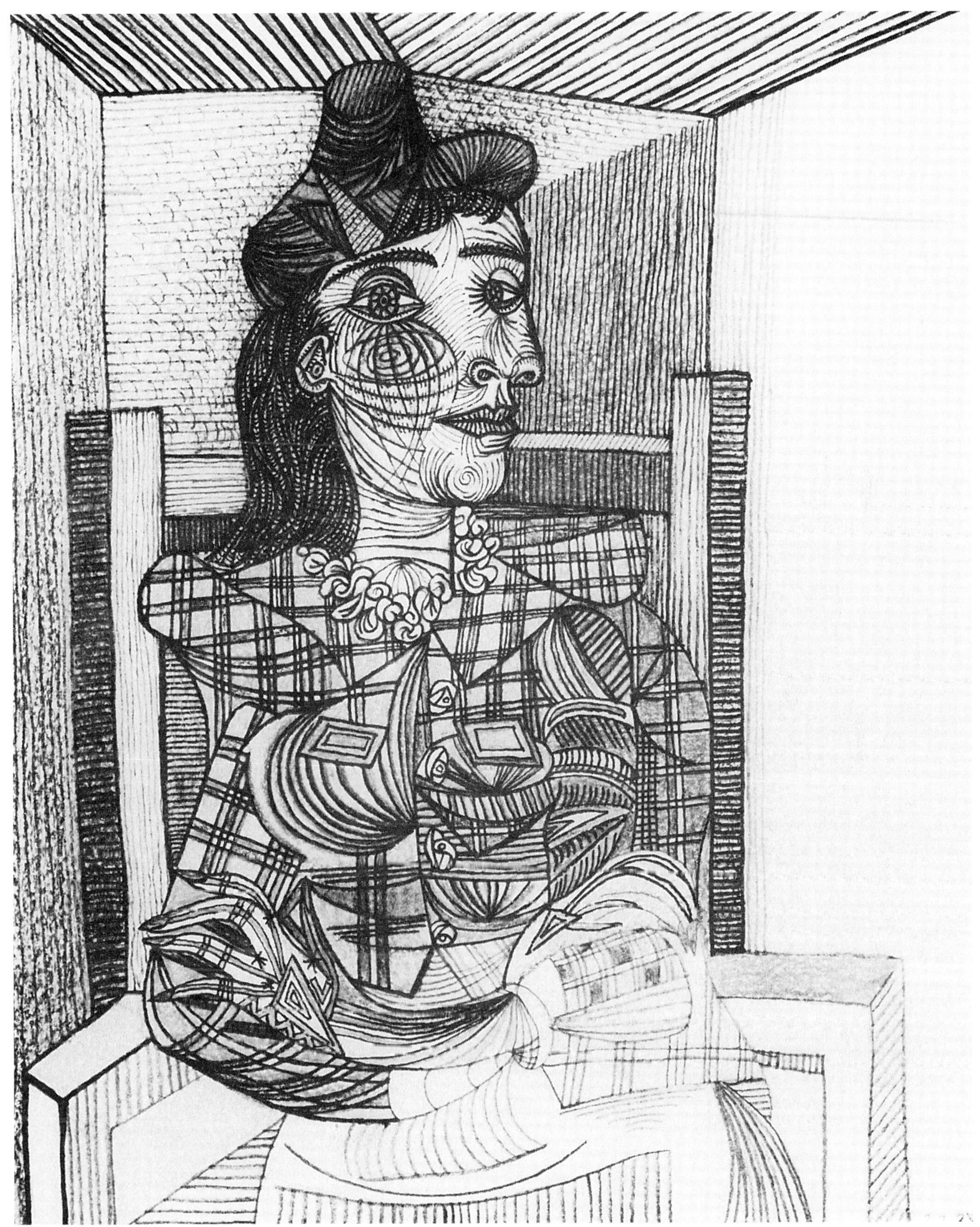

Plate 53. PABLO PICASSO

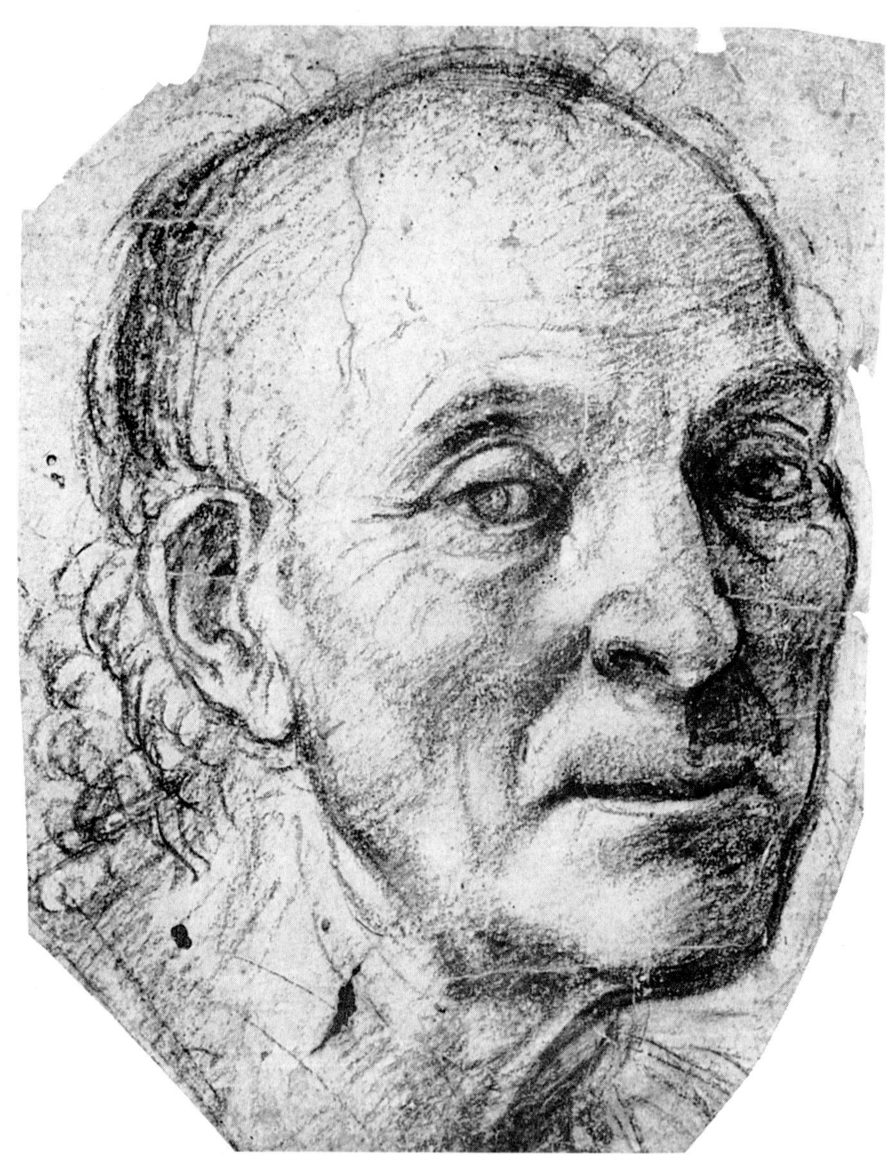

Plate 54. PIERO DI COSIMO

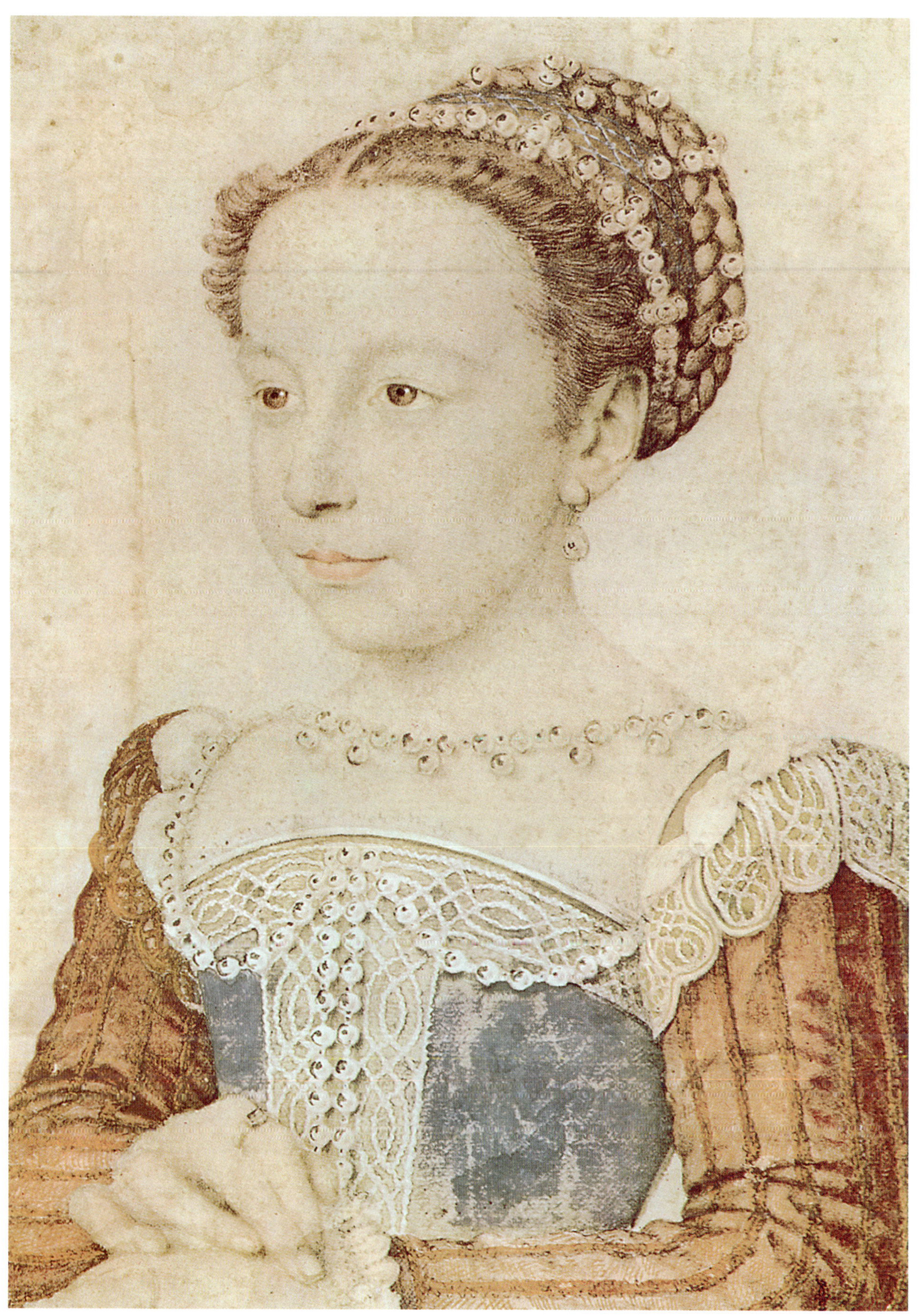

Plate 55. FRANÇOIS CLOUET

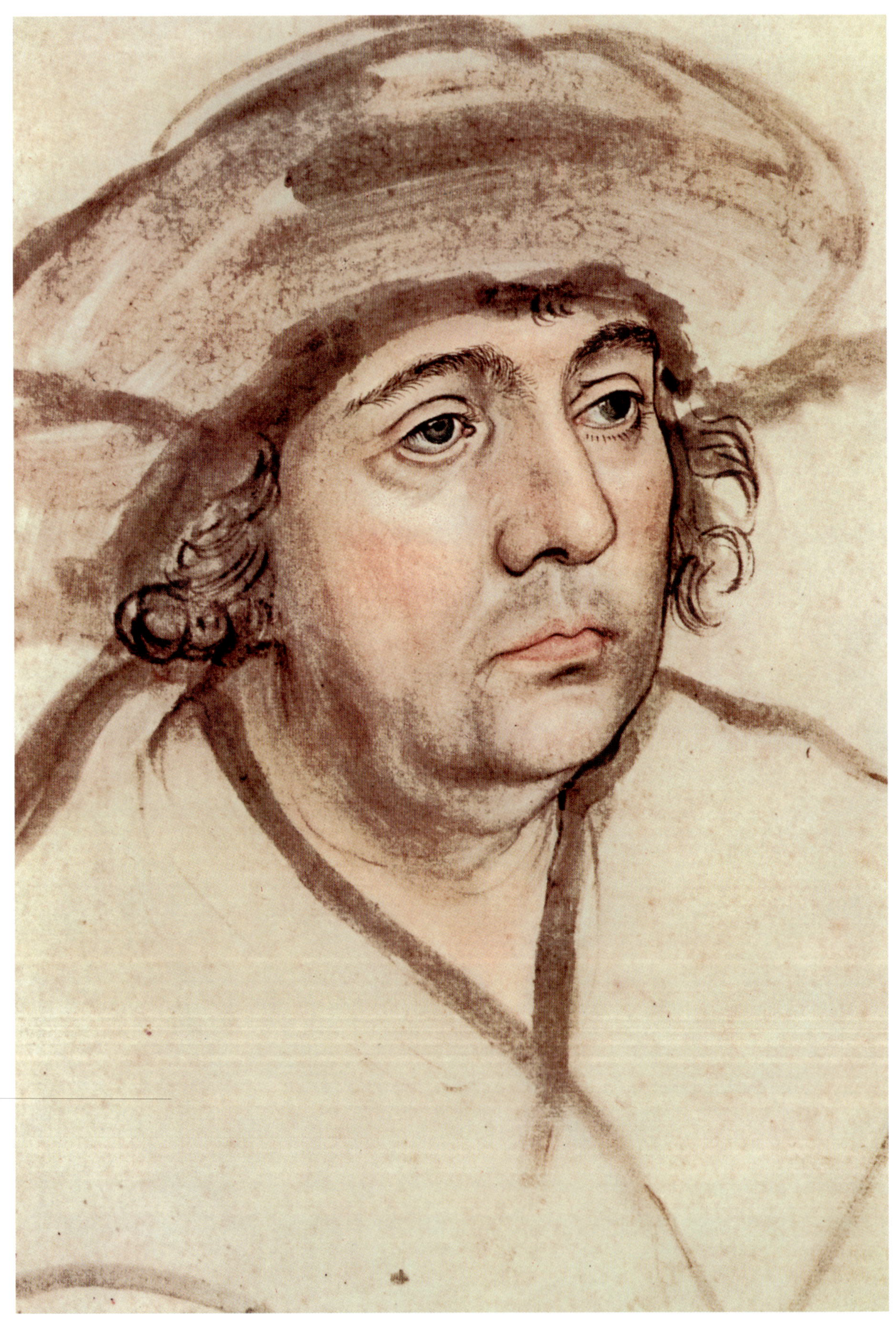

Plate 56. Lucas Cranach the Elder

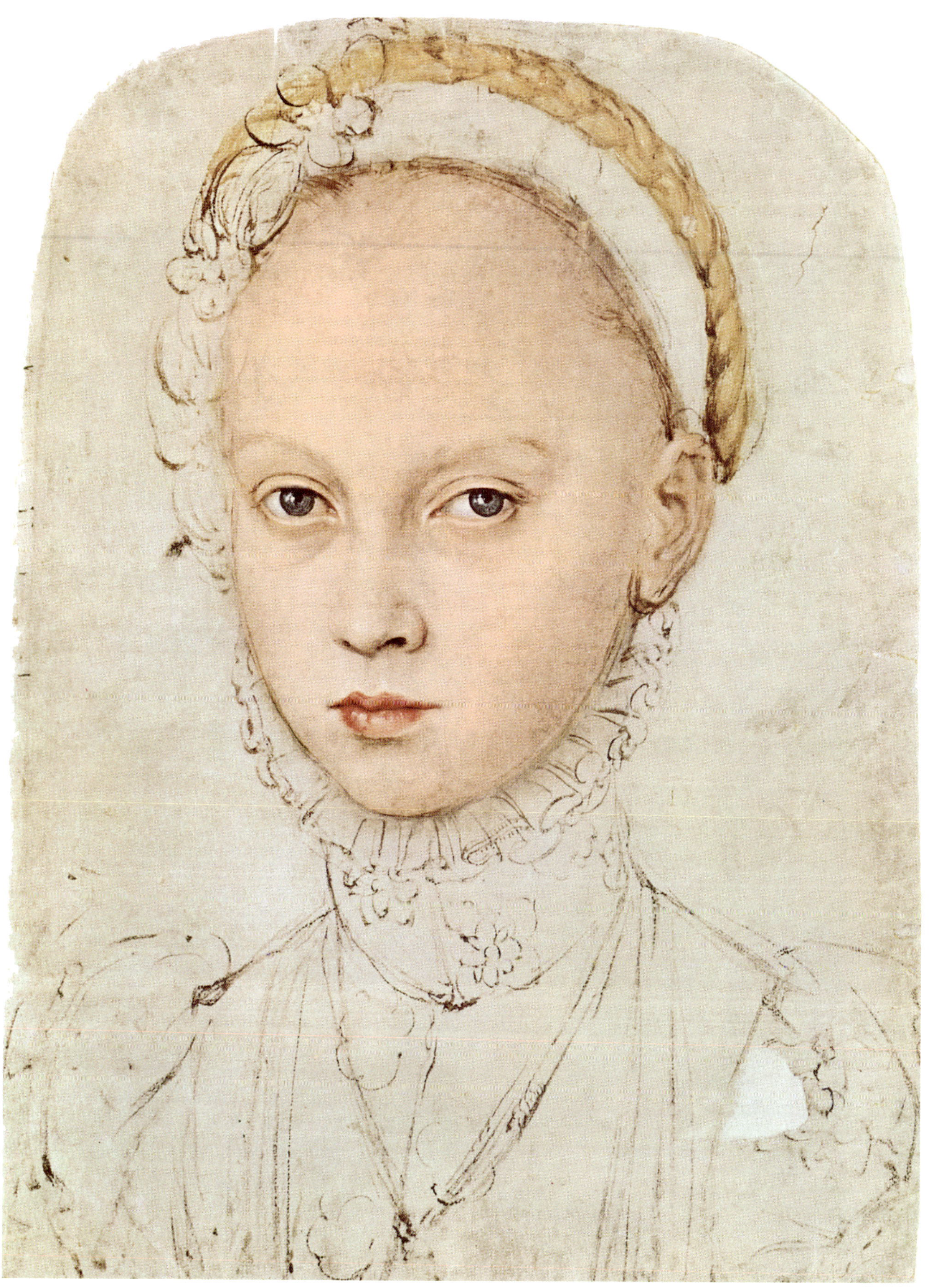

Plate 57. Lucas Cranach the Younger

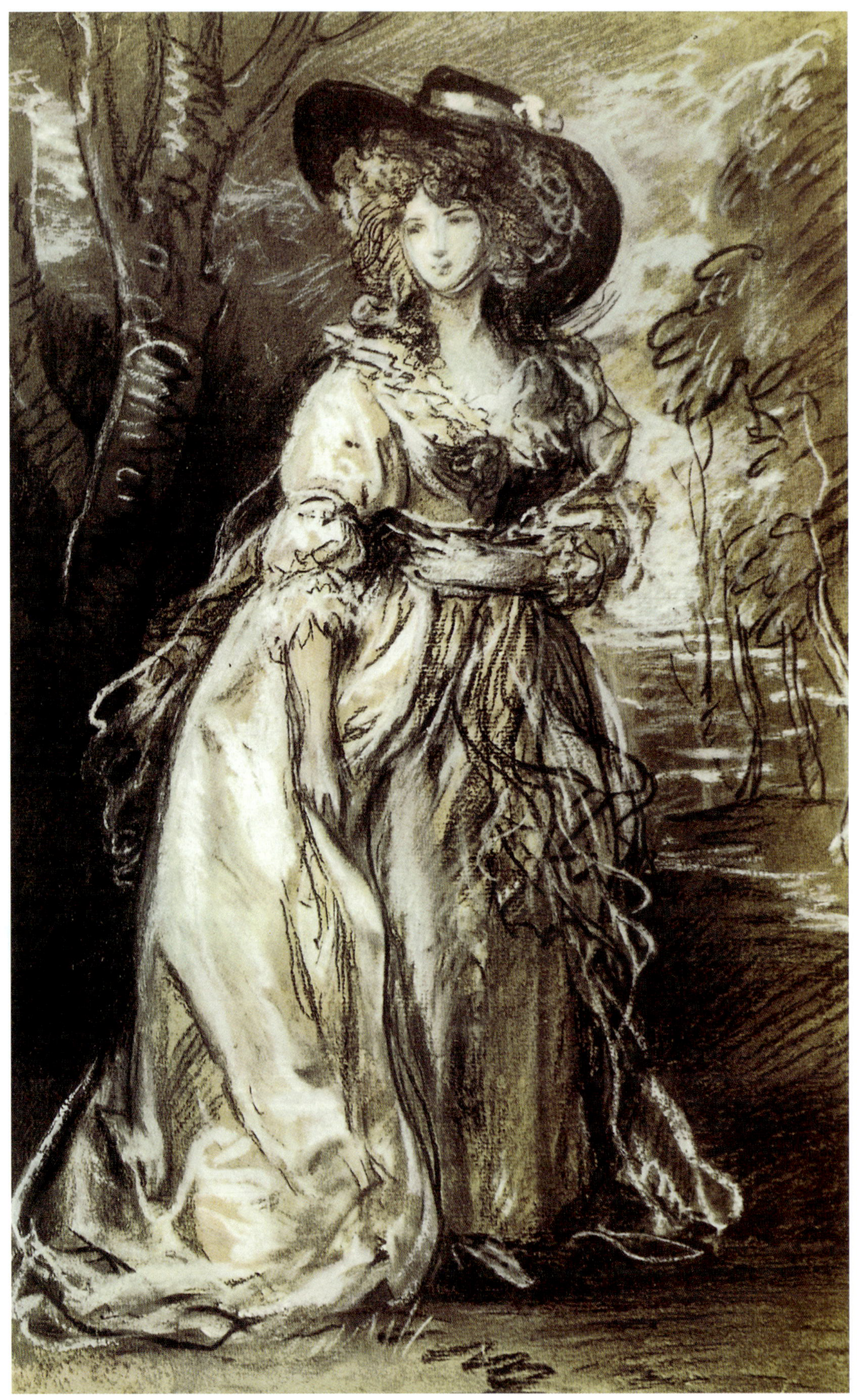

Plate 58. Thomas Gainsborough

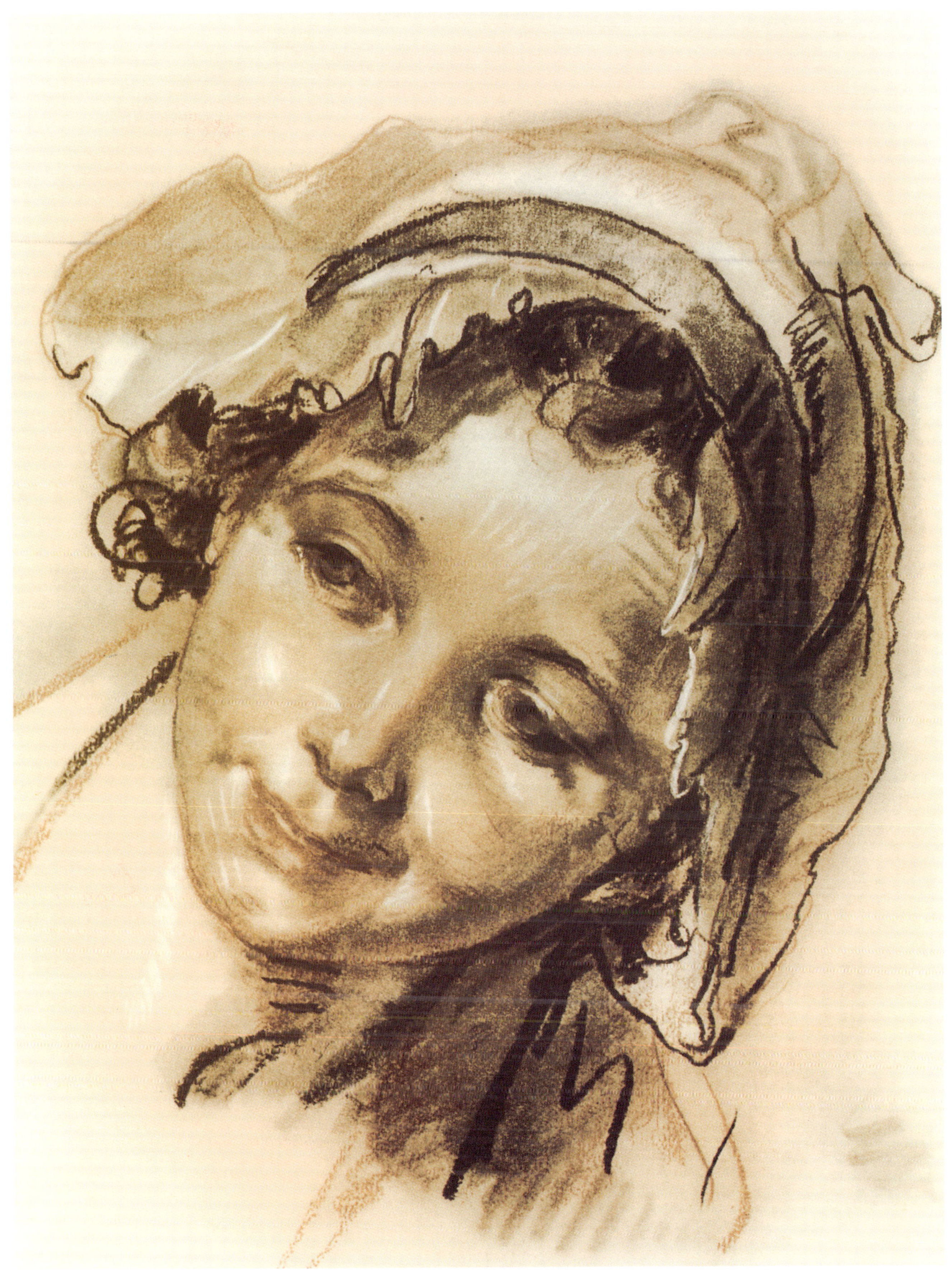

Plate 59. Jean-Baptiste Greuze

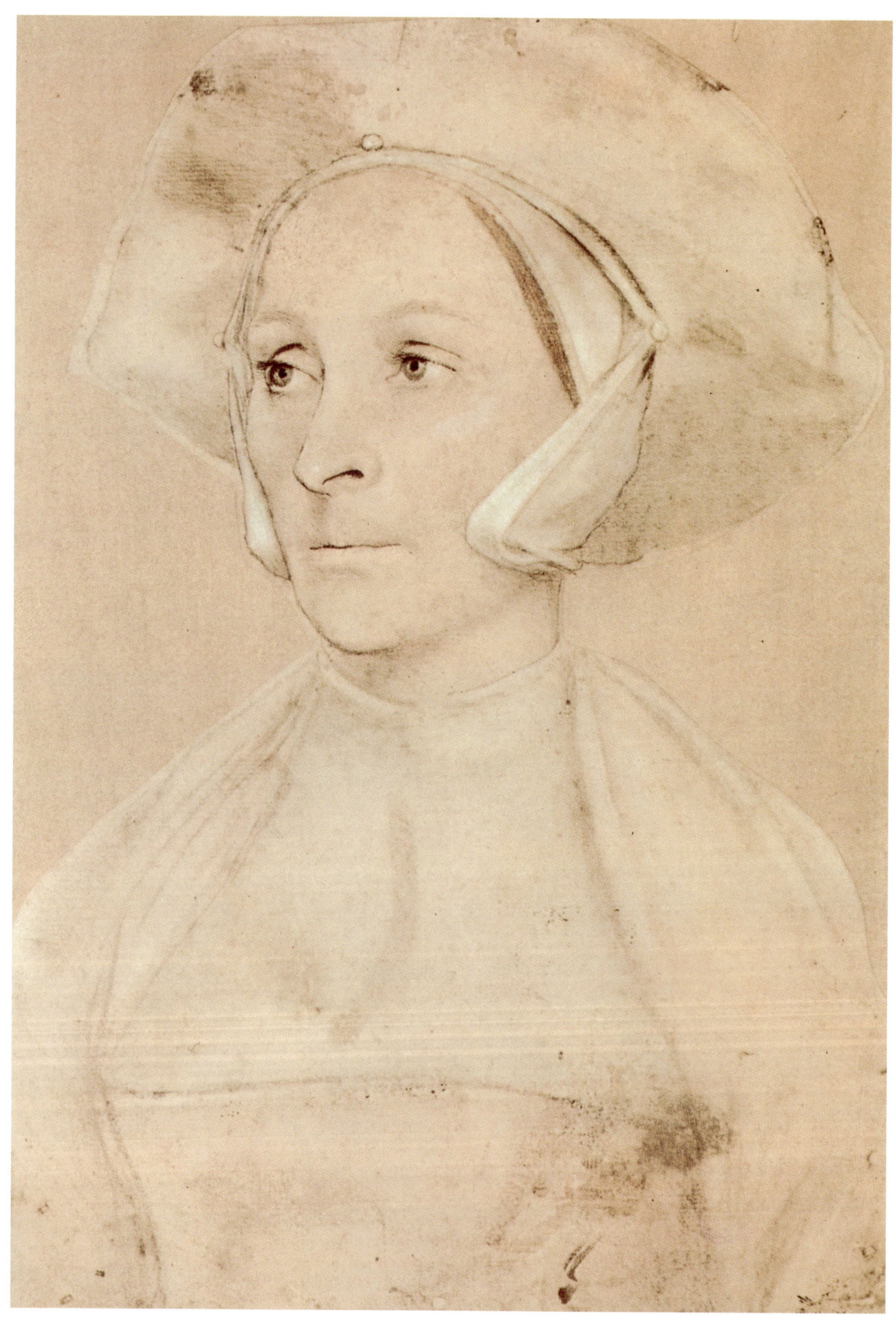

Plate 60. HANS HOLBEIN THE YOUNGER

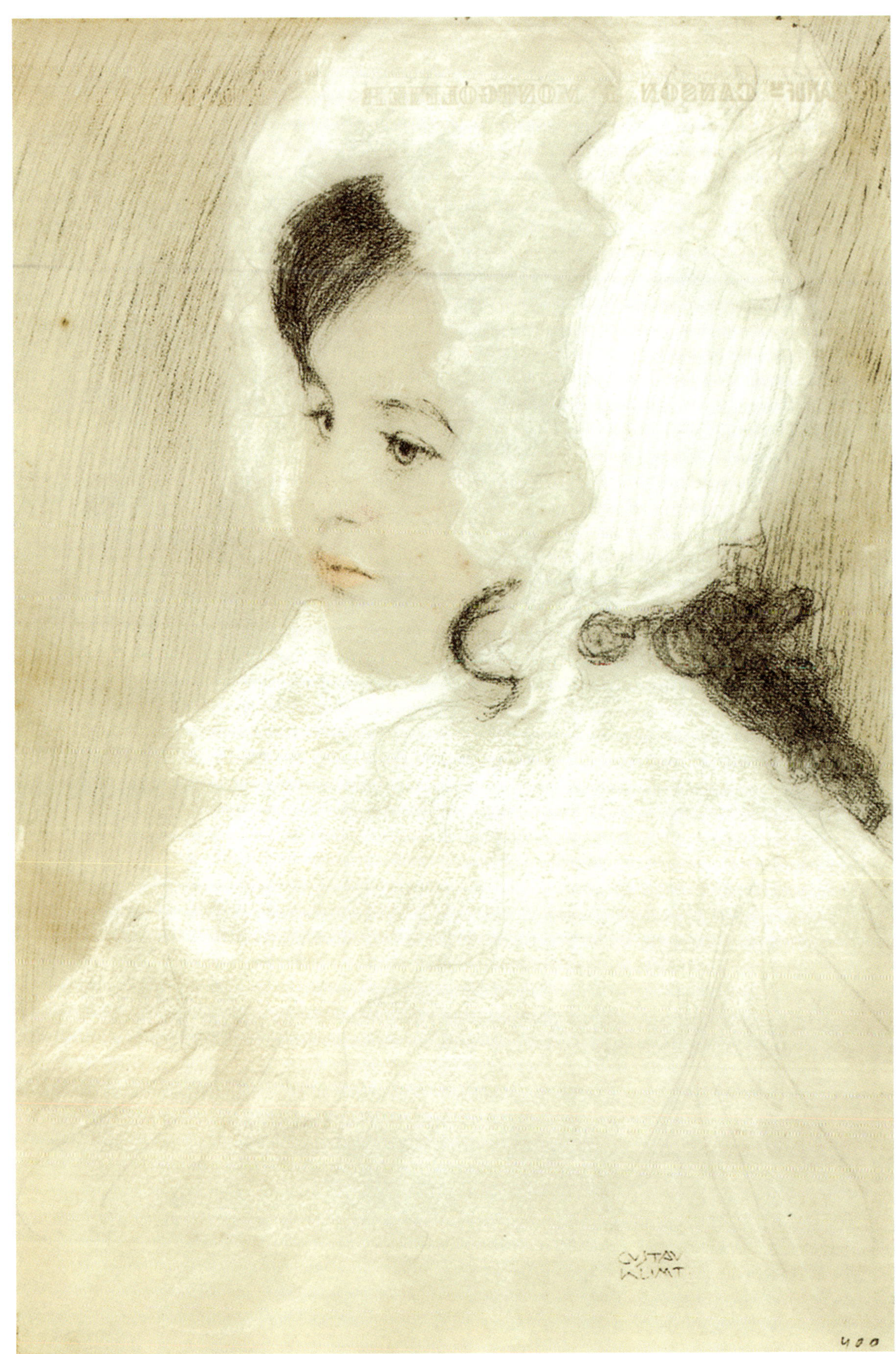

Plate 61. GUSTAVE KLIMT

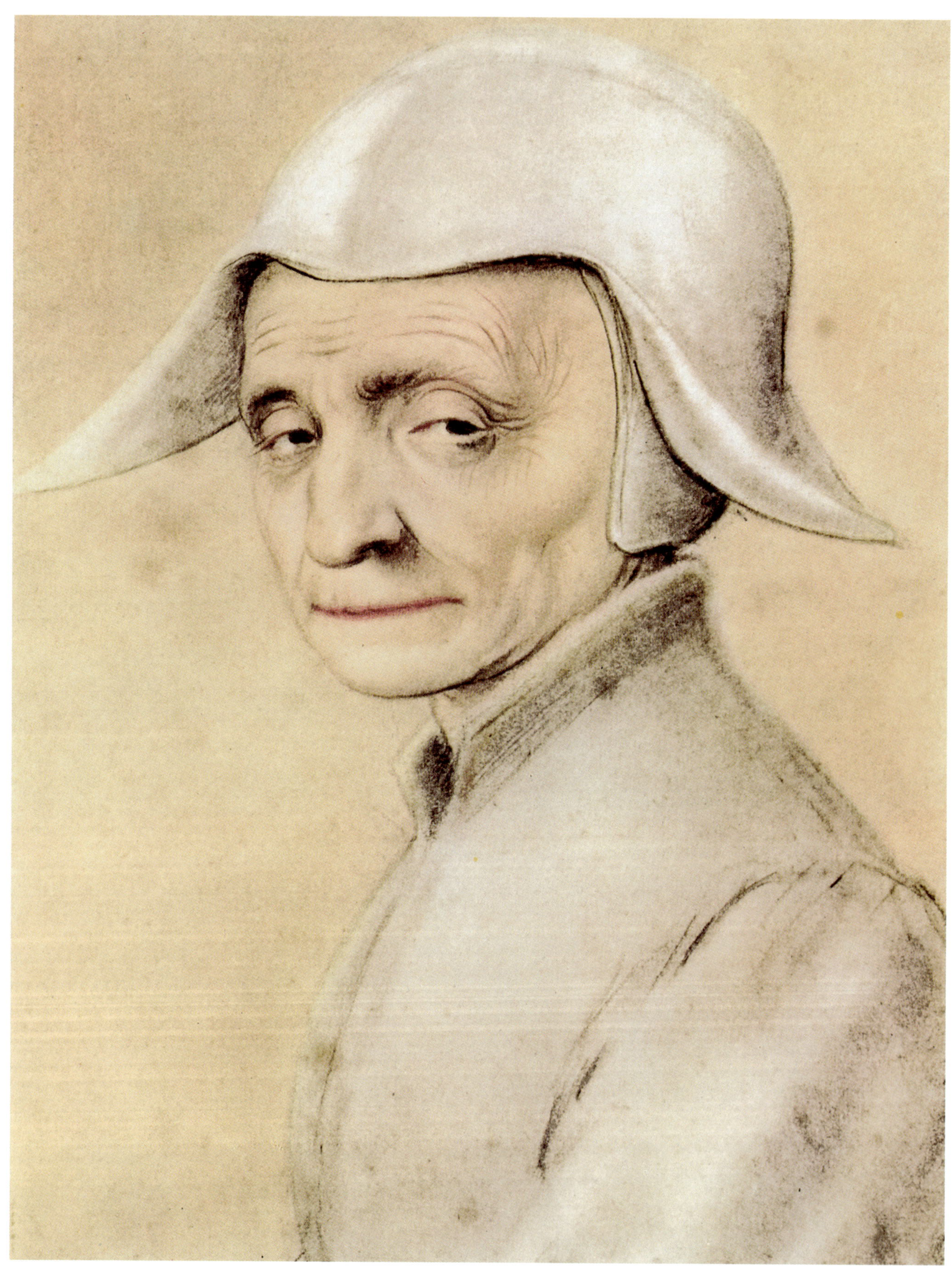

Plate 62. FRANÇOIS LAGNEAU

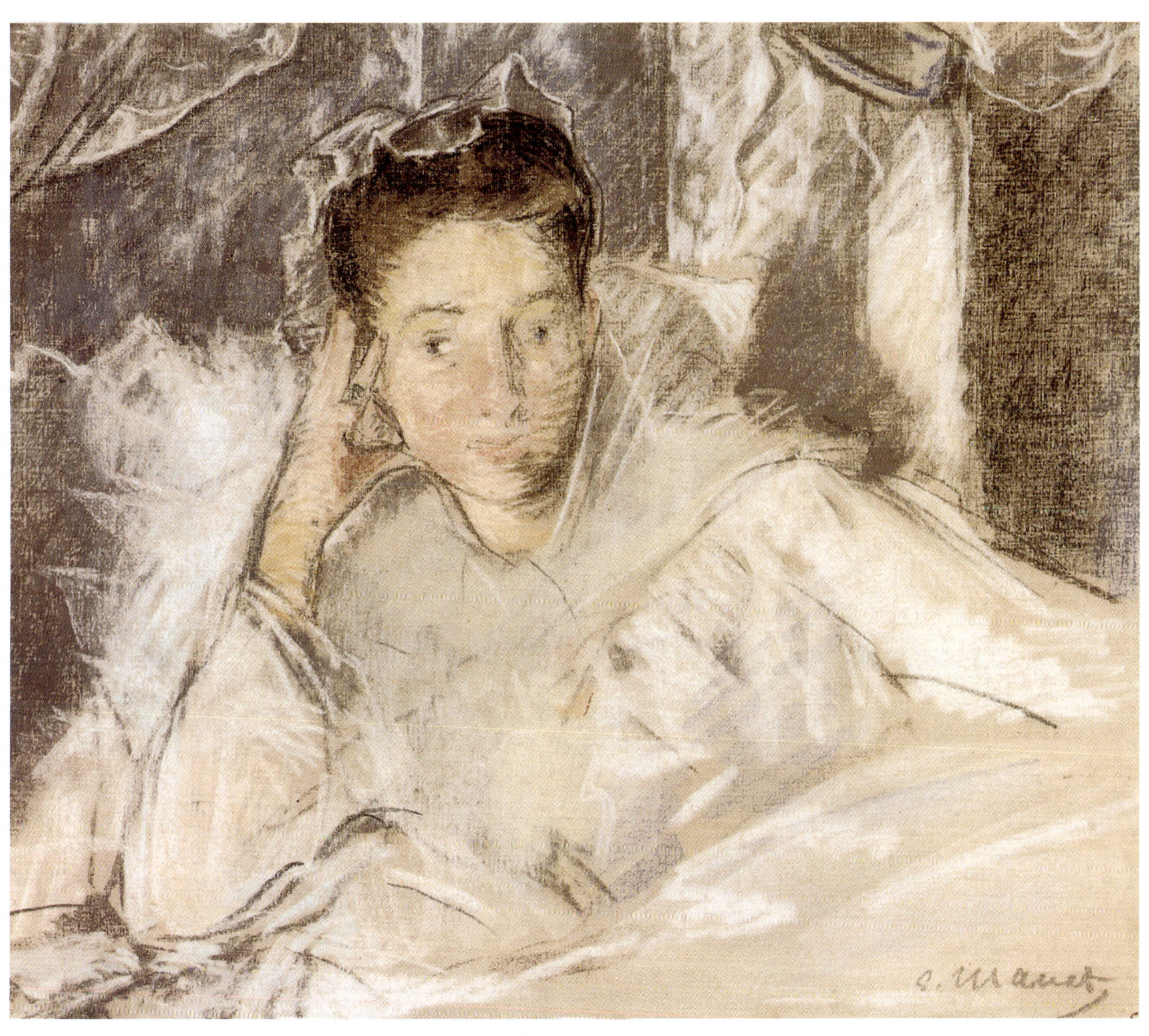

Plate 63. Édouard Manet

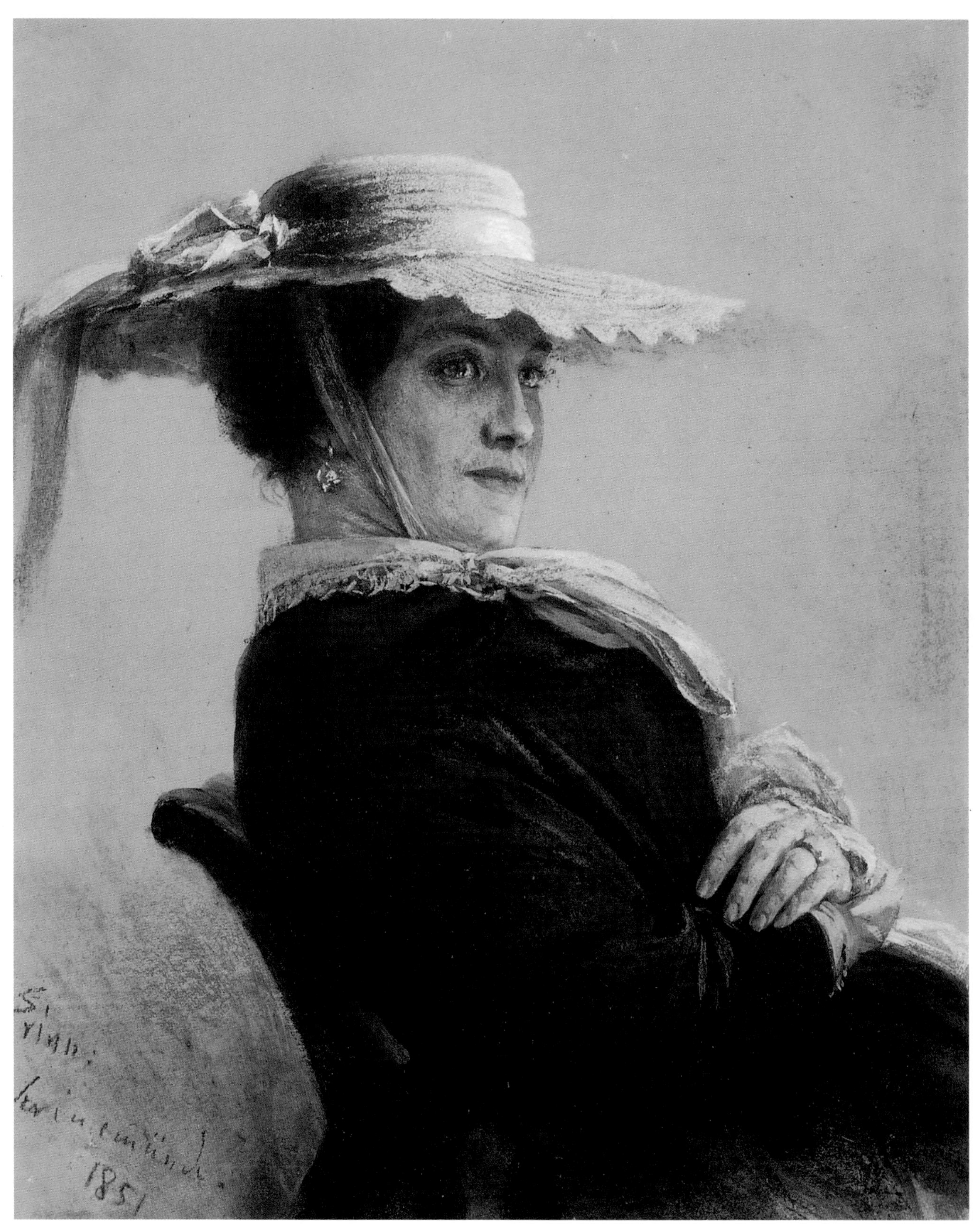

Plate 64. ADOLPH VON MENZEL

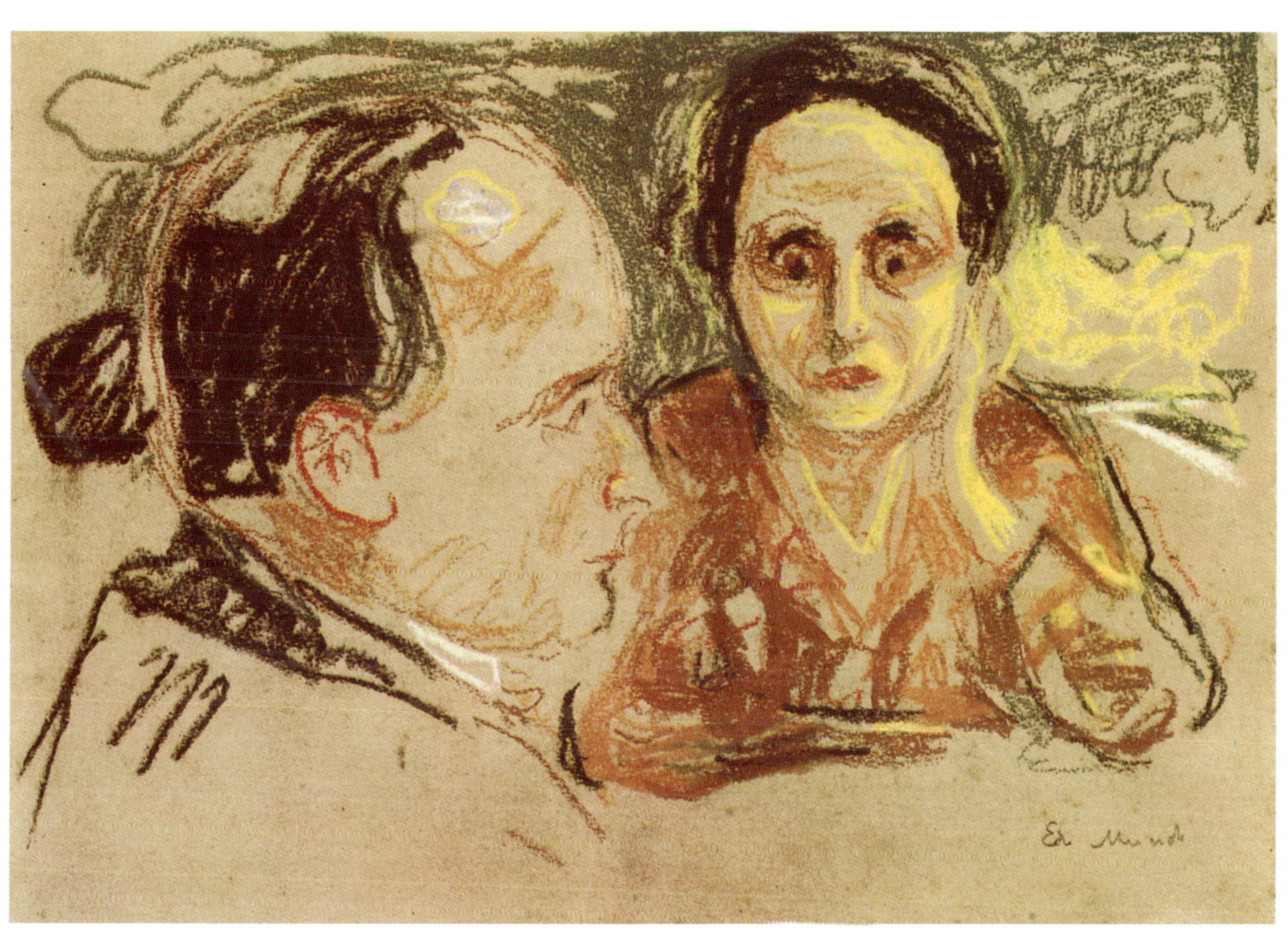

Plate 65. EDVARD MUNCH

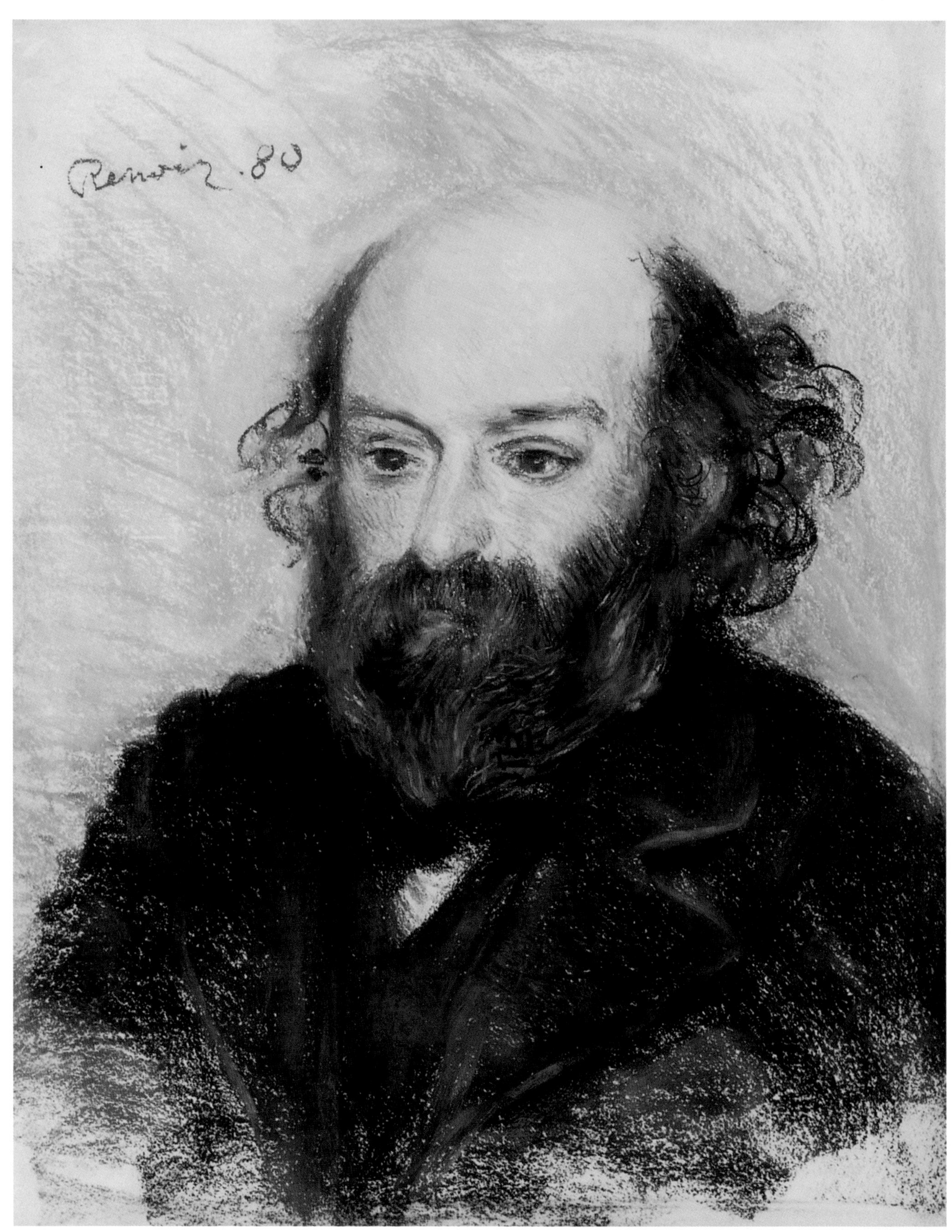

Plate 66. PIERRE-AUGUSTE RENOIR

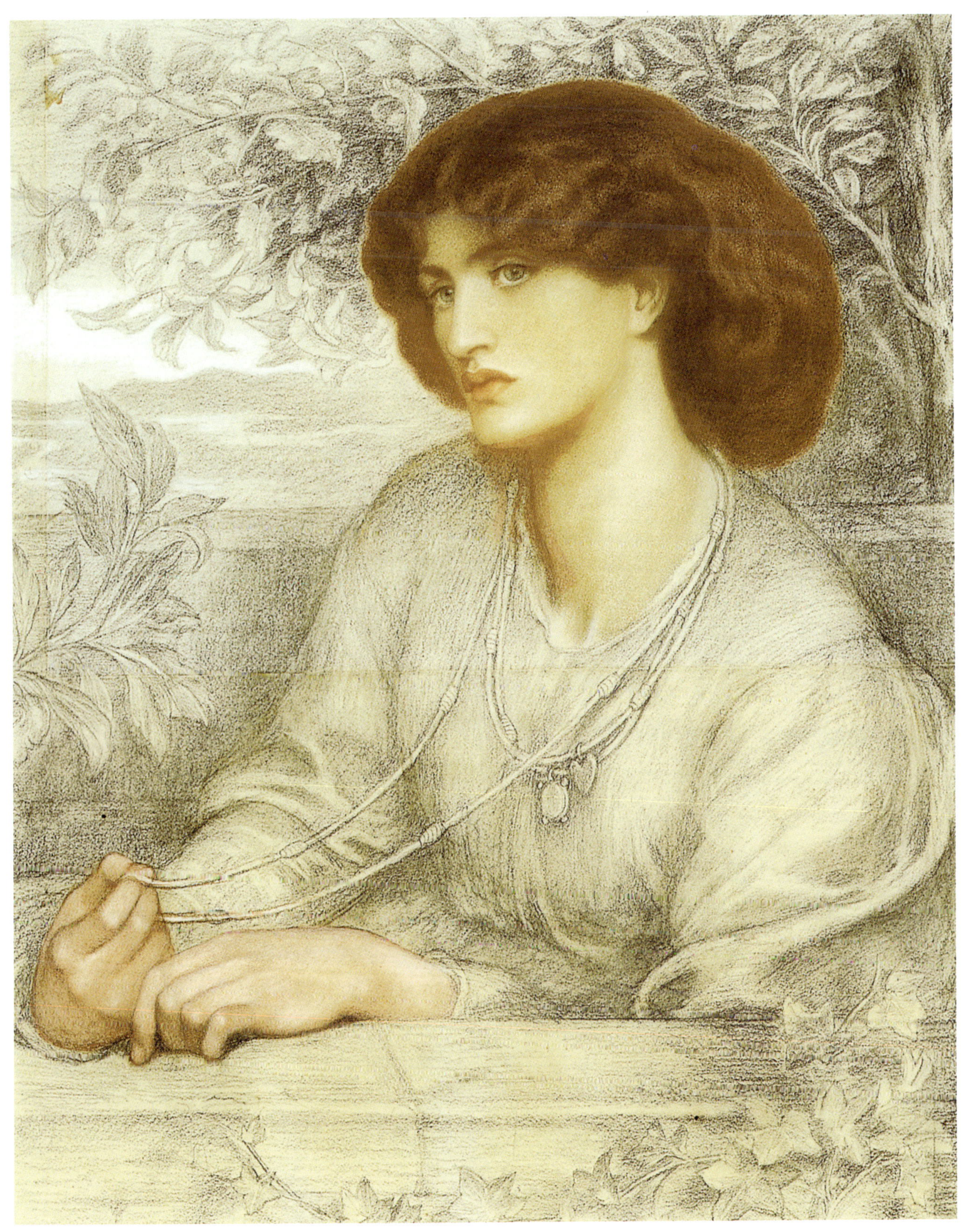

Plate 67. DANTE GABRIEL ROSSETTI

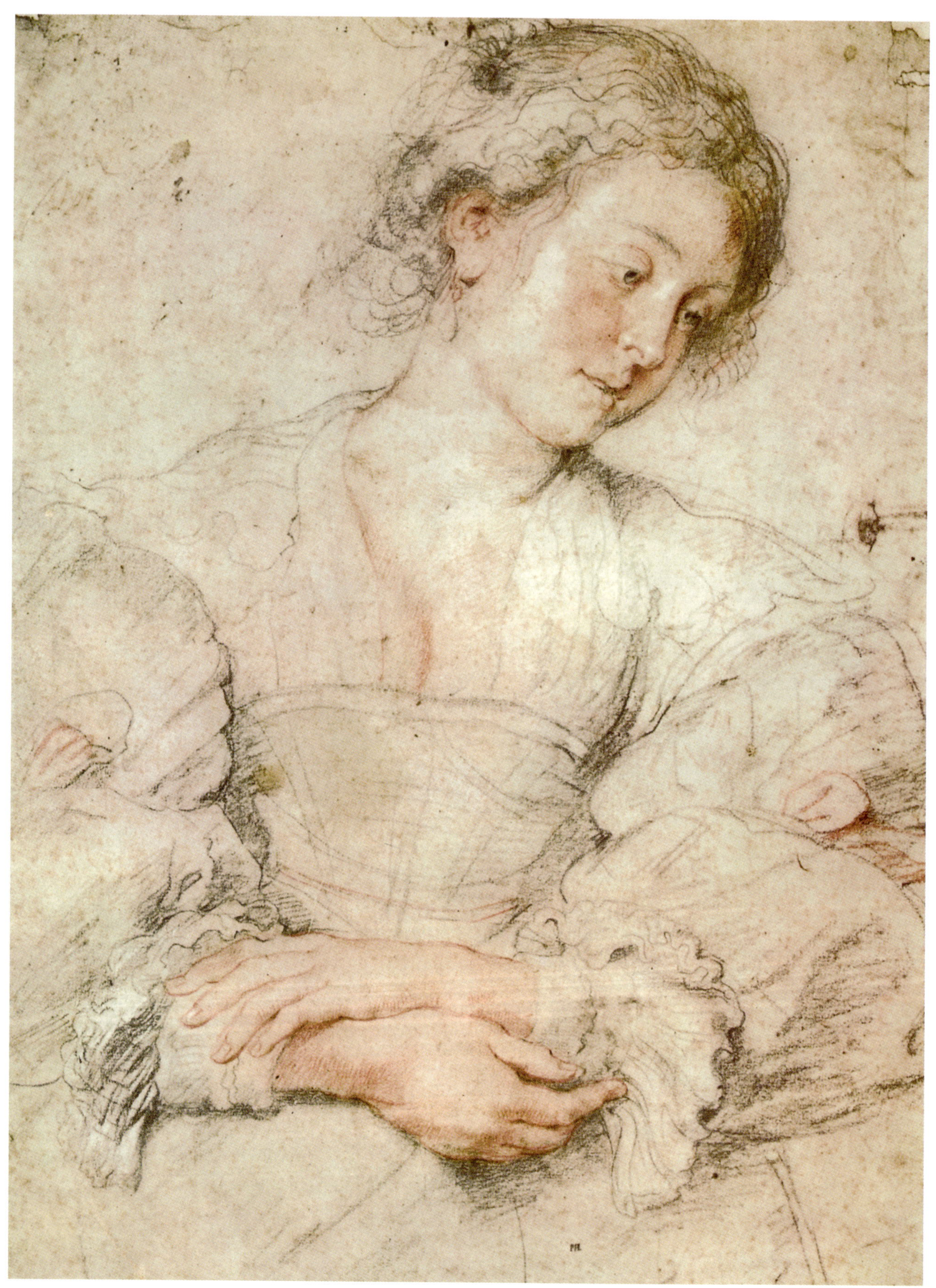

Plate 68. Peter Paul Rubens

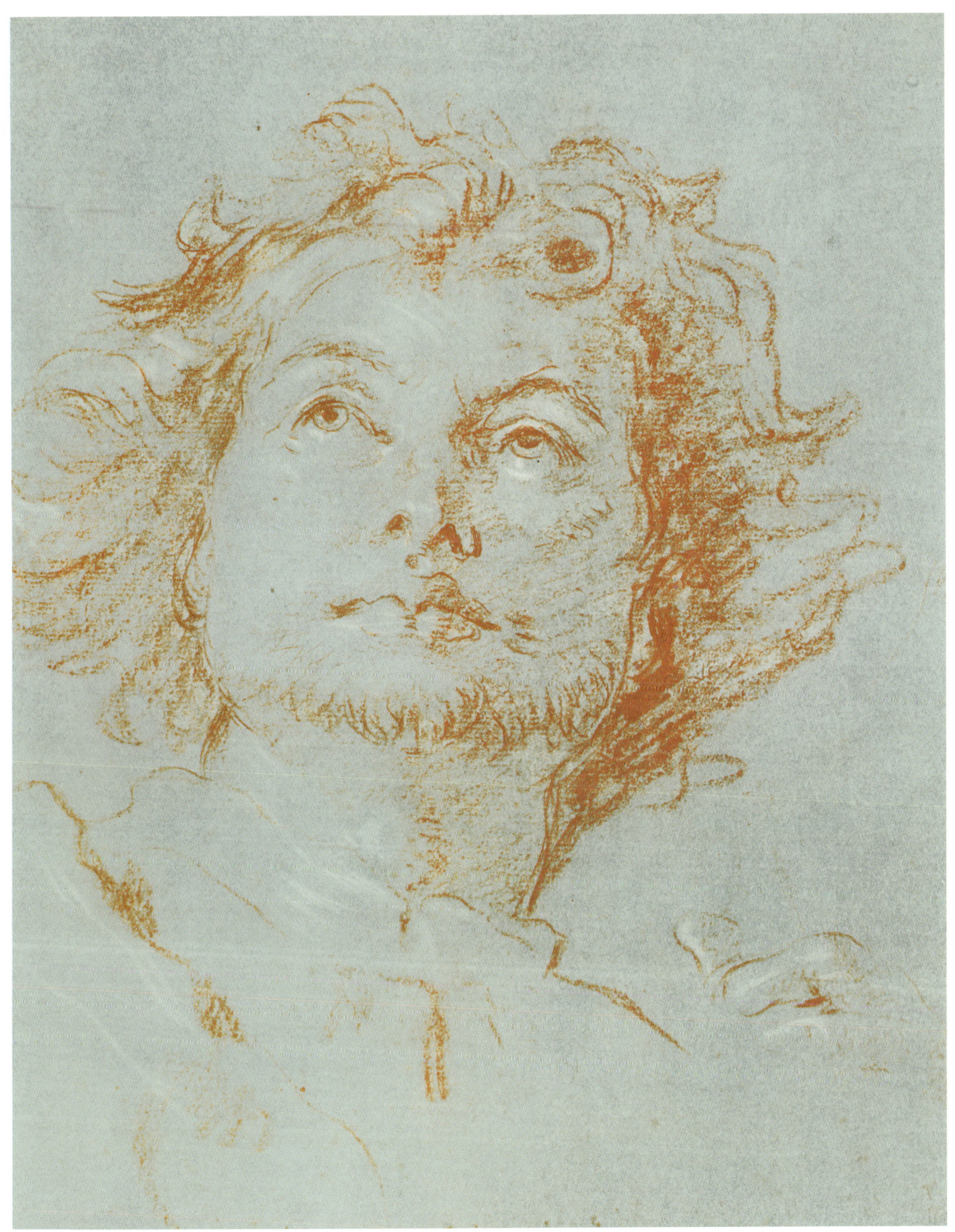

Plate 69. GIOVANNI BATTISTA TIEPOLO

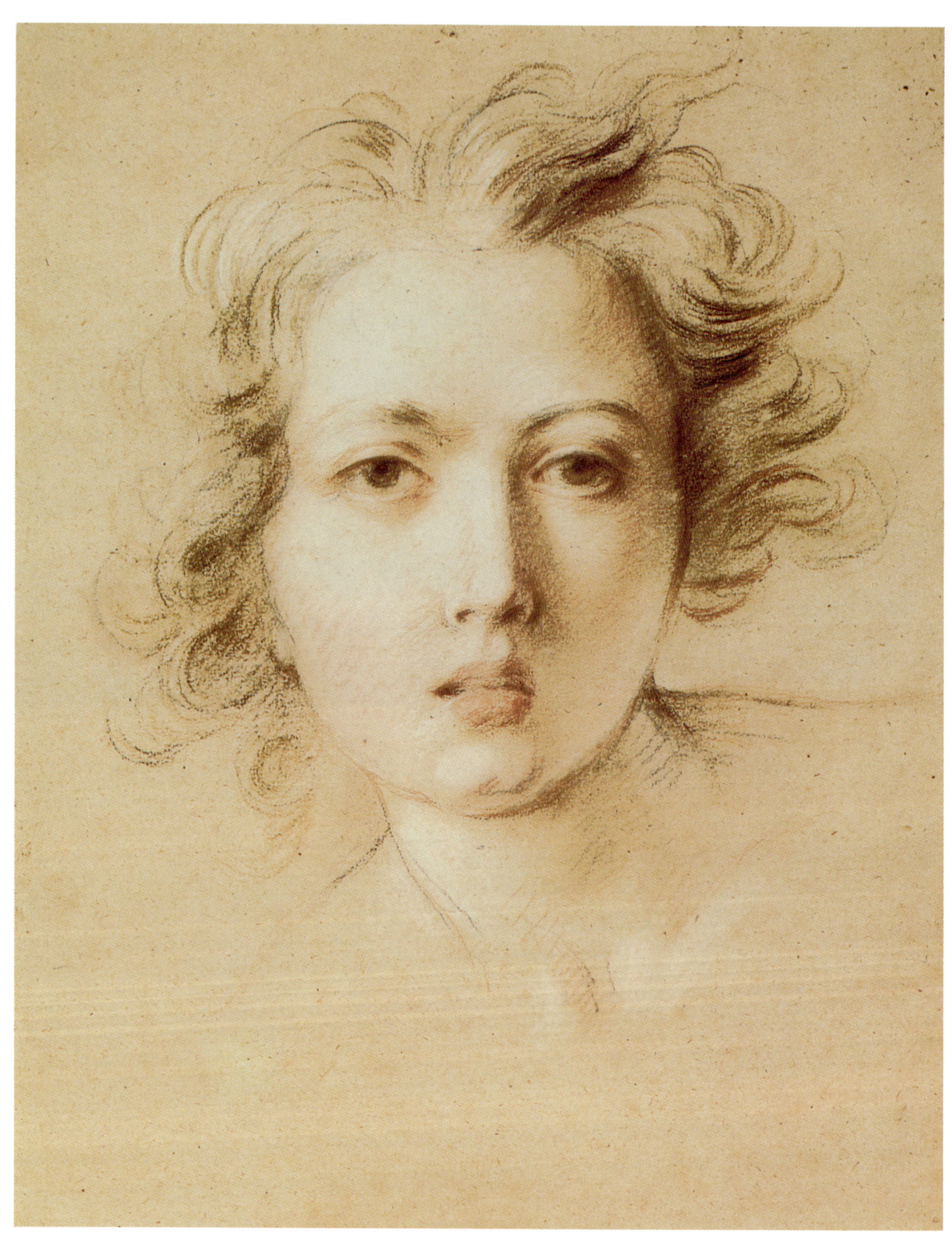

Plate 70. Attributed to John-Baptiste van Loo

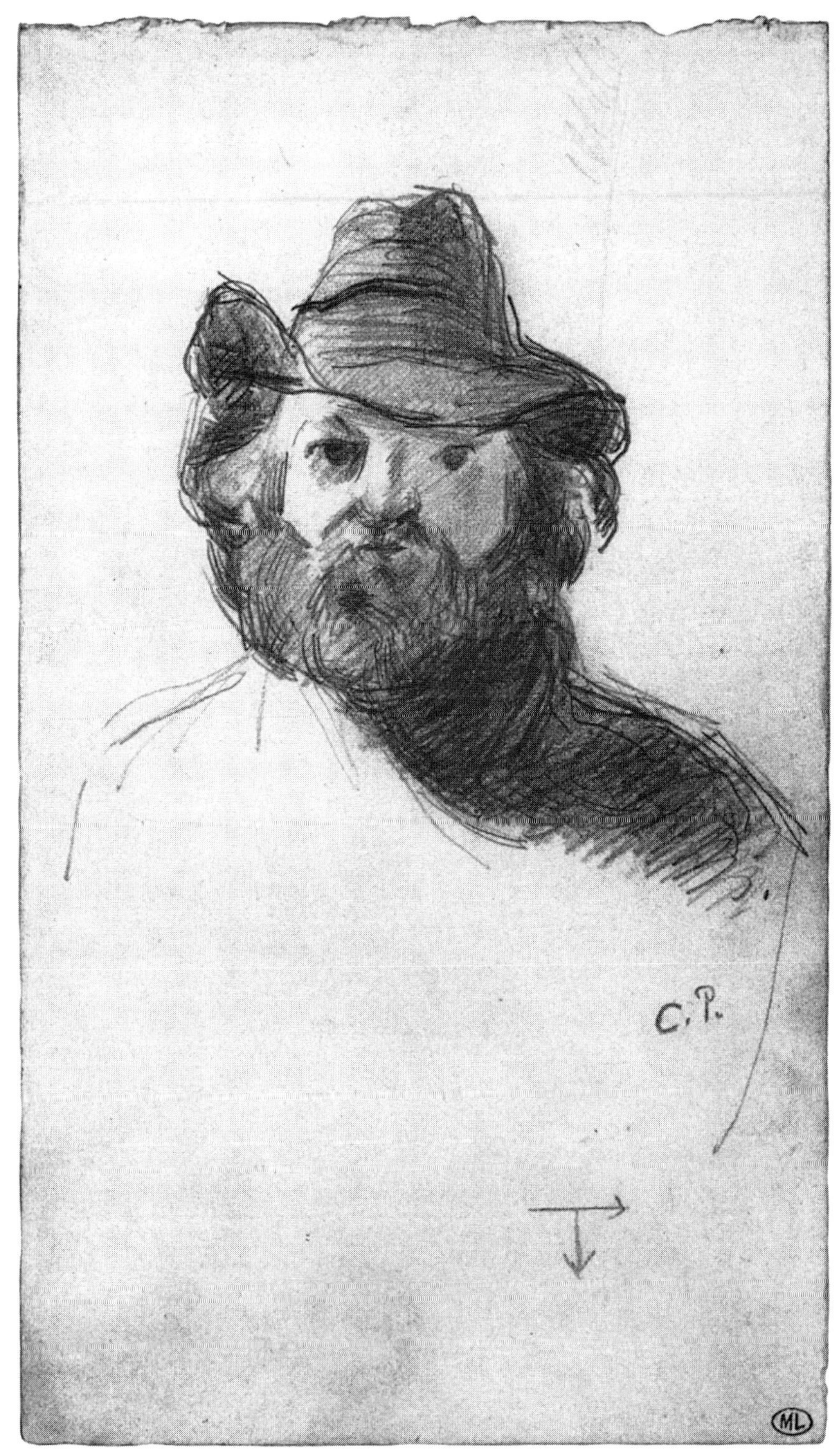

Plate 71. Camille Pissarro

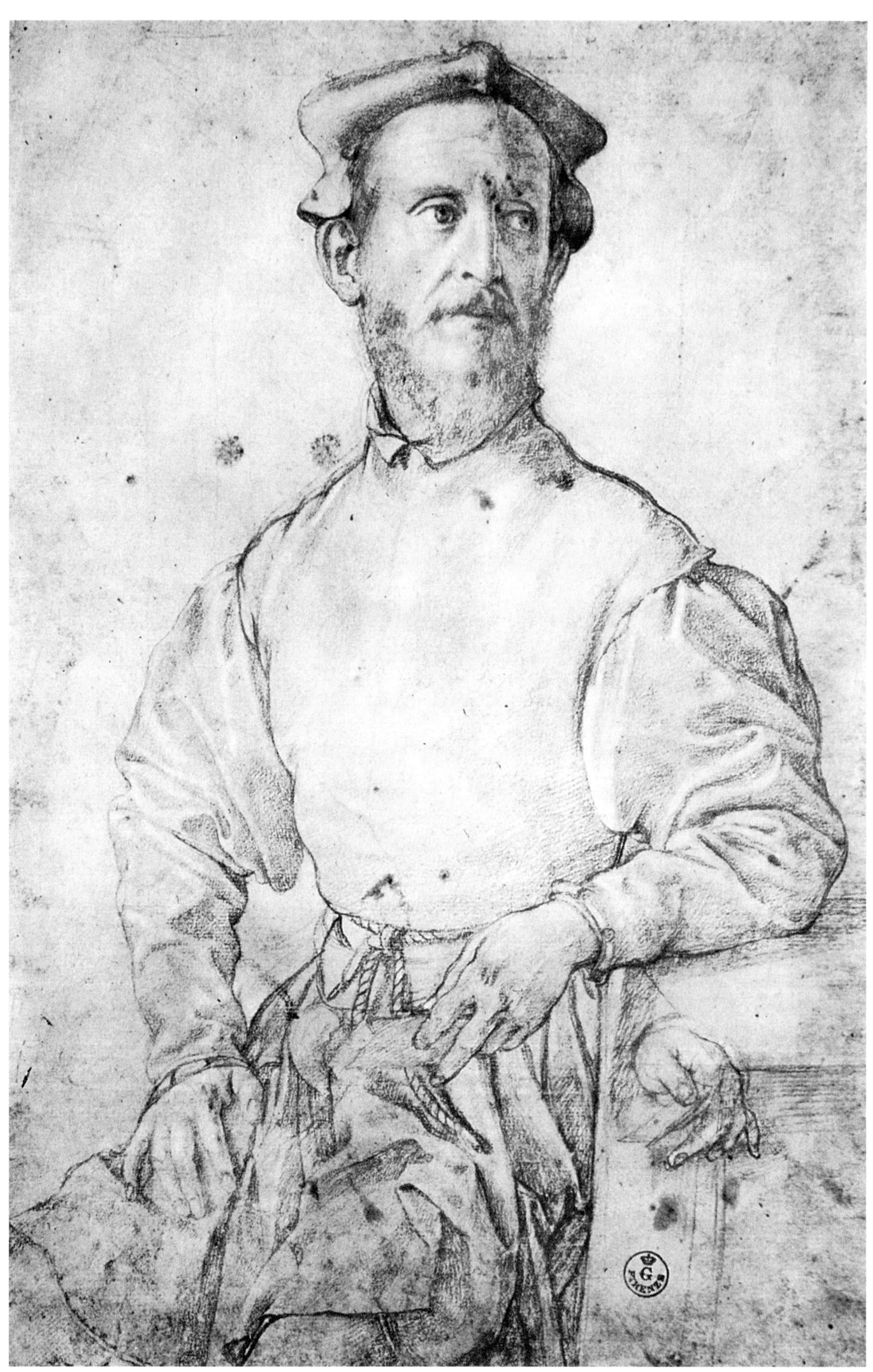

Plate 72. JACOPO DA PONTORMO

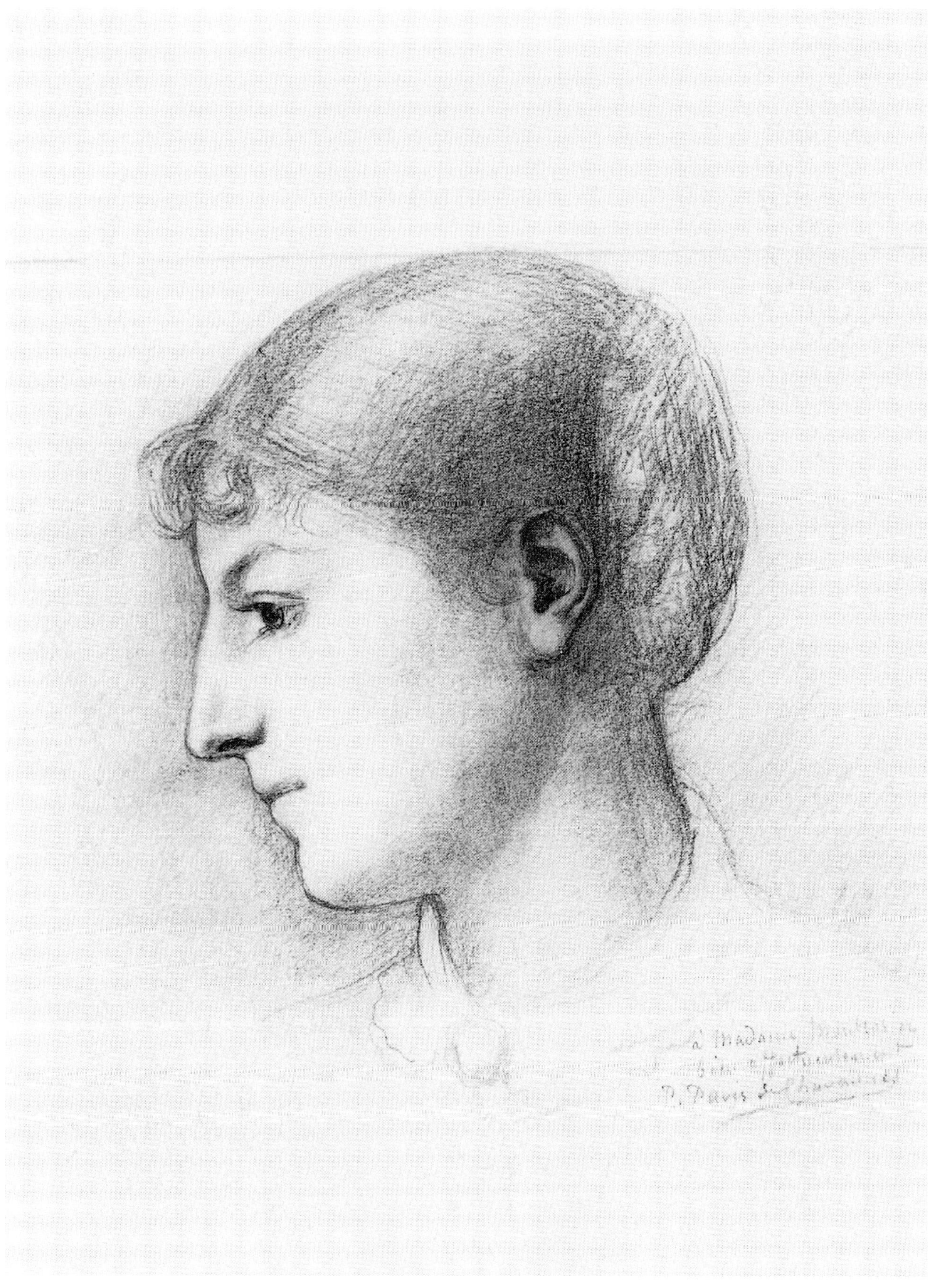

Plate 73. Pierre Puvis de Chavannes

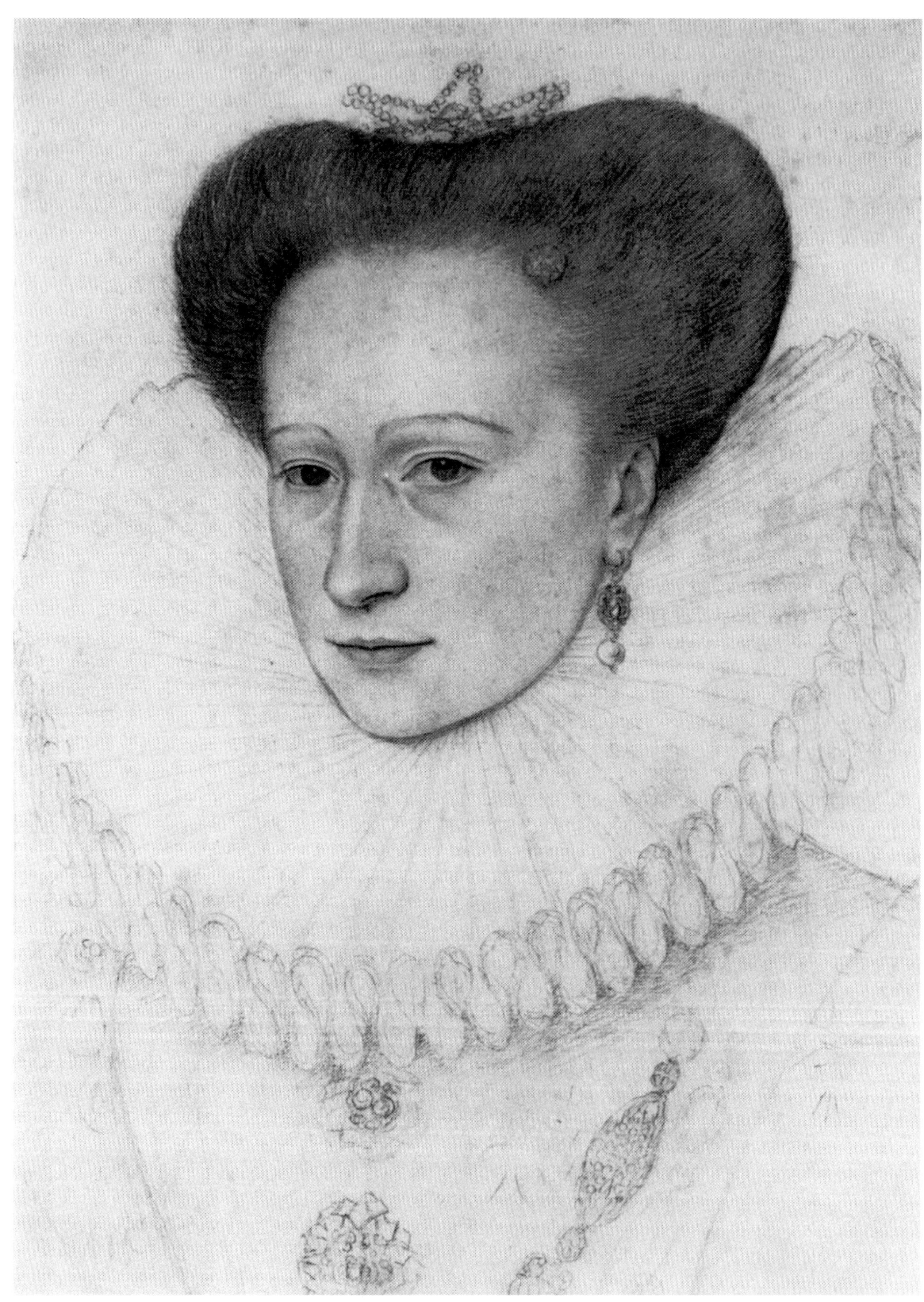

Plate 74. François Quesnel

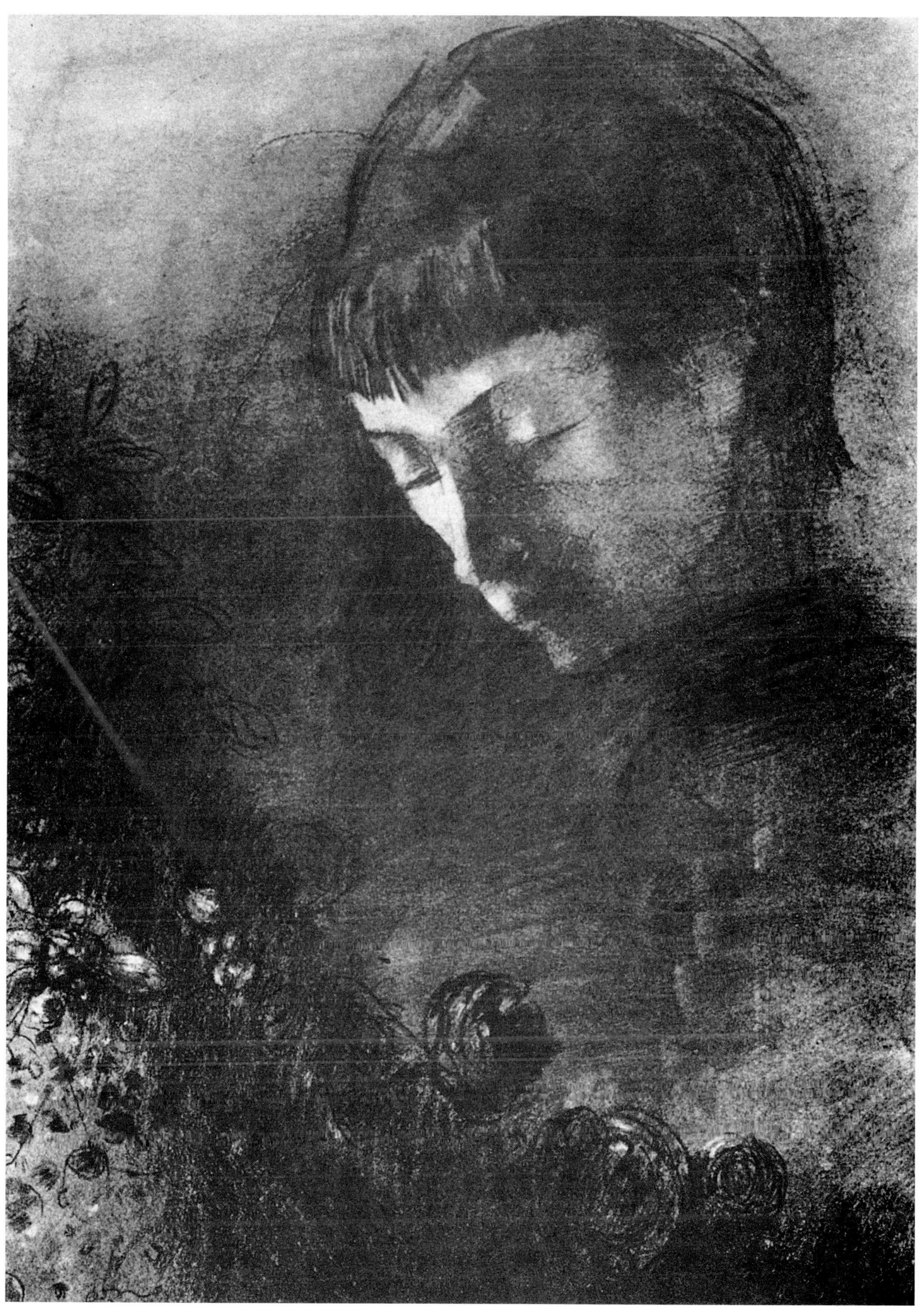

Plate 75. Odilon Redon

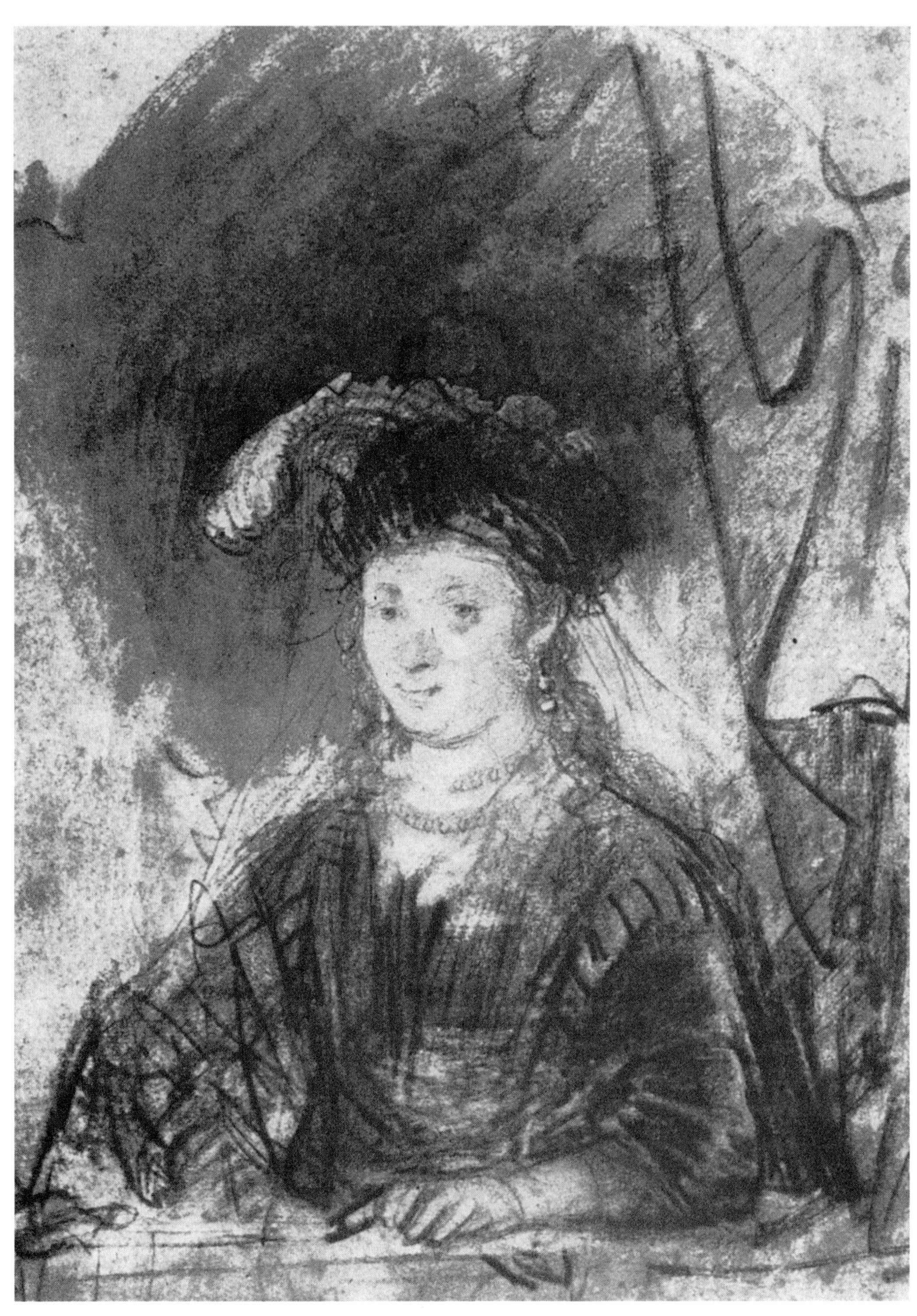

Plate 76. Rembrandt Harmensz van Rijn

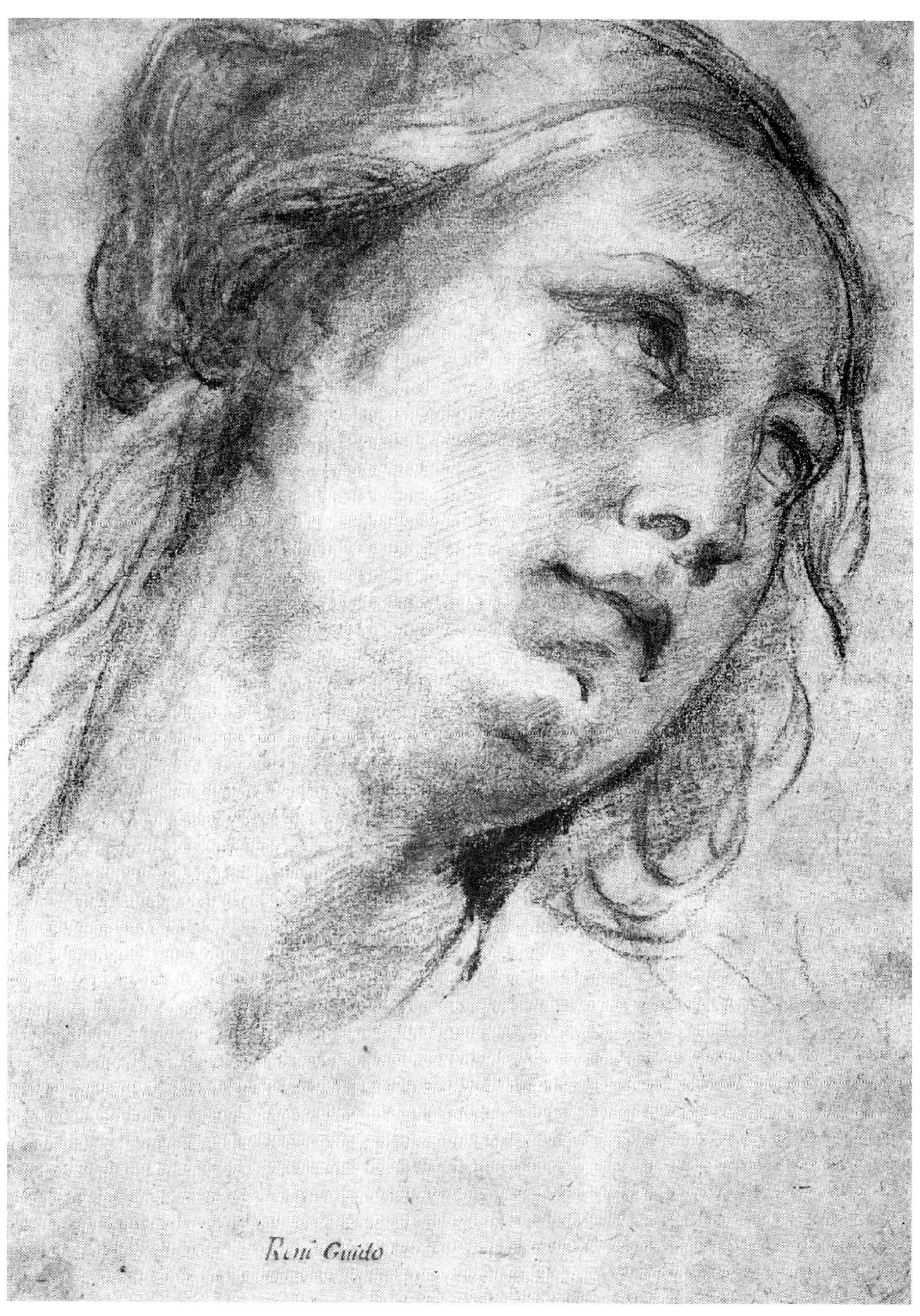

Plate 77. Guido Reni

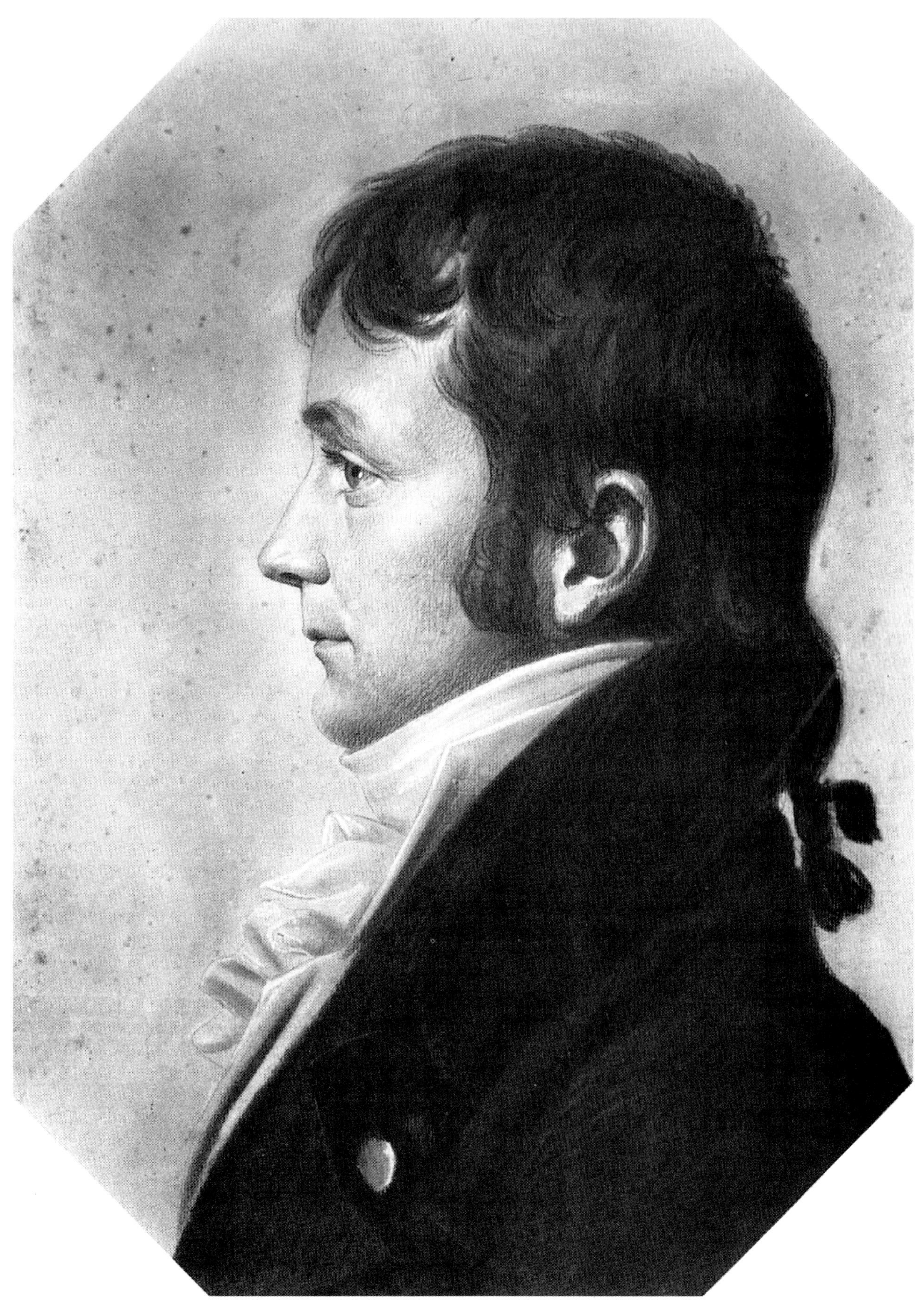

Plate 78. Charles Balthazar Julien Favret de Saint-Mémin

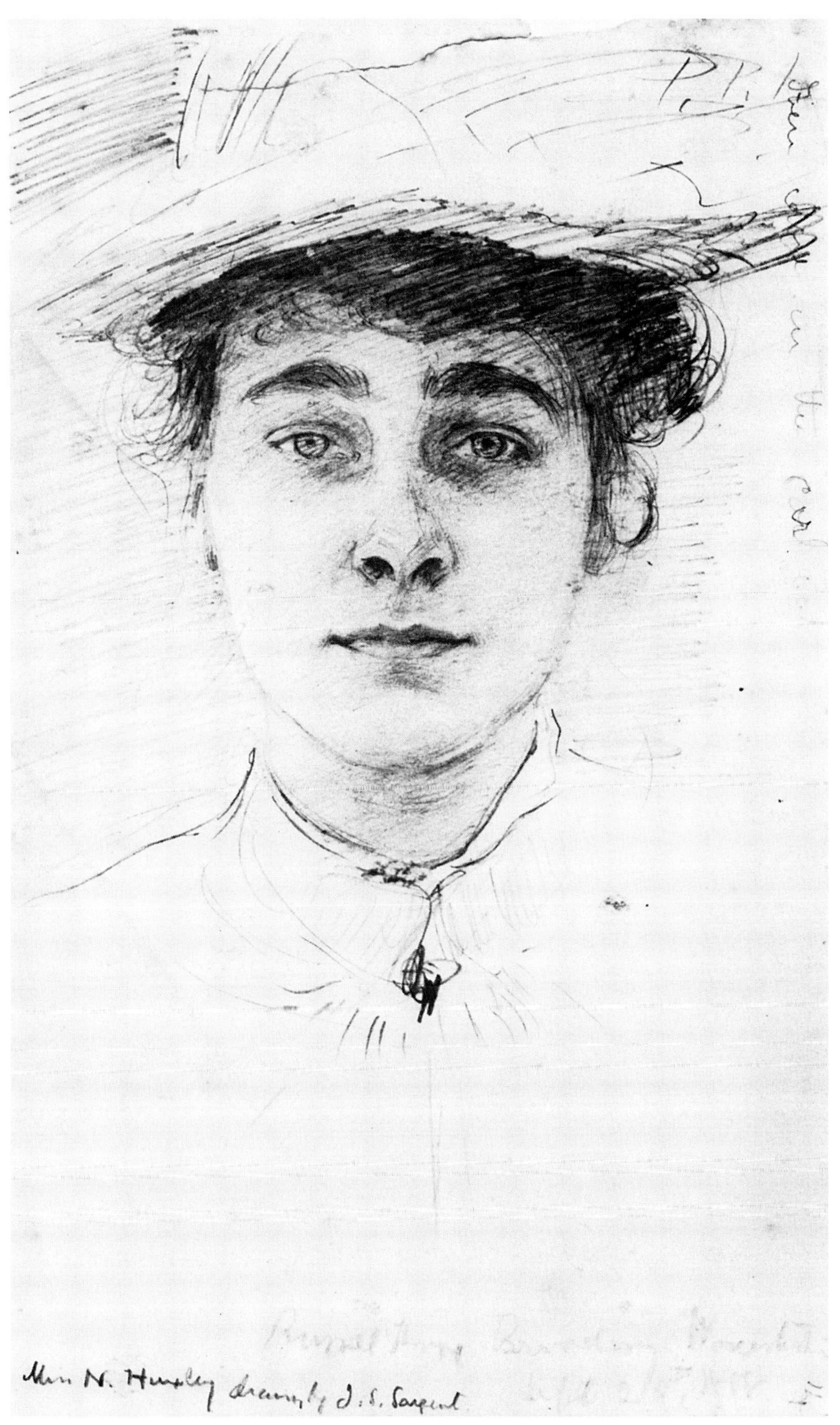

Plate 79. JOHN SINGER SARGENT

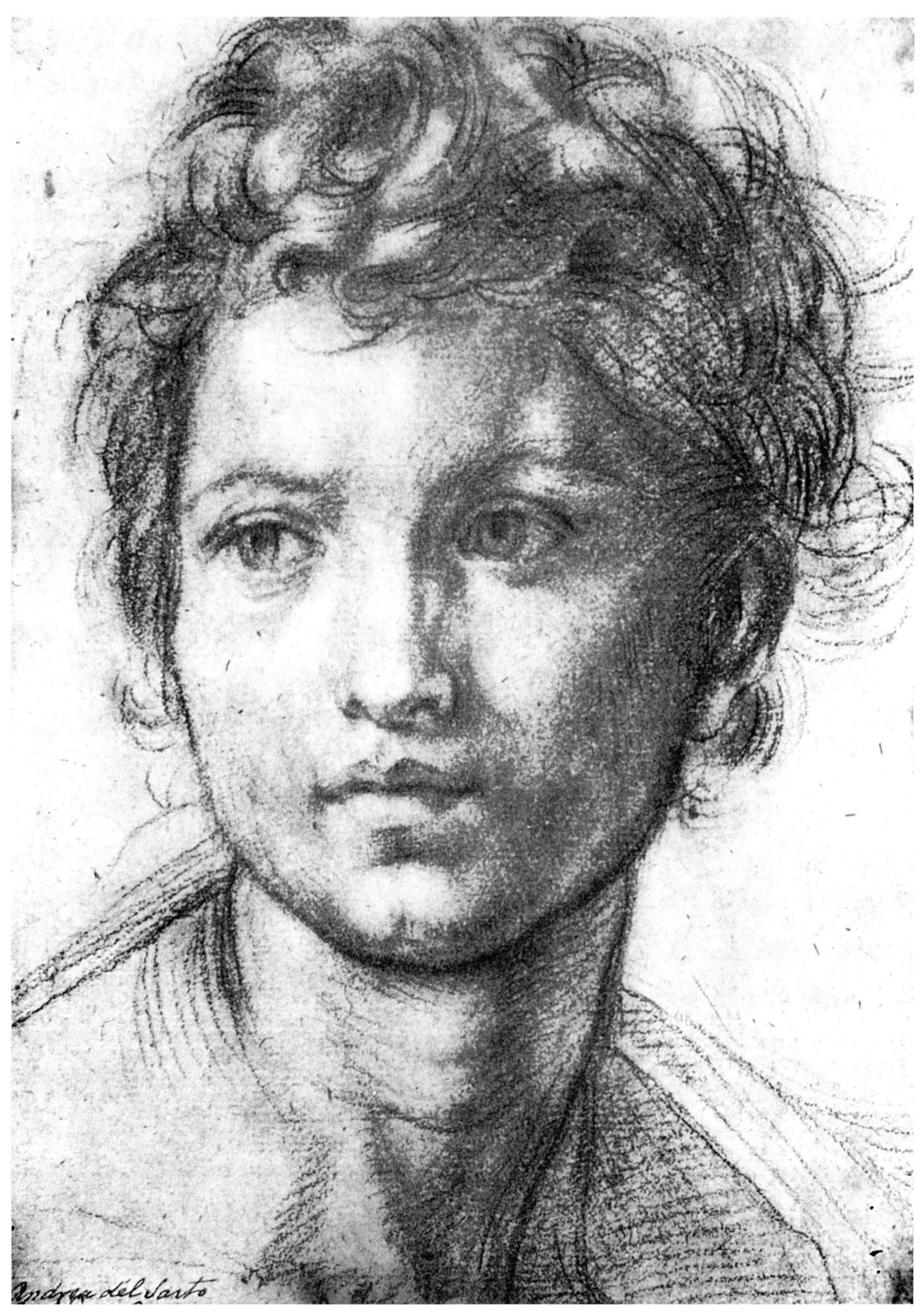

Plate 80. Andrea d'agnolo del Sarto

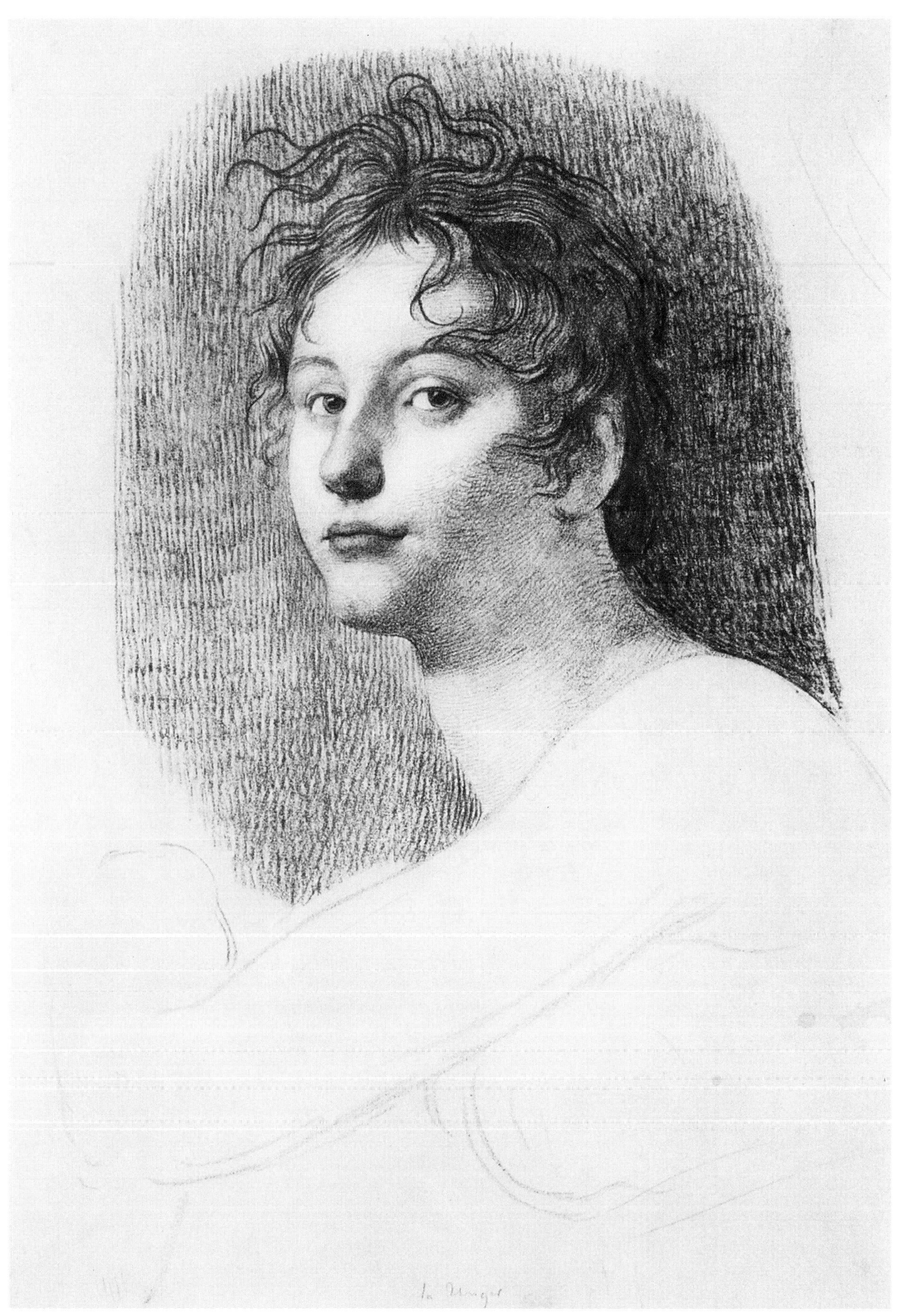

Plate 81. GOTTFRIED SCHADOW

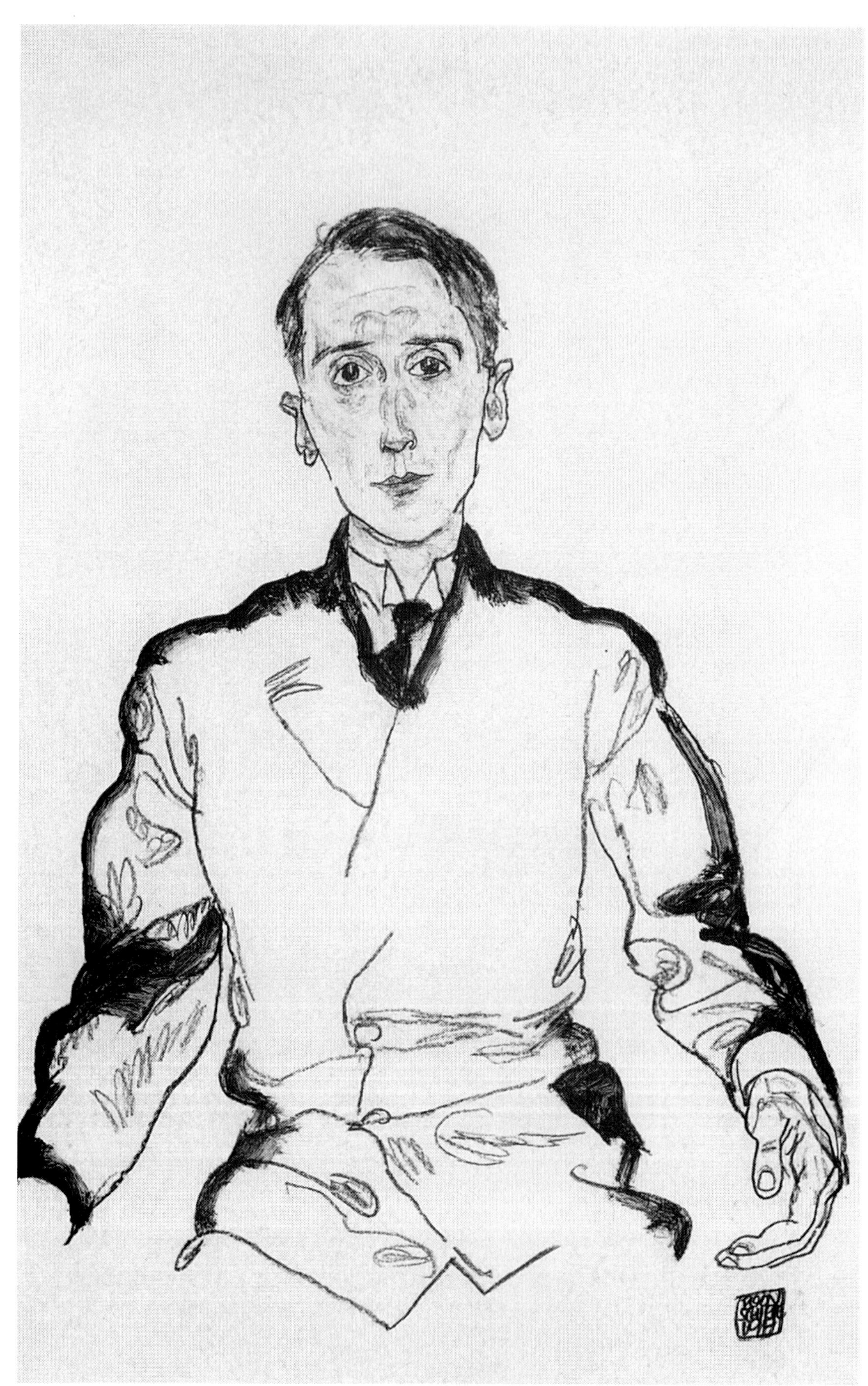

Plate 82. EGON SCHIELE

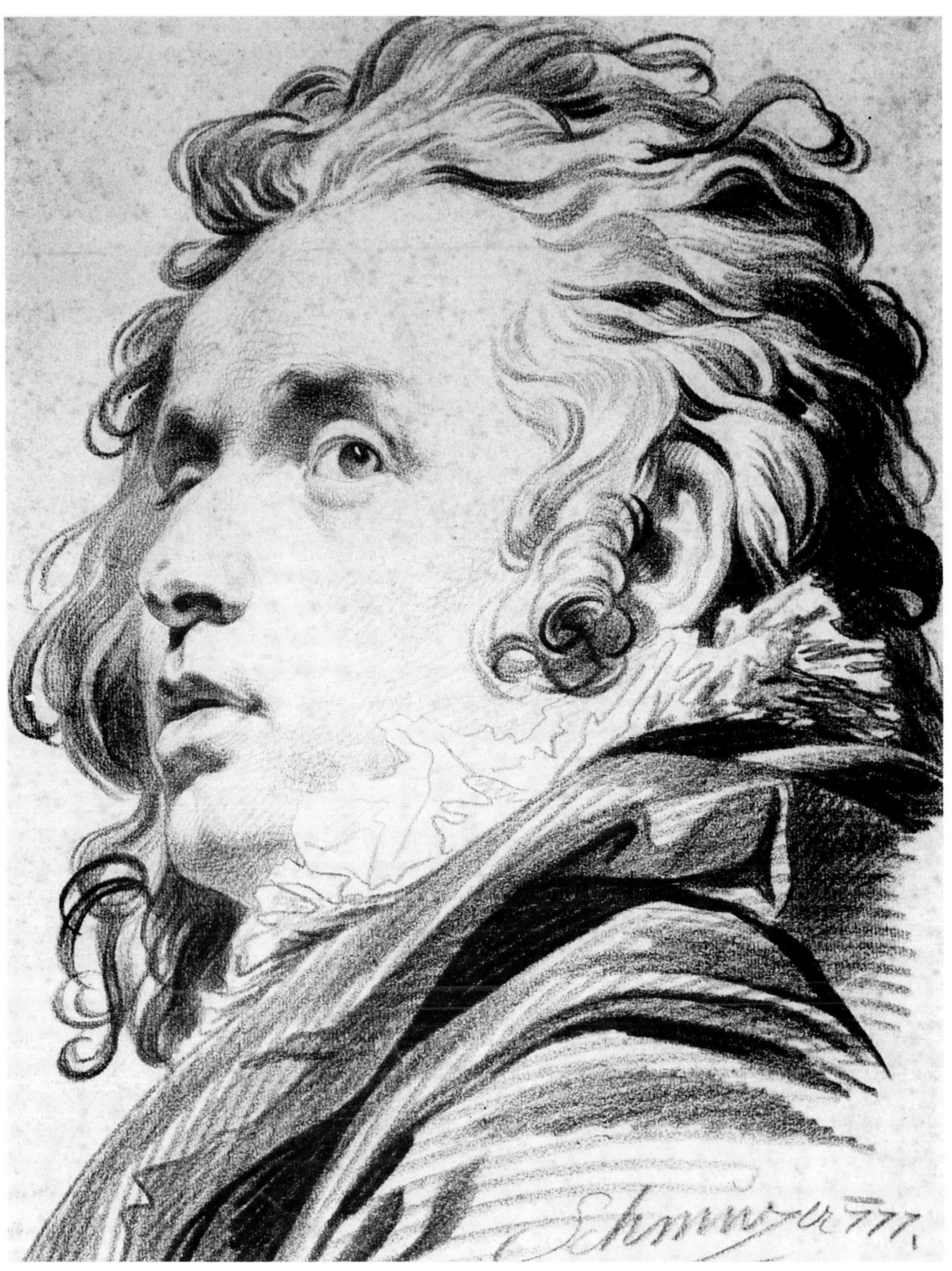

Plate 83. Jakob Mathias Schmutzer

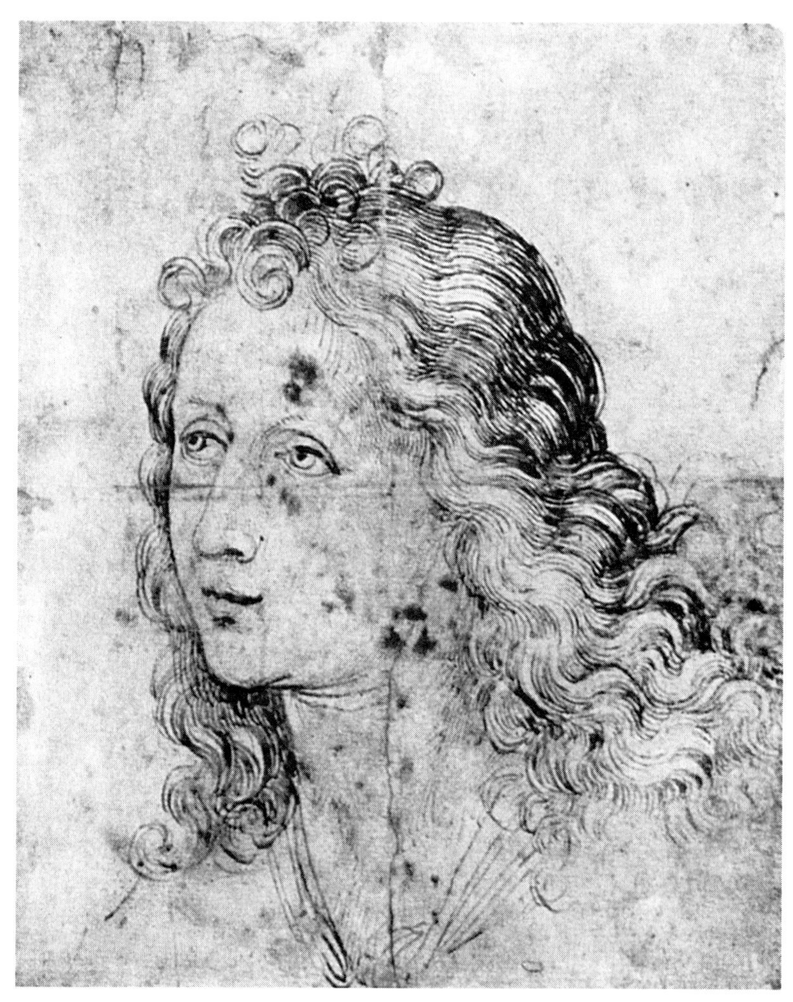

Plate 84. MARTIN SCHONGAUER

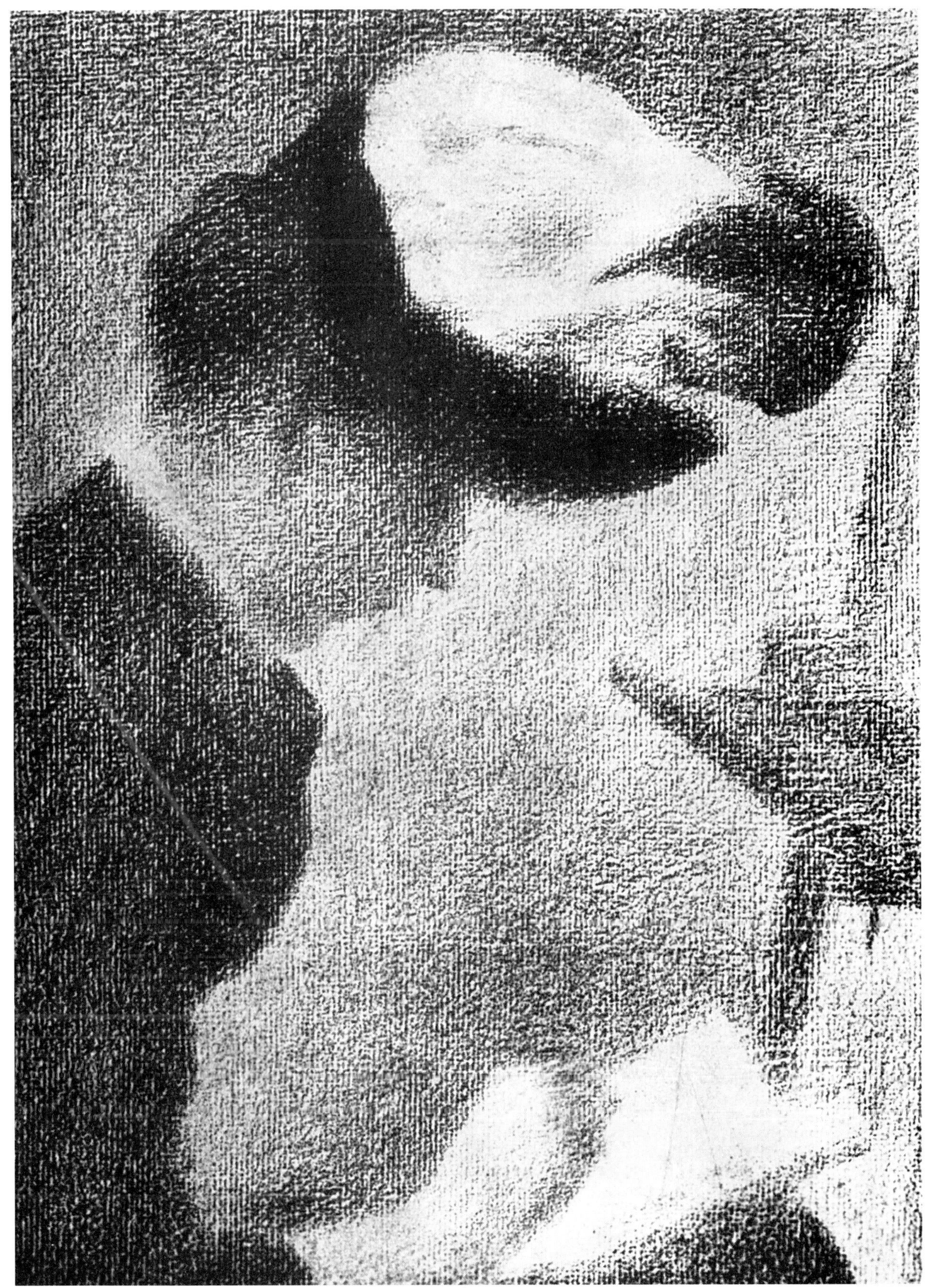

Plate 85. Georges Seurat

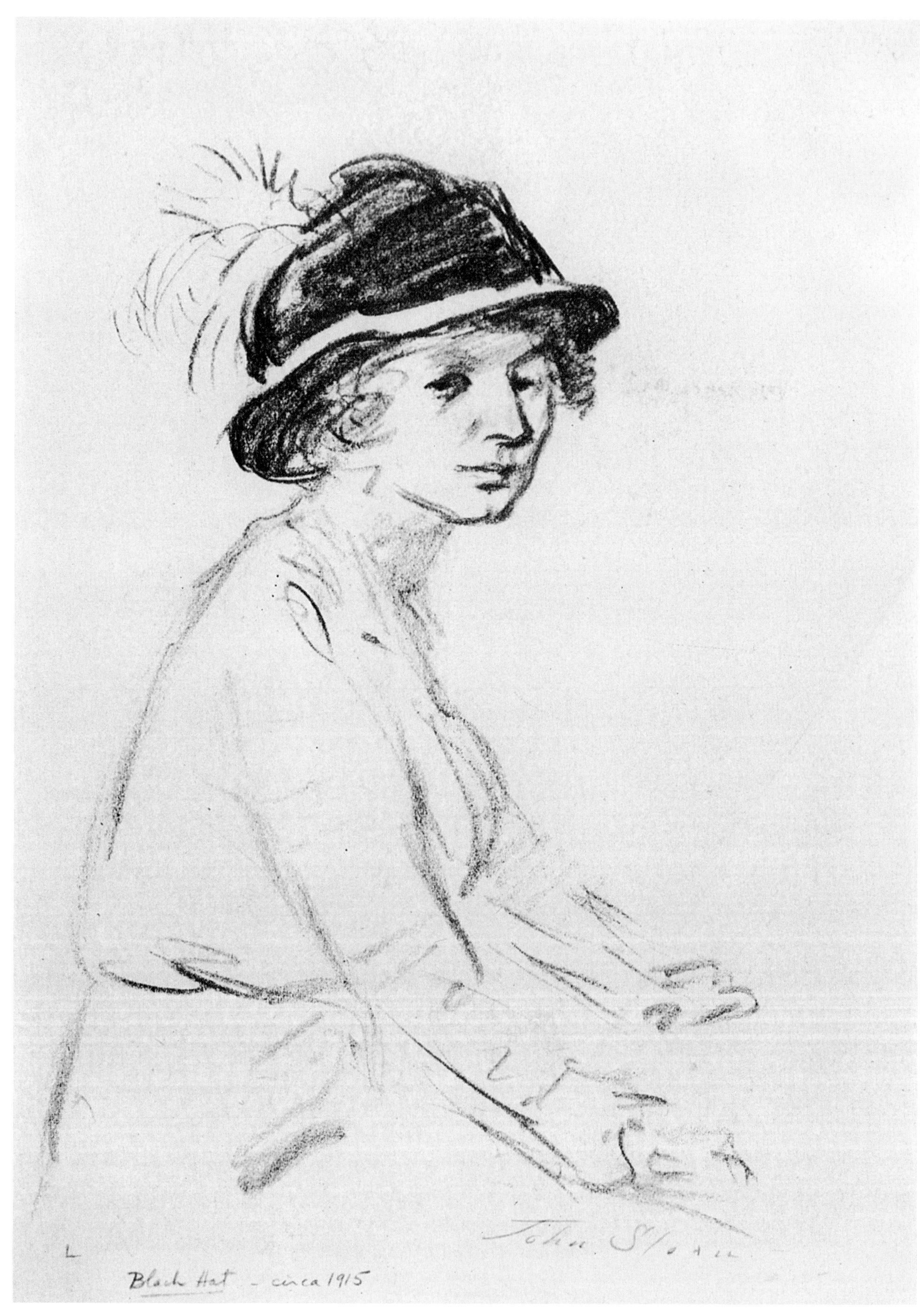

Plate 86. JOHN SLOAN

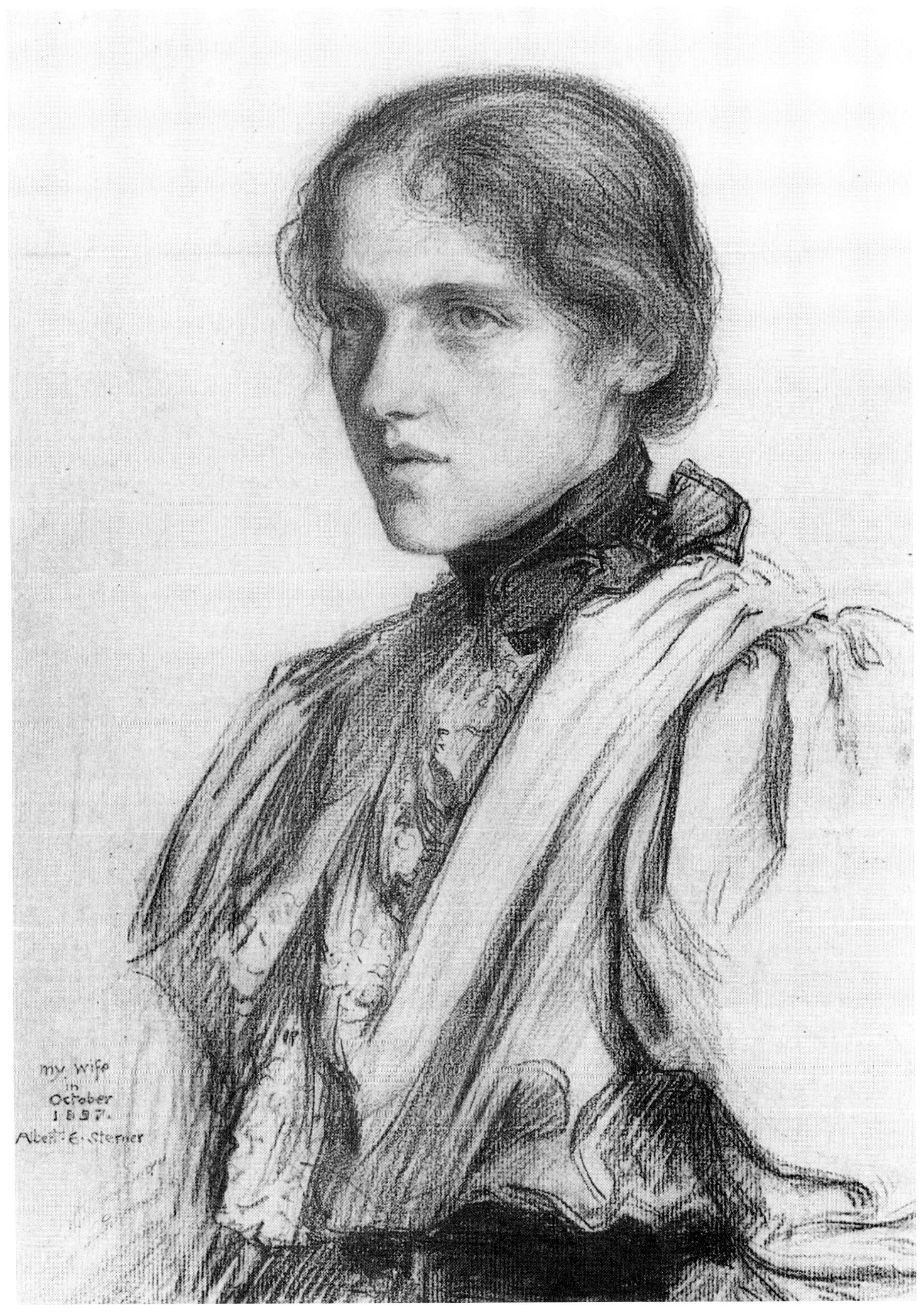

Plate 87. ALBERT EDWARD STERNER

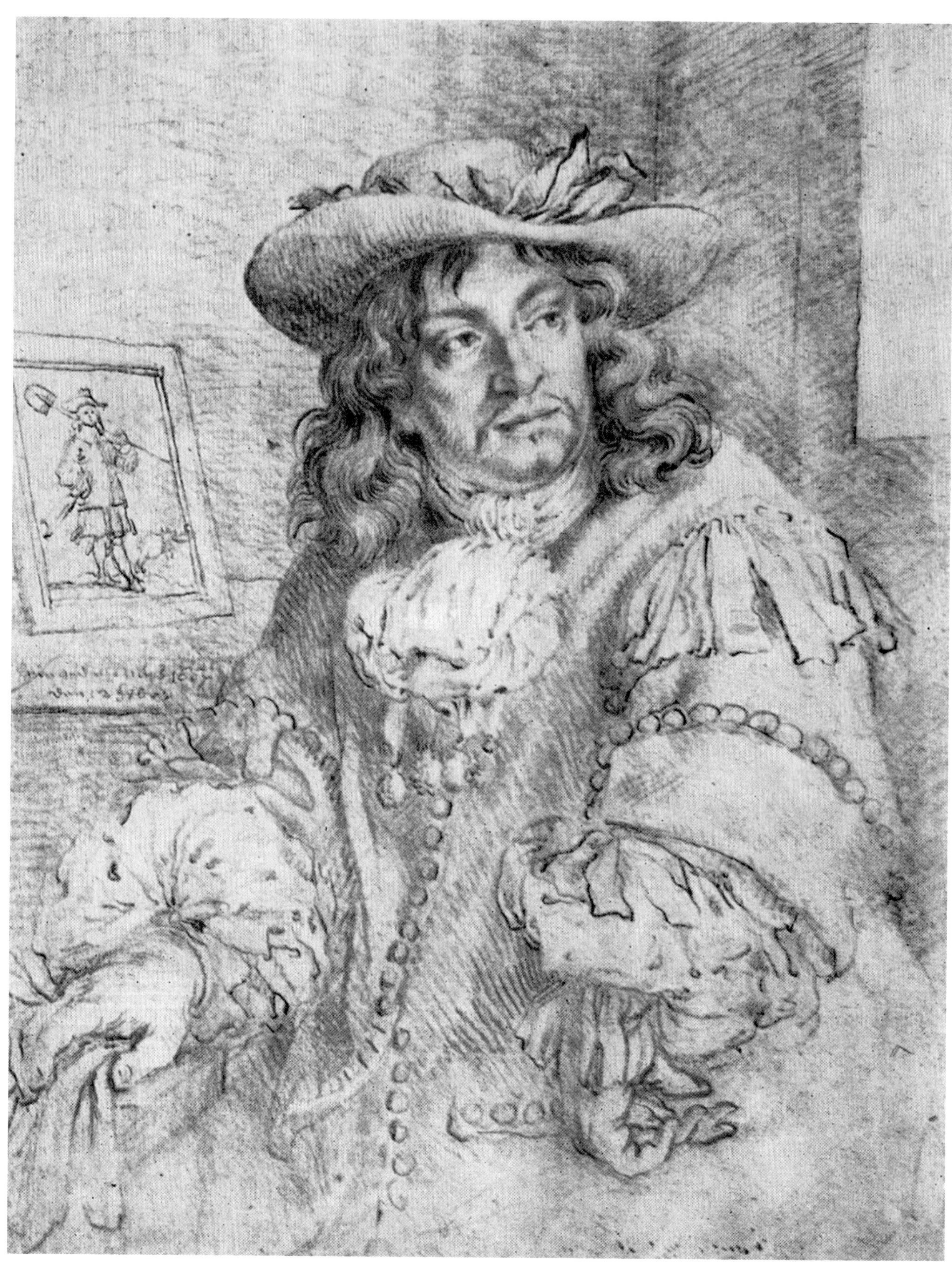

Plate 88. GEORG STRAUCH

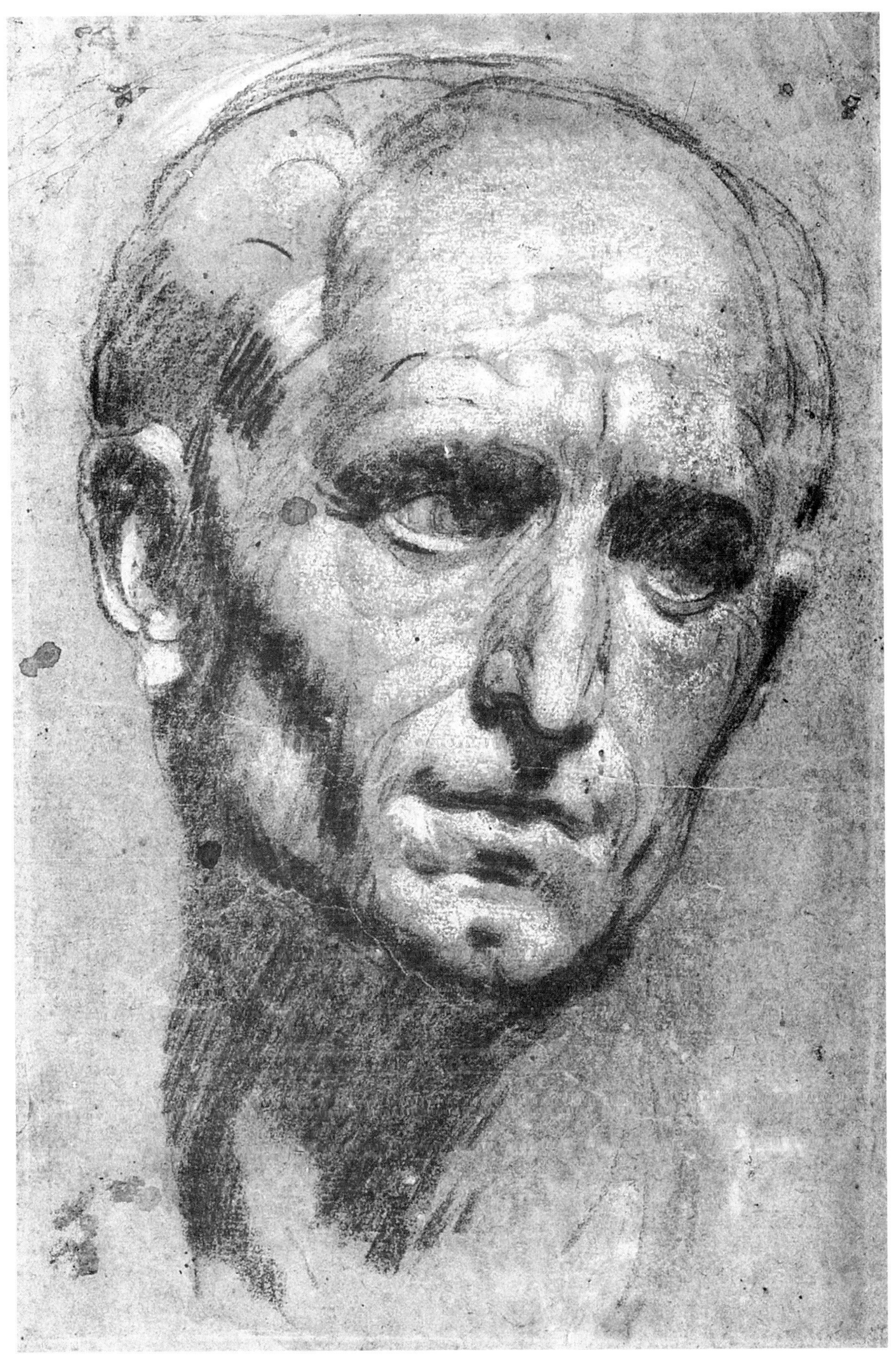

Plate 89. JACOPO TINTORETTO

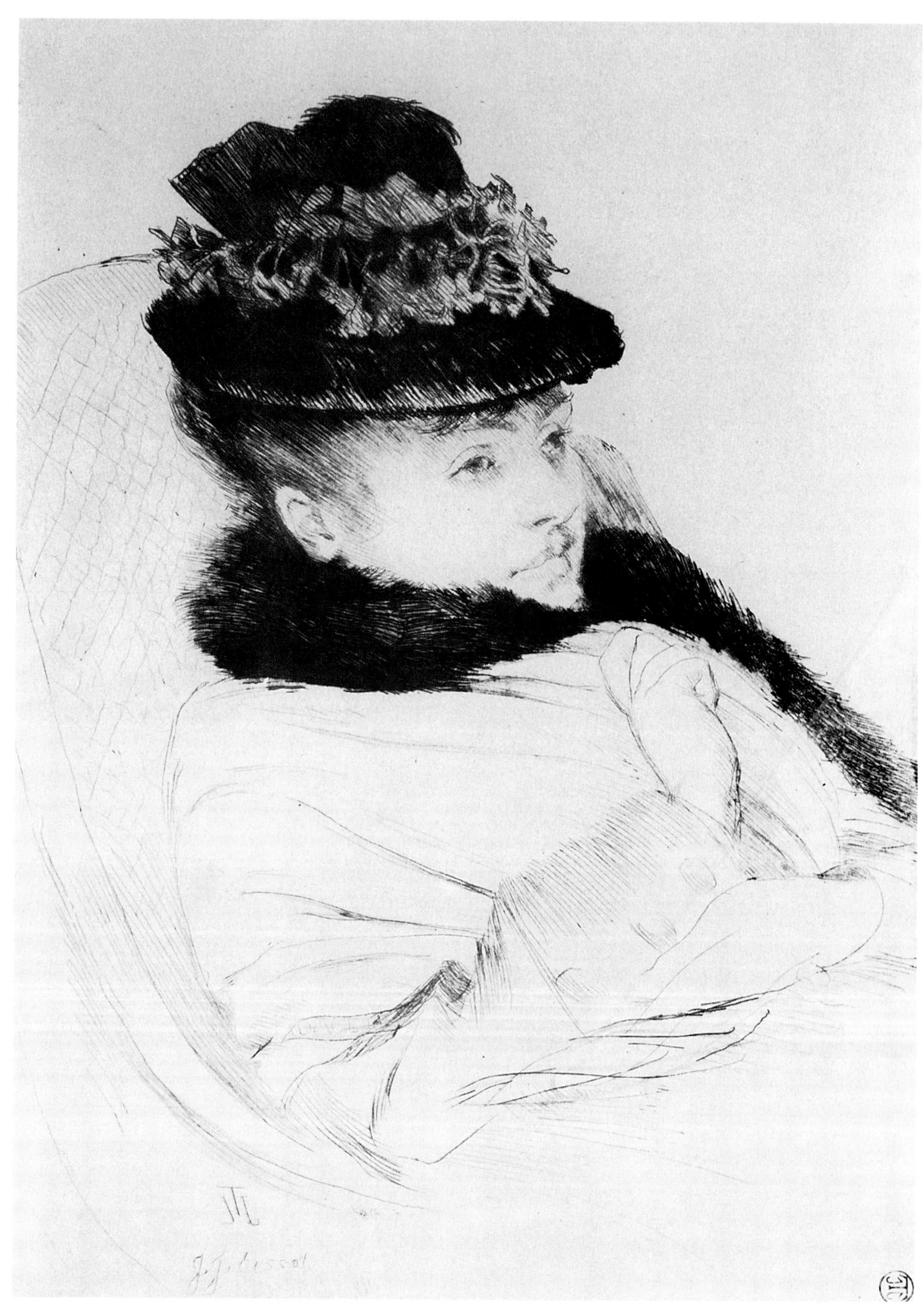

Plate 90. JAMES TISSOT

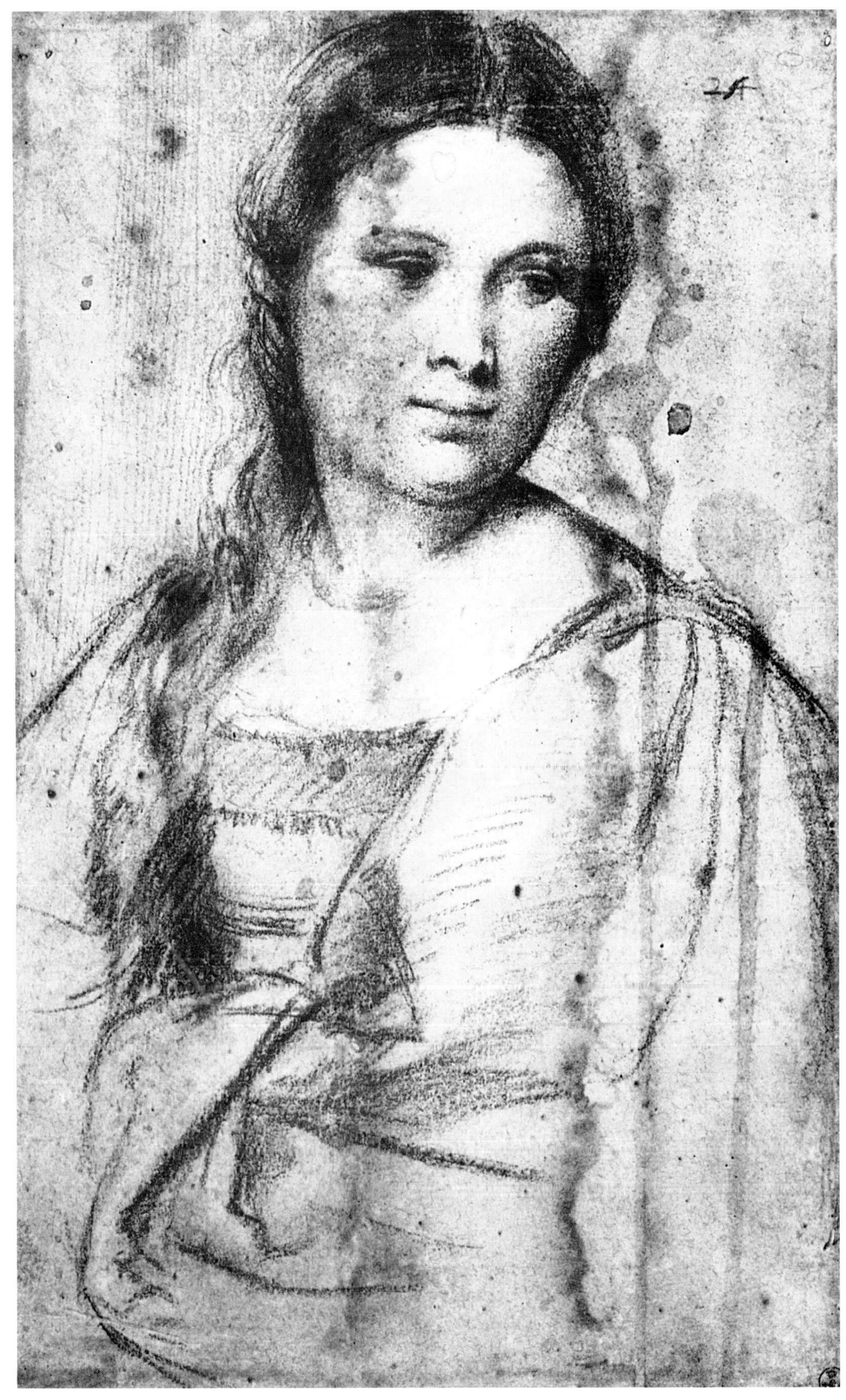

Plate 91. TITIAN (TIZIANO VECELLIO)

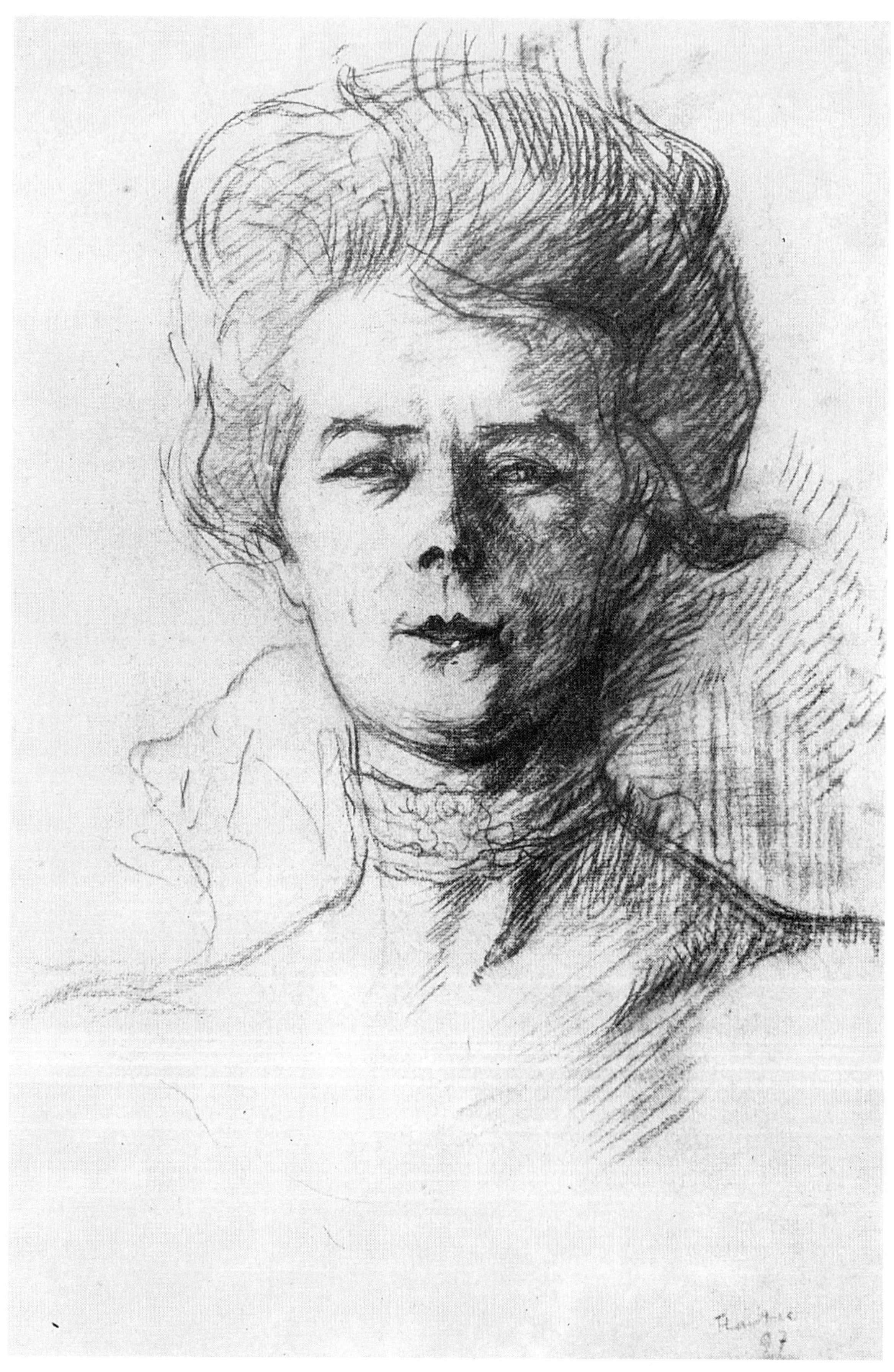

Plate 92. Henri de Toulouse-Lautrec

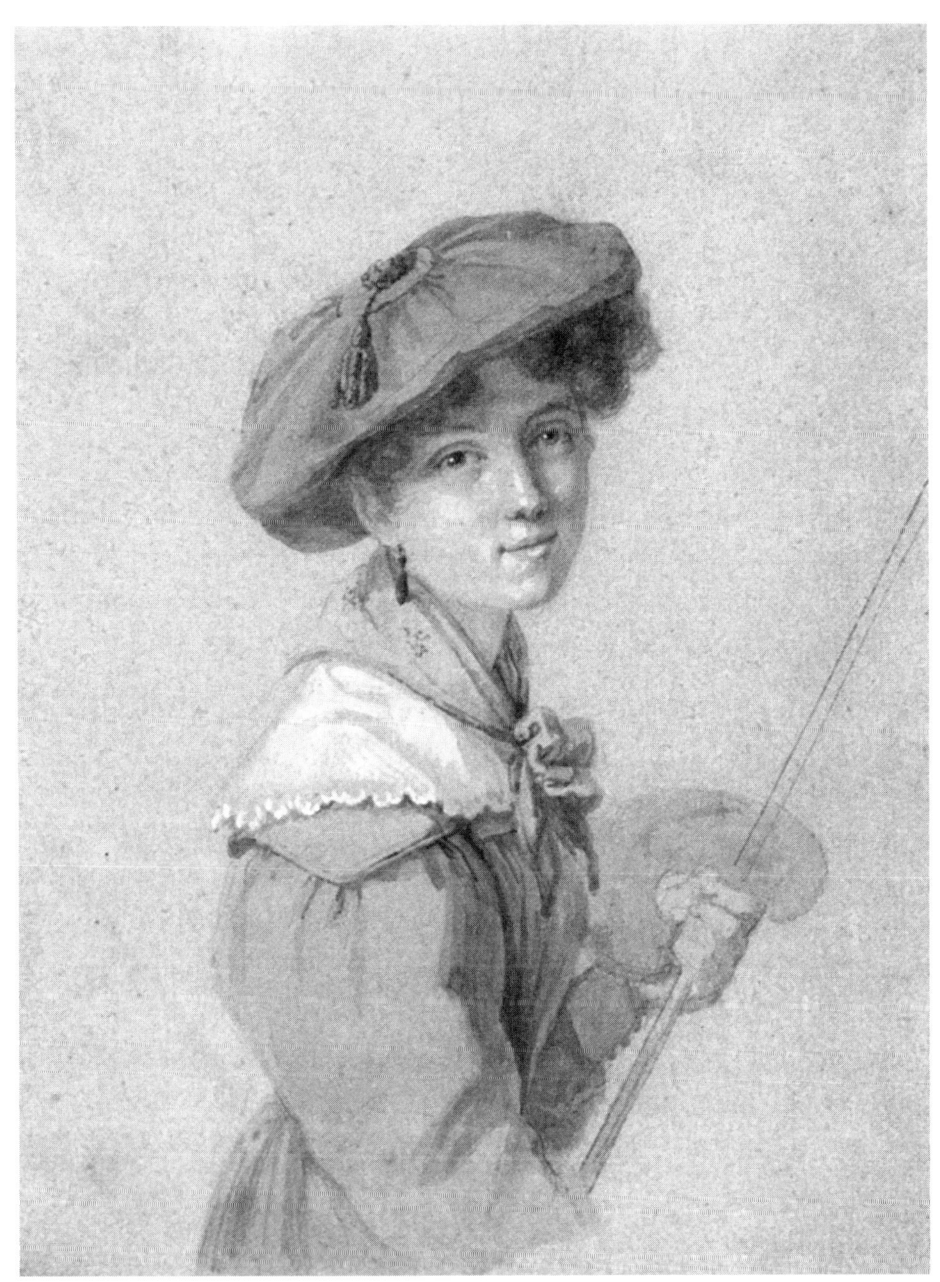

Plate 93. Attributed to EUGÉNIE TRIPIER-LE FRANC

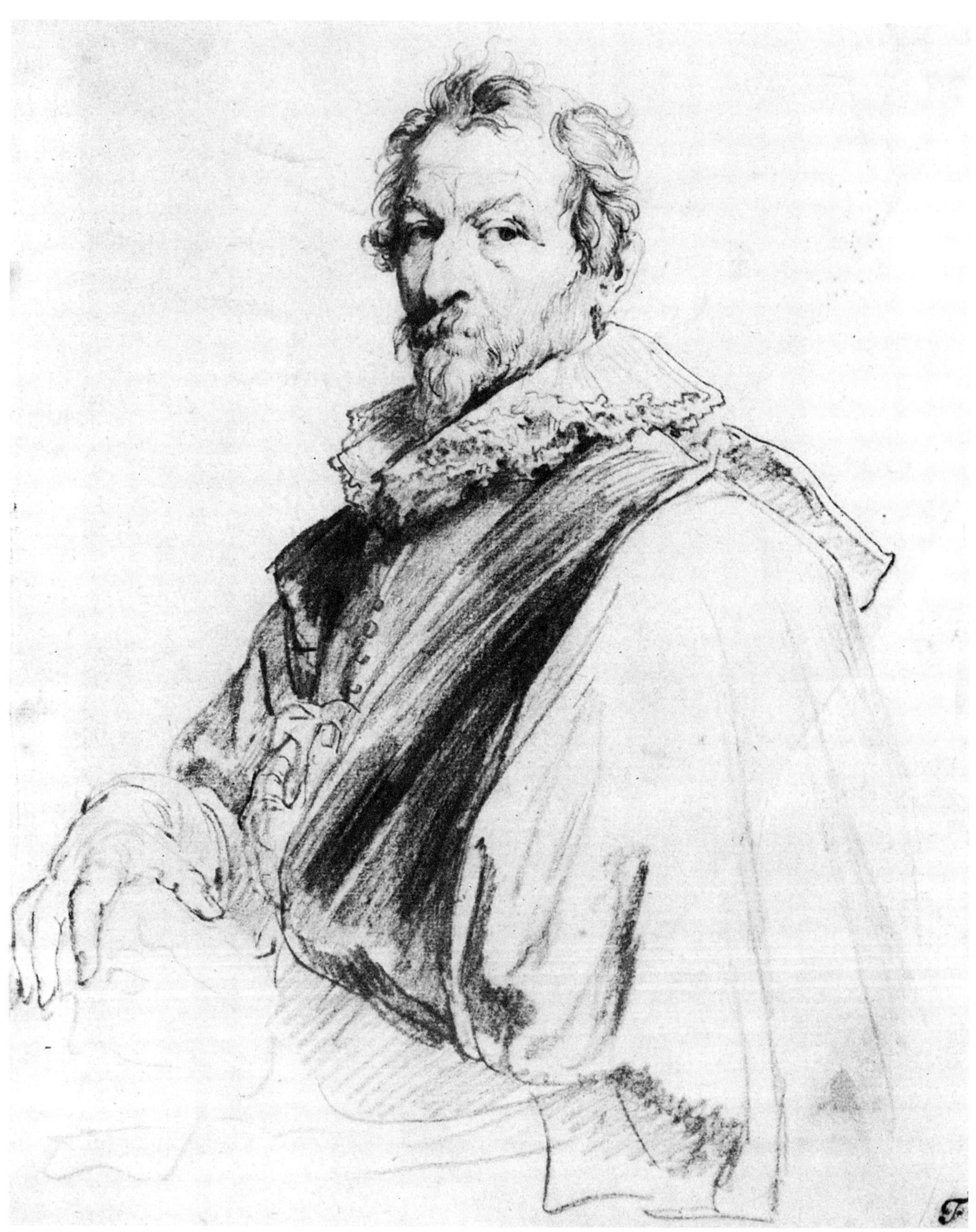

Plate 94. Anthony van Dyck

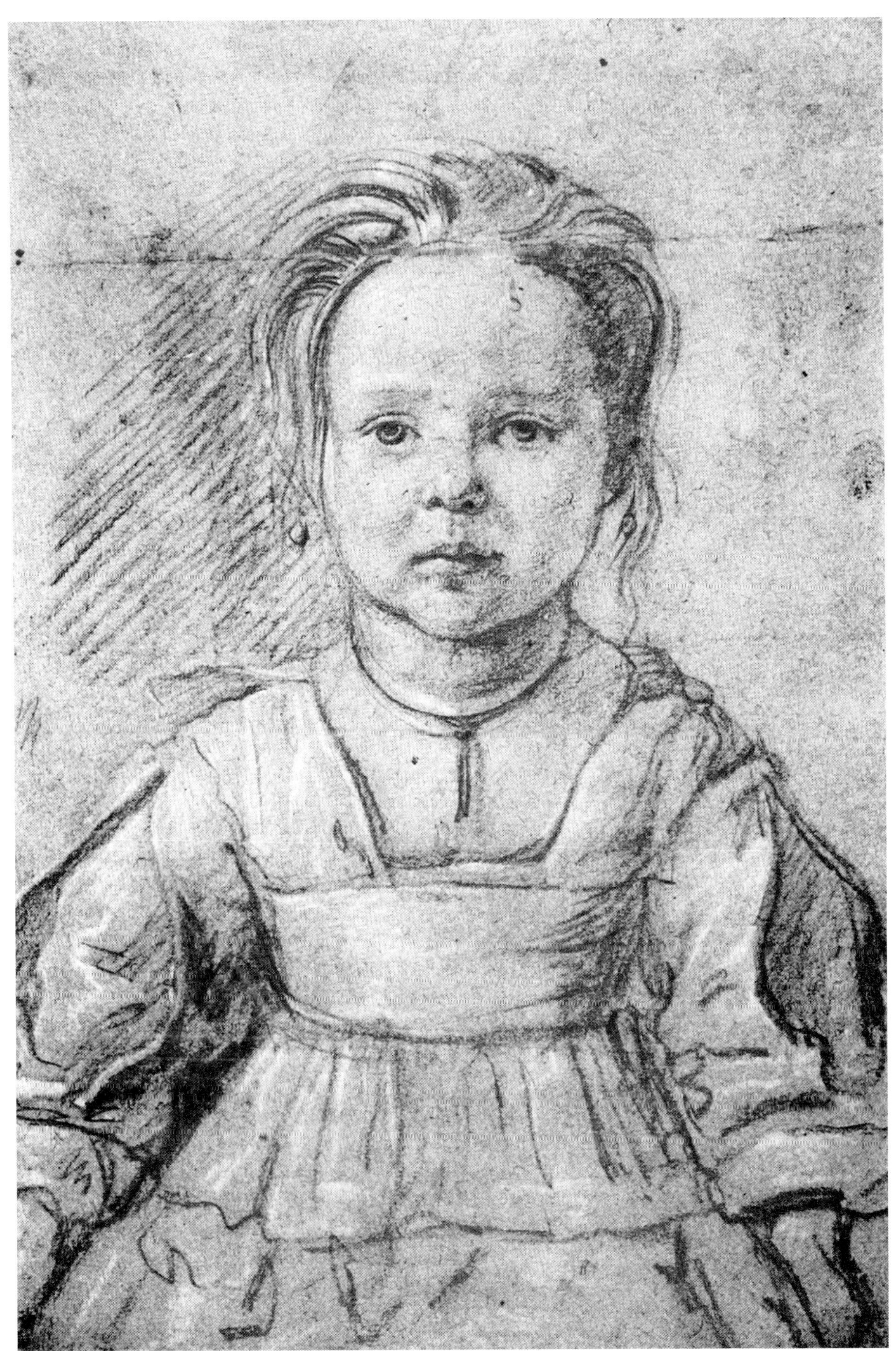

Plate 95. DIEGO VELÁZQUEZ

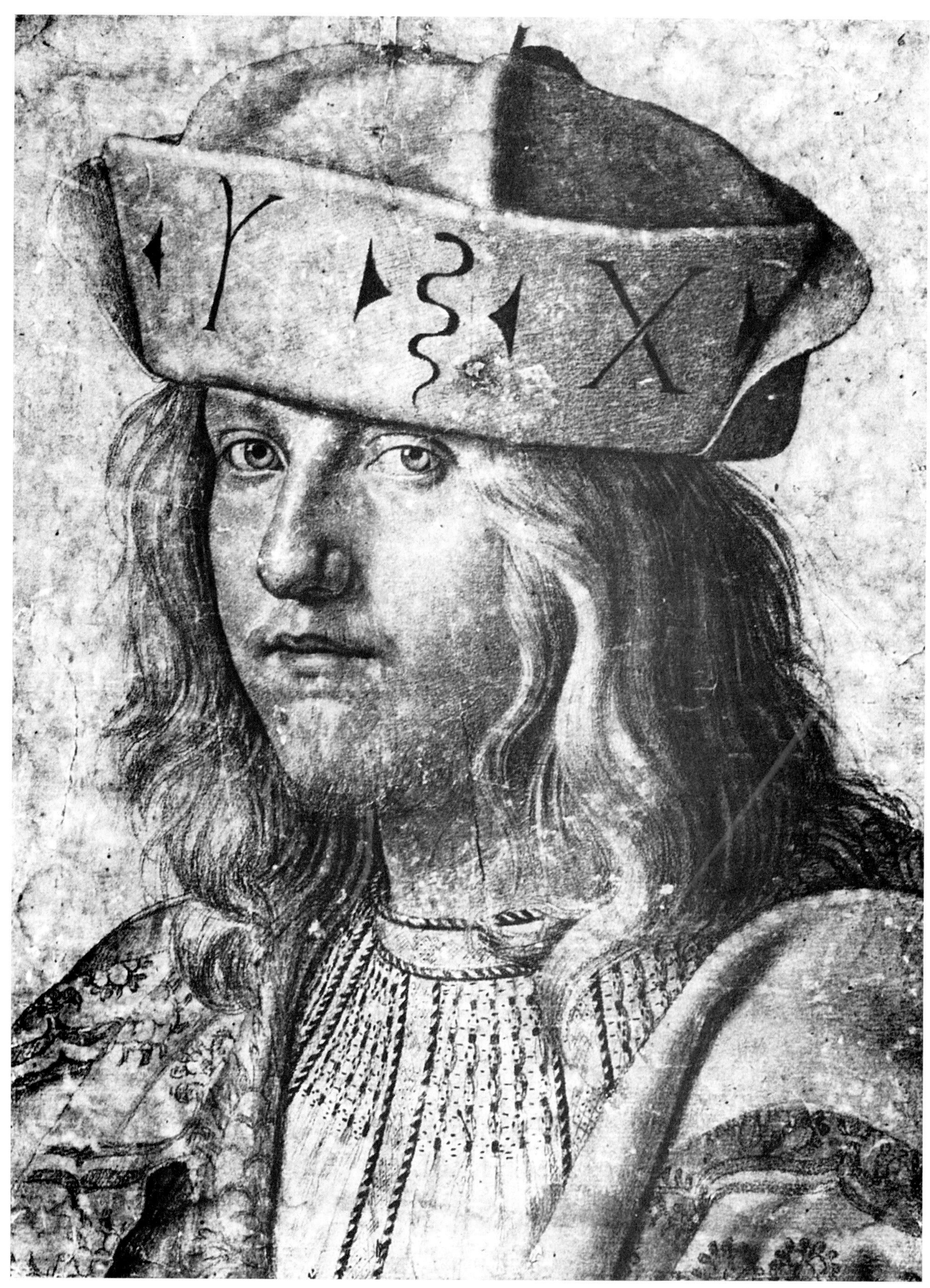

Plate 96. Bartolommeo Veneto

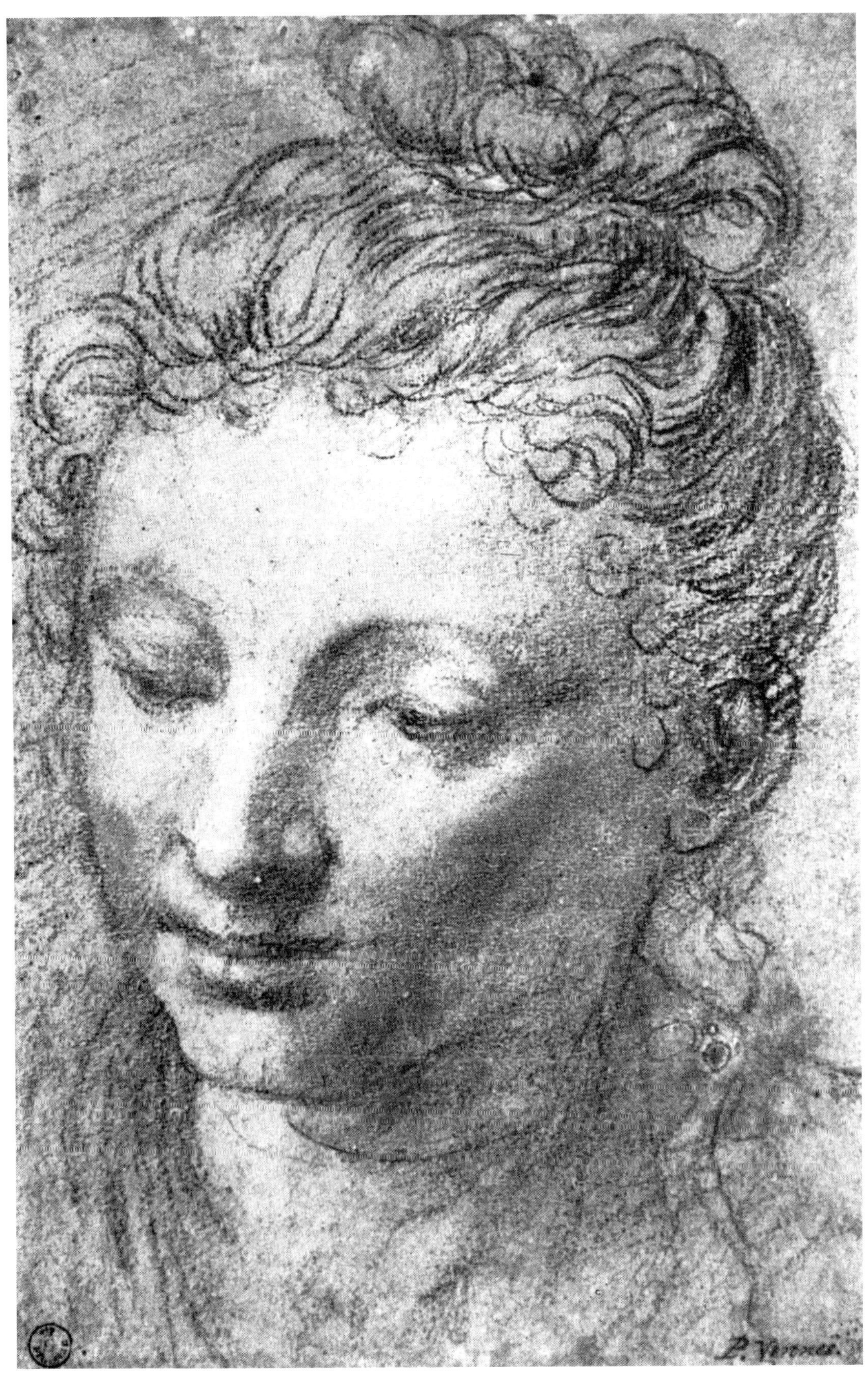

Plate 97. Veronese (Paolo Caliari)

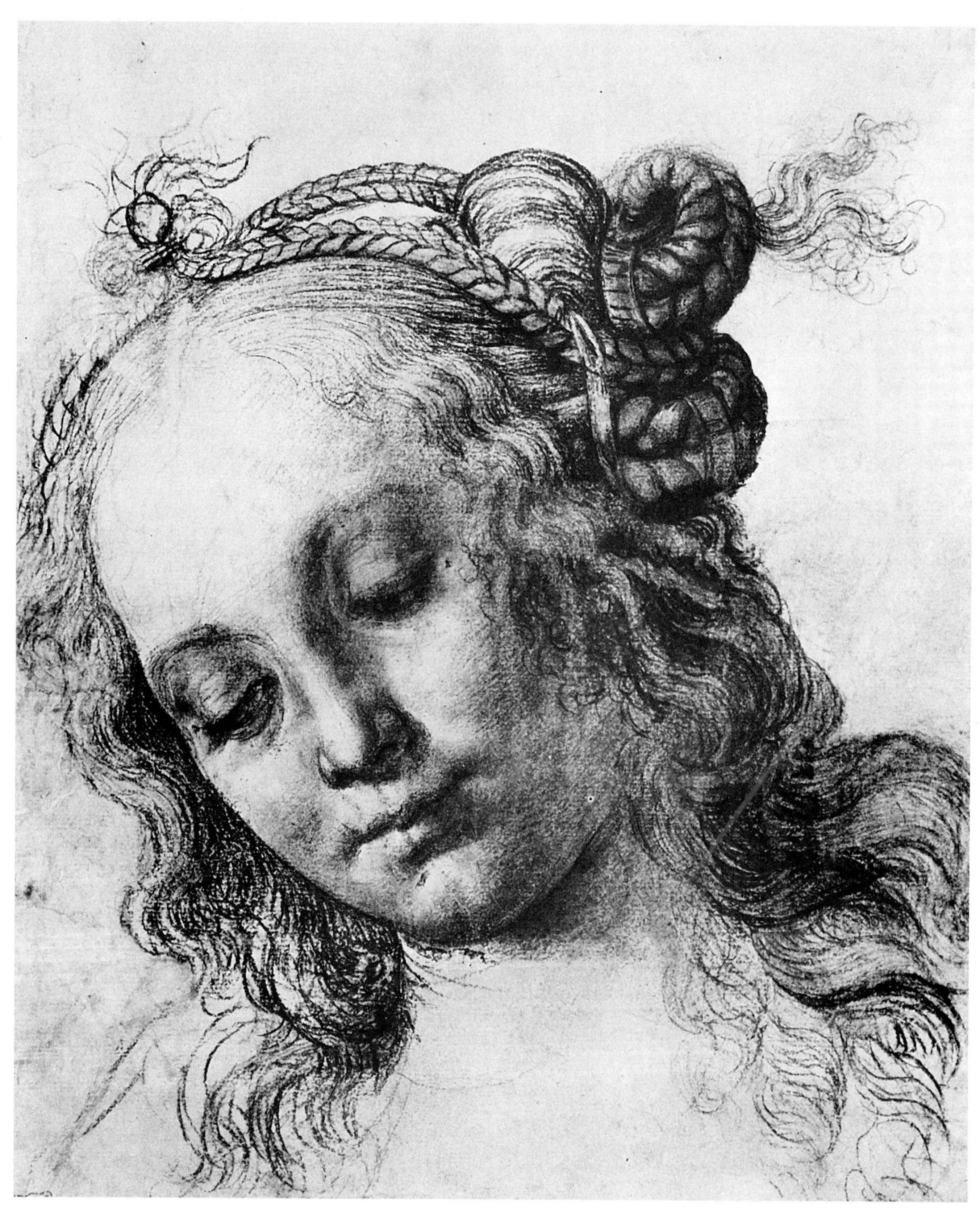

Plate 98. Andrea del Verrocchio

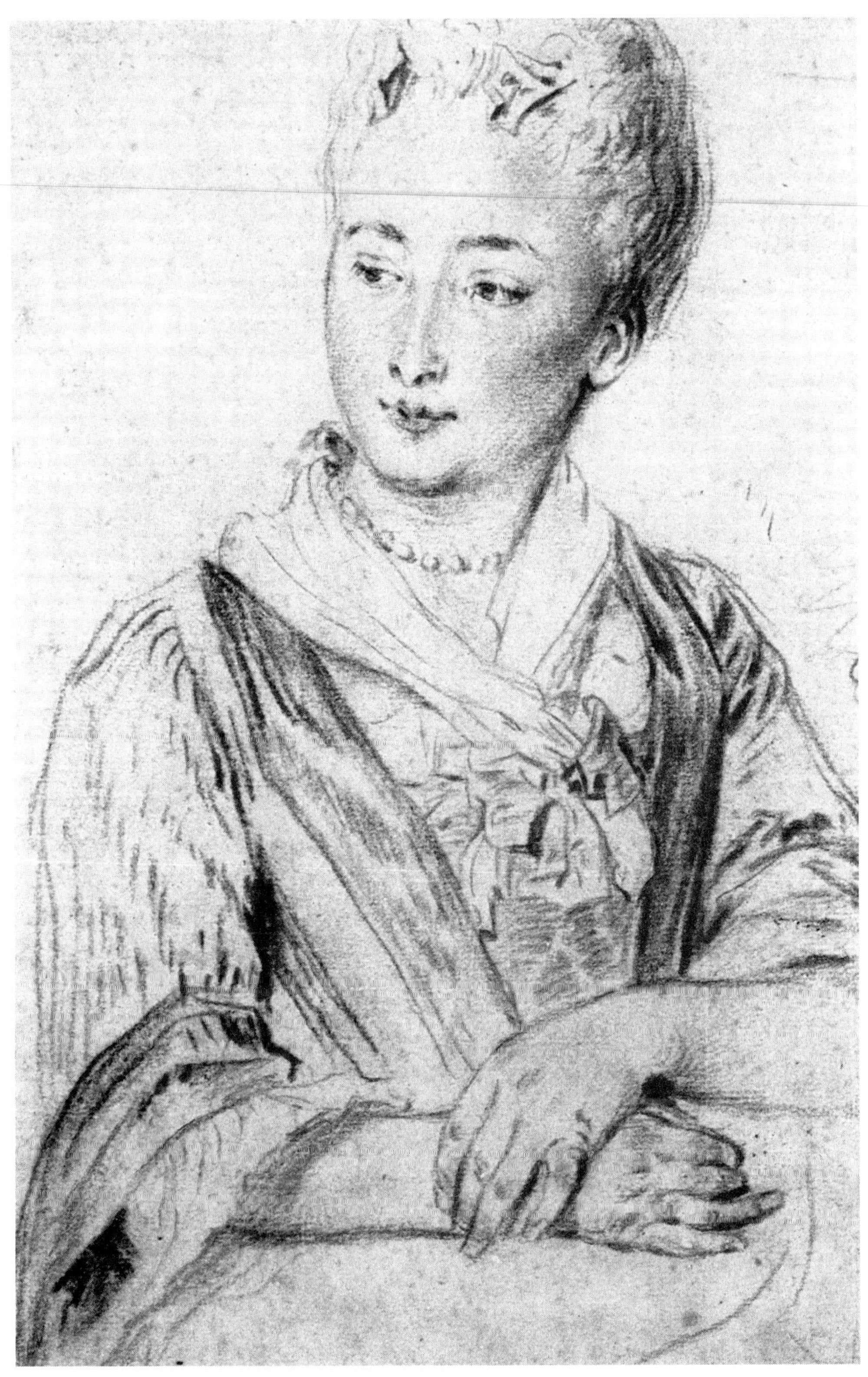

Plate 99. ANTOINE WATTEAU

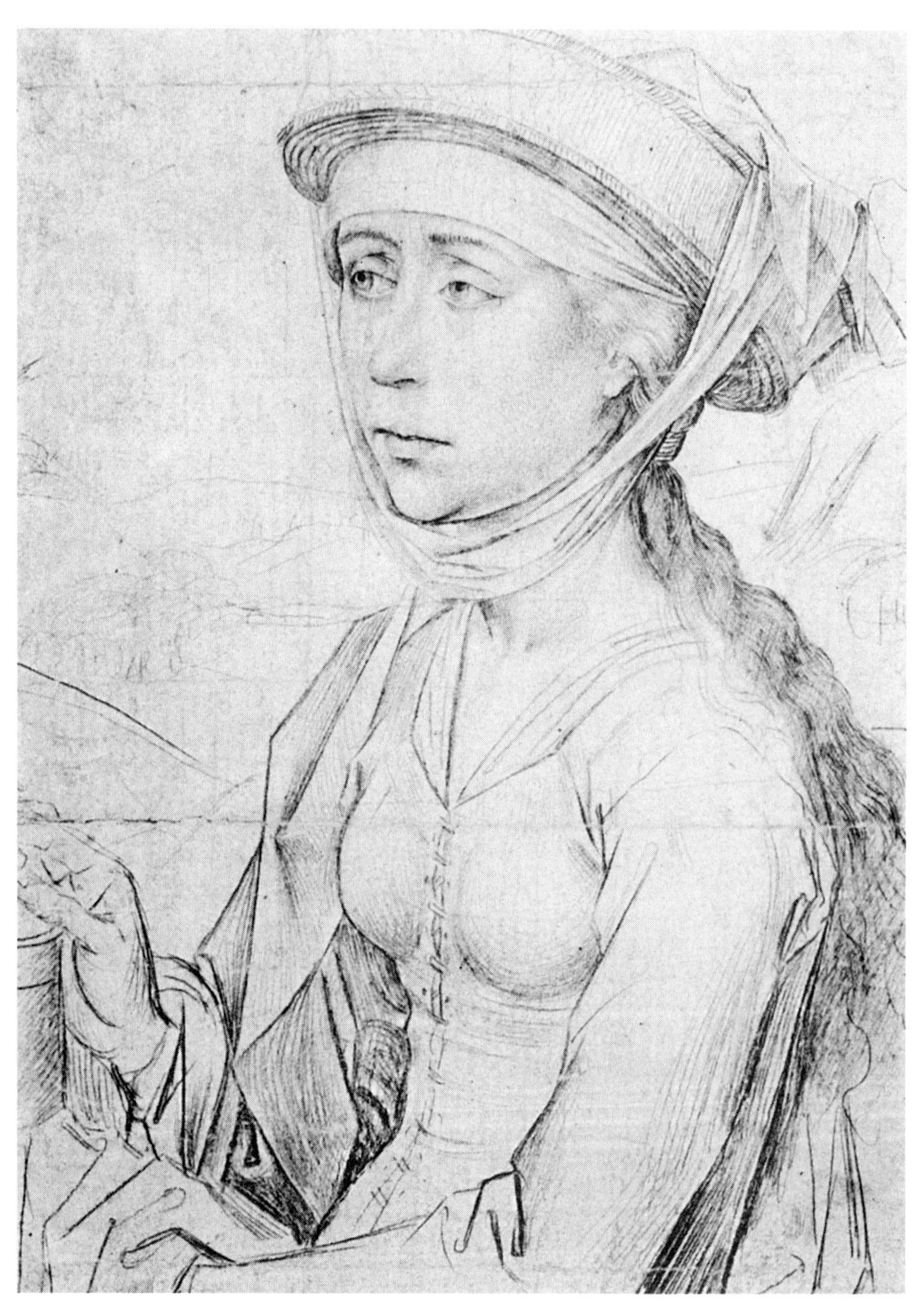

Plate 100. Rogier van der Weyden

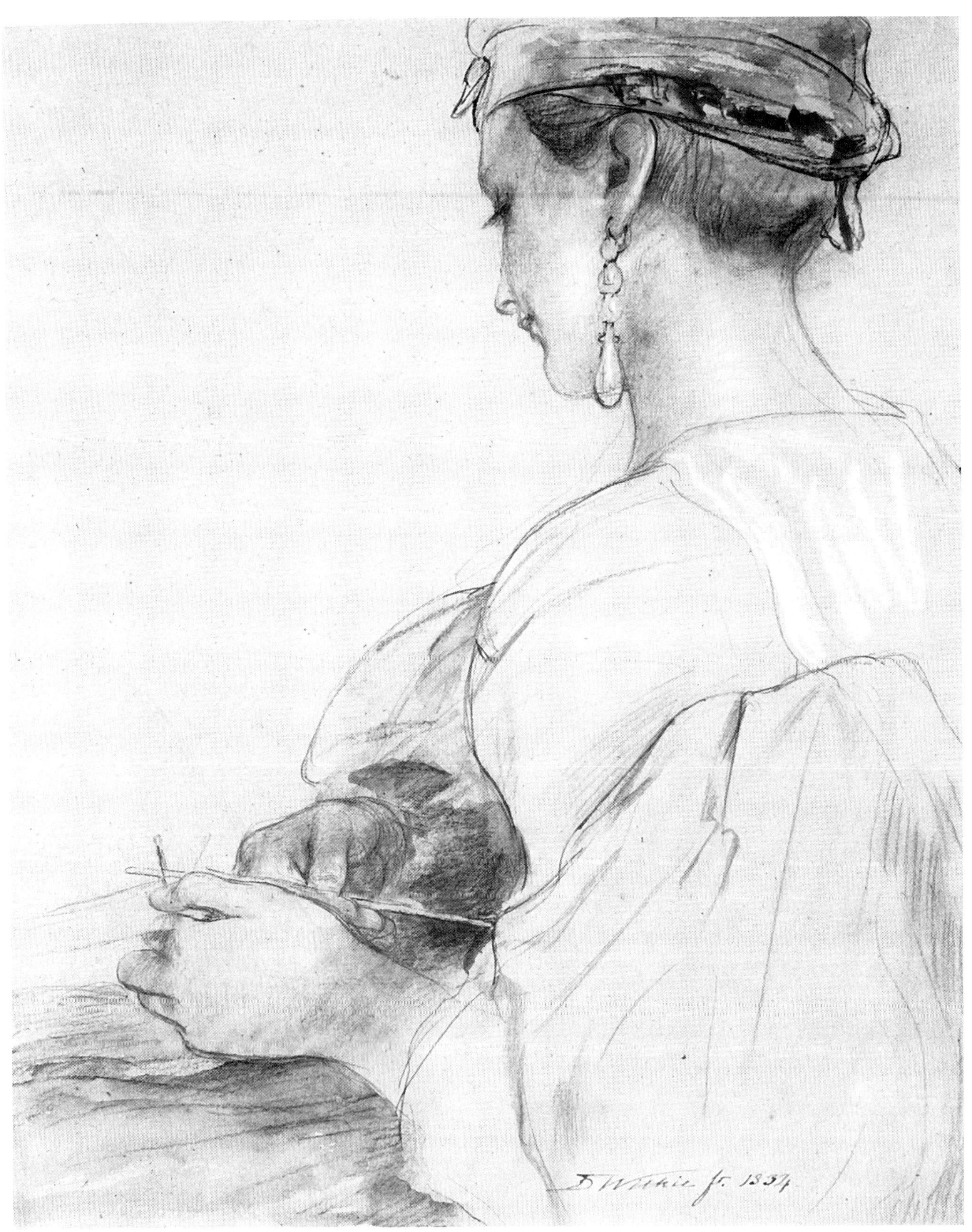

Plate 101. DAVID WILKIE